Deity Mantra and Wisdom

Deity Mantra and Wisdom

DEVELOPMENT STAGE MEDITATION IN TIBETAN BUDDHIST TANTRA

by
JIGME LINGPA,
PATRUL RINPOCHE, AND
GETSE MAHĀPAṆḌITA

Translated by the
DHARMACHAKRA TRANSLATION
COMMITTEE

SNOW LION PUBLICATIONS
Ithaca, New York
Boulder, Colorado

Snow Lion Publications
P.O. Box 6483
Ithaca, NY 14851 USA
(607) 273-8519
www.snowlionpub.com

Printed in USA on acid-free recycled paper.

ISBN-13 978-1-55939-300-3
ISBN-10 1-55939-300-9

Library of Congress Cataloging-in-Publication Data

Deity, mantra, and wisdom: development stage meditation in Tibetan Buddhist tantra by Jigme Lingpa, Patrul Rinpoche, and Getse Mahāpaṇḍita; forewords by Kyabje Trulshik Rinpoche and Chökyi Nyima Rinpoche; translated by the Dharmachakra Translation Committee.

p. cm.

Includes bibliographical references and index.
ISBN-13: 978-1-55939-300-3 (alk. paper)
ISBN-10: 1-55939-300-9 (alk. paper)
1. Rñiṅ-ma-pa (Sect) I. 'Jigs-med-gliṅ-pa Raṅ-byuṅ-rdo-rje, 1729 or 30-1798. II. O-rgyan-'jigs-med-chos-kyi-dbaṅ-po, Dpal-sprul, b.1808. III. 'Gyur-med-tshe-dbaṅ-mchog-grub, Dge-rtse Paṇḍita, b. 1764?
BQ7662.D45 2007
294.3'420423--dc22

2006029883

TABLE OF CONTENTS

"Regard all appearances, sounds, and thoughts
As the play of deity, mantra, and wisdom."

—Getse Mahāpaṇḍita Tsewang Chokdrub

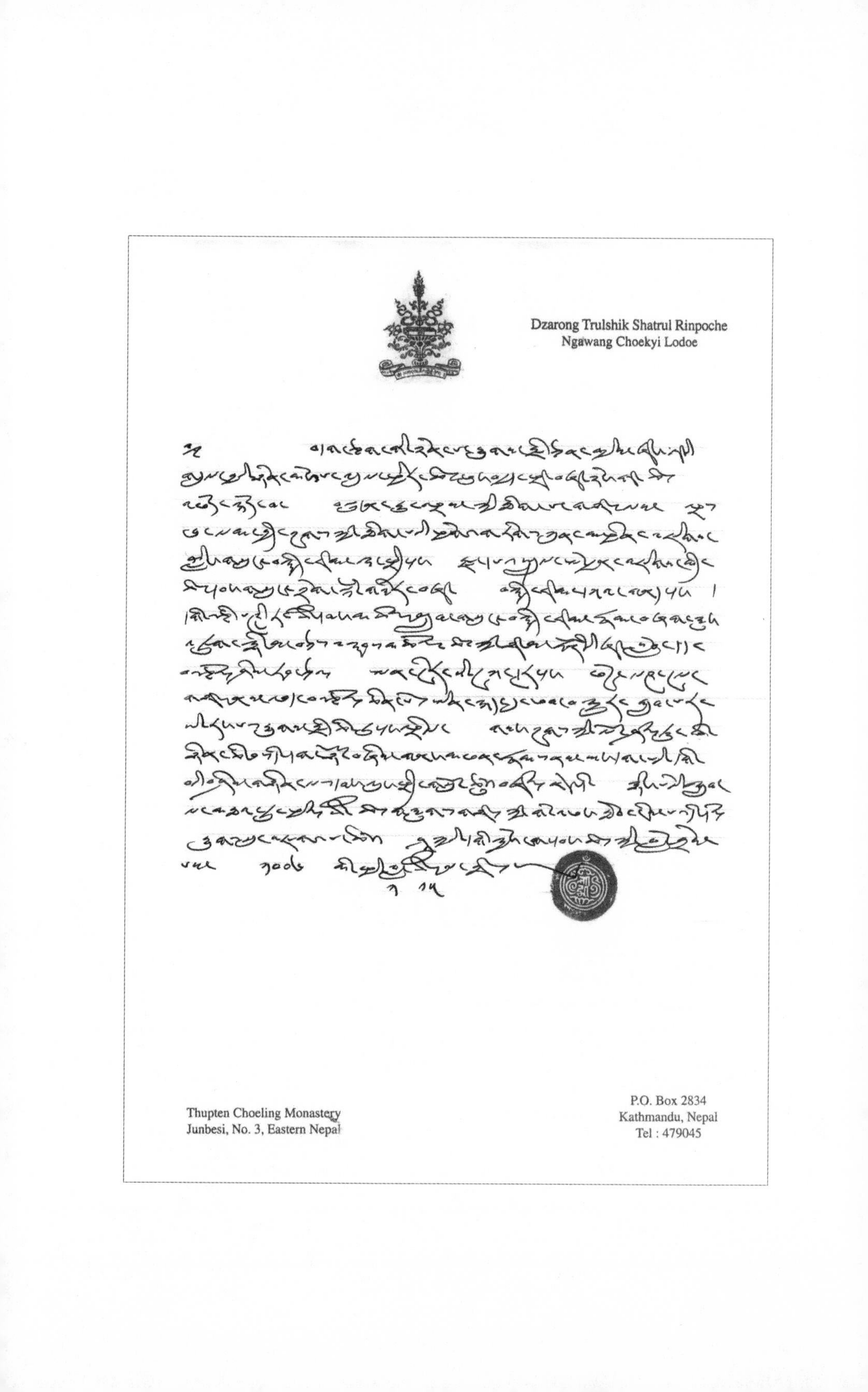

Dzarong Trulshik Shatrul Rinpoche
Ngawang Choekyi Lodoe

[illegible]

Thupten Choeling Monastery
Junbesi, No. 3, Eastern Nepal

P.O. Box 2834
Kathmandu, Nepal
Tel : 479045

FOREWORD

by Trulshik Rinpoche

As our compassionate teacher turned the wheel of Dharma in this realm he gave eighty-four thousand teachings. All of these were given to tame the afflictions of those in need of guidance. When condensed, these teachings can all be included in two vehicles, those of cause and fruition.

The texts that concern us here pertain to the Mantra Vehicle, in which the fruition is taken as the path. Here we find the omniscient Jigme Lingpa's *Instructions on the Development Stage and Deity Yoga*, Dza Patrul Urgyen Jigme Chöwang's two compositions *Four Stakes That Bind the Life-Force* and *Difficult Points in the Development Stage*, as well as Getse Mahāpaṇḍita Tsewang Chokdrub's *Husks of Unity: A Clarification of the Development Stage Rituals*. These four texts have now been translated into English by Andreas Doctor and Cortland Dahl, two devoted, committed, and knowledgeable students of the supreme refuge, Chökyi Nyima Rinpoche. In this I rejoice and offer my thanks.

The path of Secret Mantra is one of both great profit and danger. Therefore, anyone who practices these texts should receive the empowerments, reading transmissions, and instructions from an authentic spiritual teacher, doing so in the correct manner. Once the essential practice has been perfected, it is certain that both the dharmakāya and rūpakāya will be attained. For this reason, I request that these points be kept in mind.

This was written by the Buddhist monk Ngawang Chökyi Lodrö on the fifteenth day of the second month of the Fire Dog Year, 2006.

Chökyi Nyima Rinpoche, President

Dharmachakra Translation Committee
P.O. Box 21277, Boudhanath, Kathmandu, Nepal
www.dharmachakra.net

༄ སྟོན་པ་ཡང་དག་པར་རྫོགས་པའི་སངས་རྒྱས་བཅོམ་ལྡན་འདས་ཐུགས་རྗེ་ཚད་མེད་པ་དང་ལྡན་པ་དེས་བདག་སོགས་གདུལ་བྱ་རྣམས་ཀྱི་བློ་དང་འཚམས་པར་ཆོས་འཁོར་མཐའ་ཡས་པ་ཞིག་བསྐོར་བར་མཛད་པ་ལས། རྒྱུ་ལམ་དུ་བྱེད་པ་ཐུན་མོང་གི་ཐེག་པ་དང་། འབྲས་བུ་སྐུ་དང་ཡེ་ཤེས་ལམ་དུ་བྱེད་པ་གསང་སྔགས་རྡོ་རྗེ་ཐེག་པ་ཡིན་ལ། དེ་དག་རྒྱུད་སྡེ་རྒྱ་མཚོའི་དགོངས་པར་ཐུག་ཅིང་། དེ་ཡང་དབང་བཞིའི་བསྐྱེད་རྫོགས་མན་ངག་ལག་ལེན་དང་འབྲེལ་བའི་ཉམས་ལེན་ལ་འདུས་ལ། ཇི་ལྟར་ན། ལུས་རྩ་དག་ཅིང་སྨིན་པར་བྱེད་པ་བུམ་དབང་། ངག་རླུང་དག་ཅིང་སྨིན་པར་བྱེད་པ་གསང་དབང་། ཡིད་ཐིག་དག་ཅིང་སྨིན་པར་བྱེད་པ་ཤེར་དབང་། ཀུན་གཞིའི་ལས་དང་ཤེས་སྒྲིབ་དག་པར་བྱེད་པ་ཚིག་དབང་རིན་པོ་ཆེ་སོགས་ཡིན་ཅིང་། དེས་སྒྲིབ་བཞི་དག་ལམ་བཞི་འབྲིངས་སྐུ་བཞི་མངོན་དུ་འགྱུར་བར་བྱེད་པའི་མྱུར་ལམ་ཁྱད་པར་ཅན་ཡིན་པས་དེ་དག་ཐབས་བསྐྱེད་པའི་རིམ་པ་དང་། ཤེས་རབ་རྫོགས་པའི་རིམ་པར་འདུས་ཤིང་། སྣང་བ་ལྷ་གྲགས་པ་སྔགས་དྲན་རྟོག་ཡེ་ཤེས་ཀྱི་འཁོར་སོ་གསུམ་དང་མི་འབྲལ་བ་དགོས་གལ་ཤིན་ཏུ་ཆེ་ལ། དེས་ན་རིག་འཛིན་འཇིགས་མེད་གླིང་པའི་བསྐྱེད་རིམ་ལྷ་ཁྲིད། དཔལ་སྤྲུལ་ཨོ་རྒྱན་འཇིགས་མེད་ཆོས་ཀྱི་དབང་པོའི་བསྐྱེད་རིམ་ལྷའི་ཁྲིད་ཀྱི་དཀའ་གནད་དང་། སློག་སྒོམ་གཟེར་བཞི། དགེ་རྩེ་མ་ཧཱ་པཎྜི་ཏ་ཚེ་དབང་མཆོག་གྲུབ་ཀྱི་བསྐྱེད་ཚིག་ཟུང་འཇུག་སྙེ་མ་བཅས་སུ། དཀའ་གནད་མན་ངག་བྱིན་རླབས་ཀྱིས་ཕྱུག་པ་ཡོད་ན། ད་ལན་ངོས་སློབ་དང་བརྩོན་ཤེས་རབ་ཅན། ཨན་ཌེར་སི་ཌཱག་ཊར་དང་། ཀོར་ཊ་ལཱན་ཌཱལ་གཉིས་གཙོས་ཆོས་འཁོར་སྒྲ་བསྒྱུར་ཚོགས་མིས་དད་བརྩོན་ཆེན་པོས་དབྱིན་སྐད་དུ་ཕབ་བསྒྱུར་བྱས་པར་དགའ་མགུ་ཡི་རངས་ཀྱི་མེ་ཏོག་འཐོར་རྒྱུ་དང་། འདི་ལྟ་བུའི་གསང་སྔགས་རྡོ་རྗེ་ཐེག་པའི་བསྐྱེད་རྫོགས་ཟབ་གནད་ཀྱི་ཁྲིད་གཞུང་ཚུལ་བཞིན་ཉམས་སུ་བླང་བར་བྱེད་པ་ལ་བླ་མ་རྡོ་རྗེ་སློབ་དཔོན་རྟོགས་པས་བདག་རྒྱུད་གྲོལ་ཅིང་ ཐུགས་རྗེས་གཞན་རྒྱུད་གྲོལ་ནུས་པའི་མཚན་ལྡན་གྱི་དྲུང་ནས་སྨིན་བྱེད་ཀྱི་དབང་། གྲོལ་བྱེད་ཀྱི་ཁྲིད་དང་མན་ངག རྒྱབ་རྟེན་གྱི་ལུང་དང་བཅས་པ་ཐོབ་ནས་སྒྲུབ་པ་ཉམས་ལེན་ཚུལ་བཞིན་མཛད་གལ་ཆེ་བ་དང་། དེ་ལྟར་ཉམས་སུ་བླང་ཚེ་རང་ཉིད་སྐུ་བཞི་ཡེ་ཤེས་ལྔ་ལྡན་གྱི་གོ་འཕང་མངོན་དུ་འགྱུར་ཞིང་ཐུགས་རྗེས་གཞན་དོན་གཟུགས་སྐུ་གཉིས་སུ་དབང་བསྒྱུར་ནས་མཐའ་ཡས་པའི་འགྲོ་བ་འདྲེན་པའི་དེད་དཔོན་ཆེན་པོར་འགྱུར་བར་གདོན་མི་ཟ་ན་རང་གཞན་ཀུན་གྱི་ཐུགས་དམ་གྱི་མཐིལ་དམ་པར་མཛད་གལ་ཤིན་ཏུ་ཆེ་བ་མཁྱེན་གསལ་བཞིན་ཐུགས་ཉམས་སུ་བཞེས་པར་མཛད་དུ་གསོལ་ཞེས་གསོལ་བ་འདེབས་པ་པོ། ཆོས་ཀྱི་ཉི་མ་སྤྲུལ་མིང་པས་བོད་རྒྱལ་ལོ་༢༡༣༢ རབ་བྱུང་༡༧ ཤིང་བྱ། ཟླ་བ་༡༡ ཚེས་༡༨ དང་། སྤྱི་ལོ་༢༠༠༦ ཟླ་༡ ཚེས་༡༨ ཉིན་བྲིས།།

FOREWORD

by Chökyi Nyima Rinpoche

Our Teacher, the perfectly enlightened transcendent conqueror, turned a limitless number of Dharma wheels out of his boundless compassion—each of these matching the mind-set of those, including ourselves, who need his guidance. Two approaches can be found in these teachings. The first comprises the Common Vehicle, in which causes are taken as the path, while the second is the Vajra Vehicle of Secret Mantra, where the kāyas and wisdoms of the fruition are taken as the path. The latter of these two is based on the intent of the ocean of tantras.

This latter approach can also be condensed into the practices and key instructions associated with the stages of development and completion, which relate to the four empowerments. In this system, the vase empowerment purifies and ripens the body and the channels. The secret empowerment purifies and ripens speech and the energies. The wisdom empowerment purifies and ripens the mind and the essences. Finally, the precious word empowerment purifies the karma of the all-ground and the cognitive obscuration. Since this process purifies the four obscurations, completes the four paths, and actualizes the four kāyas, it constitutes a uniquely swift path. This approach, in turn, is embodied in the skillful means of the development stage and the wisdom of the completion stage. On this path, there are three notions one should never lose sight of: that appearances are the deity, sounds are mantra, and thoughts are wisdom. These points are of crucial importance.

On this topic, a wealth of intricate details, key instructions, and blessings are contained in Jigme Lingpa's *Instructions on the Development Stage*, Patrul Urgyen Jigme Chökyi Wangpo's *Difficult Points in the Development Stage* and *Four Stakes That Bind the Life-Force*, as well as Getse Mahāpaṇḍita Tsewang Chokdrub's *Husks of Unity: A Clarification of the Development Stage Rituals*. Under the auspices of the Dharmachakra Translation Committee, these four texts have now been faithfully and diligently rendered into English by two devoted, committed, and knowledgeable students of mine, Andreas Doctor and Cortland Dahl. This is a cause for strewing flowers of joy and happiness.

As these instruction manuals explain the profound key points of the Vajra Vehicle of Secret Mantra, to make proper use of them it is crucial first to seek out an authentic vajra master. Such an individual will have liberated his or her own mind through realization and be capable of liberating the minds of others through compassion. One must then receive the empowerments that mature the student, the guidance and key instructions that bring liberation, and the supportive reading transmissions from that master. Finally, the teachings should be practiced in a genuine manner.

If you practice in this way, there is no doubt that you will come to actualize the state of the four kāyas and five wisdoms and gain mastery over the two rūpakāyas that compassionately benefit others. In this capacity, you will become a great guide capable of leading limitless sentient beings. It is, therefore, of the utmost importance that everyone takes this as the very core of their practice. Since this is already well known, I request that it be applied accordingly.

This was written by Chökyi Nyima, who has been given the title of Tulku, on the fifteenth day of the eleventh month in the Wood Bird Year of the seventeenth cycle, the year 2132 of the Tibetan kings.

INTRODUCTION

The practices of the Vajra Vehicle are based on the profound content of the Buddhist tantras. In Tibet, these sacred texts were studied and practiced in two major traditions, one tracing itself to the dynastic period of the eighth and ninth centuries and another stemming from the later translation efforts that took place between the eleventh and thirteenth centuries. Due to this temporal distinction, these two traditions became known, respectively, as the Nyingma (rNying ma, Ancient) and Sarma (gSar ma, New) Schools. Although these two traditions do, at times, vary in their view on the finer details of ritual performance and textual interpretation, both are alike in summarizing the practice of Tantra under the two main headings of "development stage" (bskyed rim) and "completion stage" (rdzogs rim). For well over a thousand years, it was these two paths of Tantra that led innumerable beings to spiritual fulfillment and awakening, both in India and Tibet.

Of these two forms of tantric practice, this anthology of writings is primarily concerned with the philosophy and training of the development stage. As the texts themselves are meant as an introduction to the theory and practice of the development stage, a lengthy introduction to the topic seems unwarranted here. Moreover, those interested in the historical and philosophical matrix of development stage practice may consult some of the fine sources on these topics already available in the English language (see the Bibliography at the back of this book).

The authors of the texts contained in this anthology are some of the most well-known and influential masters in the Tibetan Buddhist tradition. Jigme Lingpa ('Jigs med gling pa, 1730-1798), Getse Mahāpaṇḍita Tsewang Chokdrub (dGe rtse mahāpaṇḍita tshe dbang mchog grub, 1761-1829), and Patrul Chökyi Wangpo (dPal sprul chos kyi dbang po,

1808-1887) are all figures that embody the ideals of erudition and spiritual accomplishment so admired in the Buddhist tradition. As all three authors trace their spiritual lineage to that of the Nyingma School, their presentation of the development stage is given according to the framework classically applied in that tradition.

Scripturally, the development stage practices of the Nyingma tradition are based on two literary genres. The first is referred to as the Transmitted Teachings (bKa' ma), a body of literature that traces itself to the first spread of Buddhism in Tibet during the dynastic era. Since the appearance of these teachings, they have been maintained in an unbroken line of study and practice. In terms of development stage practice, the most central texts of the Transmitted Teachings are the famed *Tantra of the Secret Essence* and a group of texts and practices known collectively as the Eight Great Sādhana Teachings (sGrub pa chen po bka' brgyad). These represent two divisions known, respectively, as the Collected Tantras (rGyud sde) and the Collected Sādhanas (sGrub sde). Both remain widely studied and practiced to this day.

The second major source for development stage practice in the Nyingma School is the vast, ongoing tradition of revealed Treasures (gTer ma). This tradition, which began approximately in the eleventh century and continues to this day, centers on revealed teachings of the realized master Padmasambhava. In contrast to the complex presentation found in the Transmitted Teachings, development stage practices in the Treasure tradition are often more concise and unelaborate. Despite this difference in form, however, the sādhanas of the Treasure tradition, likewise often entitled the Collected Sādhanas, remain theoretically grounded in the tradition of the Transmitted Teachings, and the *Tantra of the Secret Essence* in particular. For this reason, while the Treasure tradition has become the dominant form of *practice* in the Nyingma School, when it comes to *study*, the treatises of the Transmitted Teachings commonly take precedence. The texts contained in this anthology pertain to both of these traditions.

ON THE TEXTS

The first text in this volume, *Ladder to Akaniṣṭha: Instructions on the Development Stage and Deity Yoga*, was composed by the Treasure revealer and adept Jigme Lingpa. In terms of influence, few recent masters have had a more profound and lasting impact on the development of the Tibetan Buddhist tradition. As an itinerant yogi, Jigme Lingpa embodied the Buddhist ideals of renunciation and guru devotion, inspiring generations of practitioners with his austere lifestyle and dedication to practice. As a revealer of spiritual Treasures, he codified a collection of revelatory tantras, sādhanas, prayers, and instructions known as The Heart Essence of the Vast Expanse (Klong chen snying thig). To this day, this collection remains one of the most widely studied and practiced Treasure cycles in the Nyingma tradition. As a scholar, he composed influential works on both philosophy and practice. His treatise *Treasury of Precious Qualities*, for example, is considered one of the most thorough synopses of Buddhist philosophy and practice, while his renowned instruction manual on the Great Perfection, *Wisdom Guru*, is now a standard source for teachings on this profound topic.

In *Ladder to Akaniṣṭha*, Jigme Lingpa provides an overview of the theory and practice of the development stage, balancing philosophical inquiry with instructions on the more practical aspects of tantric meditation. The first section of the text presents the theoretical framework for development stage practice. Beginning with the four approaches one can take in the development stage, Jigme Lingpa discusses the links between the various elements found in development stage meditation, the aspects of saṃsāra they are meant to purify, and the result that ensues once the practice has been perfected. In the second section, the focus is on practice. Here, Jigme Lingpa outlines the stages of meditation, offering practical advice on how to identify and surmount obstacles and progress in practice. The text concludes with a presentation of the fruition of development stage practice. In this section, Jigme Lingpa frames his discussion around the levels of realization and the various aspects of the enlightened state.

As the basis for his presentation, Jigme Lingpa draws primarily from the Mahāyoga tantras and the commentarial literature of this tradition. Not surprisingly, his discussions often center on the *Tantra of the Secret Essence*, the most influential Mahāyoga scripture. He also gives considerable attention to less well-known texts, however, such as the *Tantra of the Perfect Secret* and the *Heruka Galpo Tantra*. In terms of philosophical interpretation, his views often mirror those of Longchenpa (Klong chen pa, 1308-1364), whom he met face-to-face in a series of three transformative visions and whose writings deeply influenced his own.

In characteristic style, Jigme Lingpa does not shy away from difficult points and controversial topics when discussing the development stage. His tendency to tackle difficult issues head-on does not always make for easy reading, but it does offer the reader an insight into the depth and subtlety of tantric theory and the difficult issues that have occupied some of the great saints and scholars of the Vajrayāna tradition. For this reason, *Ladder to Akaniṣṭha* is valuable not only as a manual on the theory and practice of the development stage, but also as an introduction to the complex tantric philosophy of the *Tantra of the Secret Essence* and the Mahāyoga tradition as a whole.

The second and third texts in this anthology, *Clarifying the Difficult Points in the Development Stage and Deity Yoga* and *The Melody of Brahma Reveling in the Three Realms: Key Points for Meditating on the Four Stakes That Bind the Life-Force*, were written by Patrul Chökyi Wangpo. Along with Jamyang Khyentse Wangpo ('Jam dbyangs mkhyen brtse'i dbang po, 1820-1892) and Do Khyentse Yeshe Dorje (mDo mkhyen brtse ye shes rdo rje, 1800-1859), Patrul was one of three main reincarnations of Jigme Lingpa. He was also the foremost student of Jigme Gyalwey Nyugu ('Jigs med rgyal ba'i myu gu, 1765-?), the latter's heart son. Patrul followed his predecessor's example and lived the life of a wandering yogi. Despite his renown as a teacher and meditator of the highest caliber, he refused to become involved in monastic institutions, focusing instead on practicing meditation in isolated locations.

Patrul Chökyi Wangpo was also a prolific writer. His compositions range from voluminous treatises on the subtleties of Buddhist philosophy, such as his five-hundred-page commentary on Maitreya's *Ornament of Clear Realization*, to pithy poems that focus on the integration of spirituality and daily life. In addition to his versatility as an author, he is also well known for his ability to present profound material in a down-to-earth, accessible manner, as evidenced in his much-loved masterpiece *Words of My Perfect Teacher*.

Clarifying the Difficult Points is a prime example of Patrul Rinpoche's ability to make complex ideas accessible. Expanding on the presentation given in *Ladder to Akaniṣṭha*, he highlights some of the more obscure issues addressed by Jigme Lingpa and clarifies the latter's presentation. In addition to his clarification of difficult issues, Patrul also stresses the importance of compassion and the view of emptiness in the context of tantric practice. Again and again, he warns of the danger of engaging in development stage meditation without a solid grounding in these two principles. Since *Clarifying the Difficult Points* is meant as a companion to *Ladder to Akaniṣṭha*, we have combined these two texts in our translation, interspersing Patrul's commentary (indicated by a grey line at the left side of the page) after the relevant sections of Jigme Lingpa's explanation.

In *The Four Stakes That Bind the Life-Force*, Patrul's explanation centers on one of the core concepts found in the development stage literature of the Nyingma tradition, as indicated by the text's title. Despite its narrow focus, this treatise addresses all aspects of the development stage, distilling the key points of this difficult subject into four main points, or "stakes," that capture the essence of this stage of practice. Though the "four stakes" presented here are a concept unique to the Nyingma School, in terms of content Patrul's explanation is relevant to all forms of development stage meditation.

The last composition included in this anthology is *Husks of Unity: A Clarification of the Development Stage Rituals* by the renowned scholar of Kathok Monastery (Kaḥ thog dgon), Getse Mahāpaṇḍita Tsewang Chokdrub. This great scholar is said to have been a reincarnation of the famed dynastic translator Nyak Jñānakumāra (gNyags jñānakumāra, 8th-9th cent.). Like Jigme Lingpa before him, Tsewang Chokdrub was deeply committed to preserving the unique teachings of the Nyingma School. As such, he wrote a catalogue to the Tantras of the Nyingma School (rNying ma rgyud 'bum), which had only recently been compiled through the efforts and connections of Jigme Lingpa at the royal house of Derge (sDe dge).

Besides this shared interest in the tantras of the Nyingma School, Tsewang Chokdrub also enjoyed a deep personal connection with Jigme Lingpa, from whom he was able to receive profound oral instructions and meditation guidance. As an expression of Tsewang Chokdrub's commitment to invigorate the study and practice of the Nyingma teachings, he founded the influential monastic study center of Getse Tralek Gon (dGe rtse bkra legs dgon), which quickly emerged as one of the primary affiliates of Kathok Monastery, housing more than one thousand monks. It was in his position as the main scholar at this monastery that Tsewang Chokdrub became known as Getse Mahāpaṇḍita. The list of Tsewang Chokdrub's publications is long and includes an extensive list of influential tantric commentaries, including an explanation of the *Tantra of the Secret Essence* itself.

As evinced by Jigme Lingpa's *Ladder to Akaniṣṭha*, the philosophy and practice of the development stage is both subtle and complex. For this reason, studying instruction manuals that apply the complexities of tantric theory to the practical experience of development stage meditation can be of great benefit to both novice as well as seasoned practitioners. This is the approach taken by Tsewang Chokdrub in his *Husks of Unity*, where the development stage is presented within the framework of practice. He begins with a description of the preliminary practices, discussing both their significance and practical application. Next, he explains visualization, mantra recitation, and meditative absorption, the three elements that form the core of development stage practice. These three elements transform one's ordinary body, speech, and mind into their awakened counterparts. Finally, Tsewang Chokdrub gives a brief description of the concluding practices of the development stage.

In contrast to Jigme Lingpa's text, where the emphasis is on the underlying *theory* of development stage practice, Tsewang Chokdrub focuses on *practical application*. There is little philosophical contemplation in his description. Instead, he offers the reader a detailed description of the various elements of development stage practice and their significance in terms of the Buddhist path. This emphasis on practical application makes Tsewang Chokdrub's text an ideal companion to Jigme Lingpa's treatise.

The four texts presented in this volume are among the most renowned and widely studied texts on the theory and practice of development stage meditation. Though they all address the same subject matter, each does so from a different angle. Together, they provide a comprehensive and balanced presentation of this profound topic. Jigme Lingpa's *Ladder to Akaniṣṭha* focuses heavily on the theoretical underpinnings of the development stage, while in terms of practical instruction, the focus is on deity visualization. Getse Mahāpaṇḍita's text, in contrast, emphasizes the various stages of sādhana practice and their practical application, areas that are barely even alluded to in Jigme Lingpa's presentation. The two remaining texts by Patrul highlight some of the core concepts in the development stage, enriching the presentations of Jigme Lingpa and Tsewang Chokdrub by offering practical advice on the most important aspects of this stage of practice.

The Translations

These texts were translated as a project of the Dharmachakra Translation Committee under the direction of Chökyi Nyima Rinpoche. Though the development stage remains one of the most widely practiced forms of meditation in the Tibetan tradition, it is also one of the most technically complex and challenging practices. It is, therefore, of crucial importance that practitioners and students of Vajrayāna Buddhism have access to the seminal texts on this subject composed by masters of the lineage. With this concern in mind, the four texts contained in this anthology were translated to make such classical expositions available to contemporary practitioners of tantric meditation.

In the Buddhist tradition, scripture is typically studied under the guidance of a spiritual teacher. Texts are therefore meant to be accompanied by the oral instructions of a qualified master. This is especially true in the case of the Vajrayāna, where the direct guidance of a teacher is considered a mandatory prerequisite to study and practice, along with the preliminary steps of receiving empowerment and reading transmission. Vajrayāna literature continually warns against engaging in tantric study and practice without having taken these critical steps.

To encourage the continuation of this tradition in the West, Chökyi Nyima Rinpoche advised us to present each of these translations "as is." For this reason, we have not added any form of commentary or annotation. This approach may, at times, make certain passages seem obscure to the uninitiated reader. Yet it is hoped that this will encourage the reader to seek personal guidance and clarification on these precious teachings from a learned and accomplished master.

While we have not added annotation to the four texts included in this book, an extensive glossary has been supplied to facilitate the reader's understanding of the core concepts and terminology found in the development stage. The glossary entries themselves are, for the most part, translated excerpts from classical commentaries on the subject. In addition, to help ensure the continuation of the oral transmission of these teachings, the original Tibetan texts have been made available for download on the website of the Dharmachakra Translation Committee (www.dharmachakra.net).

The texts included in this anthology were translated by Cortland Dahl and Andreas Doctor. *Ladder to Akaniṣṭha* and *Clarifying the Difficult Points* were translated by Cortland Dahl, *Husks of Unity* was translated by Andreas Doctor, and *The Four Stakes That Bind the Life-Force* came about as the result of our combined efforts. Once completed by the primary translator, each translation was read and checked against the original Tibetan by the other. The extended glossary at the back of the book was compiled and translated by Cortland Dahl.

ACKNOWLEDGMENTS

While producing these translations, we have been fortunate to receive support from a number of learned and accomplished masters. To the following lamas we would like to offer our sincere thanks for the transmissions, clarifications, inspiration, and blessings they so generously shared. It was Chökyi Nyima Rinpoche who first requested these translations and, throughout our efforts, he has directed the project with wisdom and kindness and been a great source of inspiration. In addition, Kyabje Trulshik Rinpoche, Tsike Chokling Rinpoche, Ringu Tulku Rinpoche, Dzongsar Khyentse Rinpoche, Khentrul Lodro Thaye Rinpoche, and Lopön Jigme Rinpoche kindly granted their blessings and guidance to our work. Khenpo Sherab Sangpo, Khenpo Tashi Palden, and Shechen Khenpo Gendun Rinchen generously shared their knowledge and expertise and helped clarify a number of obscure issues. Finally, from the lotsāwas Erik Pema Kunsang and Matthieu Ricard we were fortunate to receive much advice and help in translating a number of difficult passages.

We also wish to thank Thomas Doctor, Heidi Köppl, Dan Martin, and Dhondup Tsering for their thoughtful suggestions and advice, James Hopkins for his many helpful linguistic remarks, Steven Rhodes at Snow Lion Publications for skillfully editing the manuscript, and Laura Dainty for proofreading the final text. Rafael Ortet kindly lent his artistic gifts to the layout and design of this book. Financial support to the project was generously offered by George MacDonald, the Rimé Foundation, and the Khyentse Foundation.

We sincerely regret and apologize for any errors and mistakes this book may contain. They are exclusively our own, caused by our limited understanding of this profound topic. Whatever merit, direct and indirect, may arise from this publication we dedicate to the welfare of all beings.

Cortland Dahl and Andreas Doctor
Boudhanath, Nepal
The Month of Saga Dawa, 2006

LADDER TO AKANIṢṬHA

Instructions on the Development Stage and Deity Yoga

by **Jigme Lingpa**

&

Clarifying the Difficult Points in the Development Stage and Deity Yoga

by **Patrul Chökyi Wangpo**

Homage to the transcendent conqueror, glorious Vajrasattva!

Clear potential—utterly pure by nature and obscuration free;
The union of appearance and emptiness, wisdom's illusory display—
So this state of the three kāyas may be discovered with ease,
I will now explain the practical approach of deity yoga meditation.

Sentient beings wander through a succession of deluded states due to the temporary impurity of their fundamental nature. The development stage practice of deity yoga establishes this very condition as the enlightened body, speech, and mind of the tathāgatas—a secret and inconceivable dimension of existence. Here, I pledge to set forth a thorough presentation of this topic, entitled *Ladder to Akaniṣṭha.*

This work contains three main topics:

I. The unerring cause: the basis for development stage practice
II. The undeluded condition: the path of meditation
III. The pure fruition: attaining the unified state

I

The Unerring Cause:

THE BASIS FOR DEVELOPMENT STAGE PRACTICE

Stages of the Path states:

> A treasury, a complete stream, with interest,
> Skill in tantra and activity, key instructions,
> And warmth—a teacher with eight qualities.

As indicated here, one should begin by studying closely with a vajra master that has these eight traits and serving him or her well in the three ways. The next step is to mature one's being thoroughly by receiving the entire range of empowerments: the beneficial outer empowerments, the inner empowerments of potentiality, and the profound secret empowerments. From that point on, the various pledges and samaya vows need to be maintained and one may engage in the deity practices of the development stage.

This section contains two divisions, the teachings on: 1) purifying the habitual tendencies associated with the four types of birth and 2) the three absorptions, the basis for the development process.

A. Four Types of Development and Four Types of Birth

Generally speaking, the key point of all paths of the Great Vehicle is to purify the nature of saṃsāra—the truths of suffering and its source—and bring the fruitional state of buddhahood onto the path. Though the truth of suffering comes in various forms, they are all rooted in birth. Furthermore, all forms of suffering can be subsumed under birth and death. For these reasons, there are two stages that purify this twofold process of birth and death: the development stage and the completion stage. The entire textual tradition of Secret Mantra pertains to these two practices.

Outlining the approach of the development stage, the *Glorious Magical Web* states:

> To purify the four types of birth
> There are four types of development:
> The very elaborate and elaborate,
> The simple and the completely simple.

As shown here, there are four types of birth. These four, in turn, correspond to the four types of development stage practice: concise, intermediate, extensive, and very extensive.

1. The Concise Approach of Complete Simplicity

Those of the very highest acumen practice the development stage ritual of complete simplicity by developing the mind's inner potential. This potential is linked with the universal view of the king of vehicles, the natural and supreme yāna. The momentum that ensues from this process allows one to train in the indivisibility of development and completion. Without having to verbalize anything, the mind's nature is visualized in its innate state, as the complete form of the deity. This occurs in a manner similar to the way a reflection can appear suddenly in a mirror. The following passage illustrates this approach:

> The deity is you and you are the deity.
> You and the deity arise together.
> Since samaya and wisdom are nondual,
> There is no need to invite the deity,
> Nor to request it to take its seat.
> Self-emanated and self-empowered,
> Awareness itself is the Three Roots.

In this form of development stage practice, the nature of the deity is inherently and perfectly present within illusory wisdom. This purifies miraculous birth. Explaining further, the omniscient Longchenpa writes:

In the same way that miraculous birth occurs instantaneously,
There is no need to start from nothing and then meditate
On development and completion in stages.

2. The Intermediate, Simple Approach

The truth of nondual wisdom-space allows those of superior acumen to practice the simple development stage using an instantaneous approach. In this style of practice, deities are perfected by bringing their essence to mind; they are not developed using words. A progressive approach may also be practiced, in which case appearances arise naturally as the form of the deity within the expanse of Samantabhadrī—the great, empty basic space of knowledge. Thus, one takes on an illusory, divine form that is unified and nondual. On this topic, the *Tantra of the Natural Arising of Awareness* states:

What is instantaneous practice?
The deity is not developed,
But perfected, its essence recalled.
How does one practice in stages?
By entering successively
Into basic space and wisdom.

As indicated here, the support and supported, the celestial palace and divine nature, are visualized in a perfect and complete manner either by having their individual names verbalized or by merely remembering their essence. This type of development stage purifies the habitual patterns associated with birth through heat and moisture and involves the recognition of the inseparability of bliss and emptiness.

3 & 4. The Extensive, Elaborate Approach and the Very Extensive, Very Elaborate Approach

The very extensive, very elaborate development stage purifies egg birth and is for those who are more conceptual. In this context, the causal heruka arises as the resultant vajra holder, whereupon one meditates on the various aspects of *one's own children* and *another's child*. In the Eight Great Sādhana Teachings, it is taught that there are five steps involved in *making others one's child*: 1) light from the causal seed syllable radiates outwards and is drawn back in, generating the primary male and female consorts; 2) the buddhas of the ten directions are invoked and dissolve into space; 3) sentient beings are summoned and their obscurations purified; 4) the greatness of nonduality is proclaimed; and 5) the deities are drawn out from space and established within the maṇḍala.

Making oneself the child of another has eight parts: 1) the primary male and female consorts dissolve and transform into the causal seed syllable; 2) the male and female consorts develop from this seed syllable; 3) syllables are generated from the male consort's realization; 4) light emanates from the female consort and supplicates the deity; 5) all maṇḍalas dissolve into oneself as the male and female consorts, producing the pride of having become the wisdom being; 6) the male and female consorts join and the maṇḍala is generated in space; 7) one's own forty-two concepts become deities and are drawn outwards; and 8) the wisdom beings are invited, sealed, and so on.

> While the concise and intermediate stages are easy to understand, in the very extensive stage of practice outlined above we encounter topics such as *one's own children* and *another's child.* The following passage approaches this topic from the point of view of the Collected Tantras. Referring to *one's own children,* the *Magical Web* states:
>
> > Knowing the fruition itself to be the path,
> > Truly innate and without conflict,
> > Meditate on all maṇḍalas and spheres,
> > Without exception, as your children.
>
> And concerning *another's child*:
>
> > If minds engage and merge inseparably
> > By one supplicating the other,
> > What is the point of becoming a child?
>
> Alternately, the *Dagger Tantra* explains *another's child* by stating:
>
> > Just as what appears from the power of the buddhas,
> > From the ritual of spontaneity
> > And the completion of its branches
> > Come the wise—the children of the buddhas.

And on *one's own children*:

> Children and wives arise
> From the phenomena of saṃsāra.

While according to the Eight Great Sādhana Teachings:

> There are five ways of making others your child.

Although this topic is fairly clear in each individual text, there does not appear to be any clear explanation that presents exactly what *one's own children* and *another's child* actually mean. Consequently, this topic can appear difficult to explain. Once this matter is investigated, however, the first and last of the texts just mentioned can be understood to teach that the basis of development is the reality of the self—buddha nature. Thus, by visualizing the form of this causal vajra holder, the "other"—all of the clinging and appearances that we apprehend within saṃsāra and nirvāṇa, along with the intermediate state—is gathered in and then "made a child" by being extracted from the womb. This process is referred to as "making another one's own child."

In *making oneself the child of another*, the appearances and apprehensions of saṃsāra and nirvāṇa (the "other") are visualized as the primary deity of the maṇḍala (the vajra holder). This transforms all the accumulated grasping one has towards the aggregates, elements, and sense fields into a seed syllable, which is then "made a child" by being extracted from the womb. In this way, one becomes "the child of another."

The middle passage teaches that saṃsāric sentient beings are completely and perfectly enlightened as the buddhas of the three times. Here, sentient beings are referred to as "oneself" and buddhas as "other." Making oneself "the child of the buddhas" occurs by generating oneself as the primary deity of the maṇḍala by perfecting practices such as the ritual of spontaneity and the five ritual branches.

Making another one's own child, on the other hand, refers to a process in which everything that appears as the host of deities within the maṇḍala circle is the "other" and all saṃsāric sentient beings "oneself." The sequence in which each of these comes into existence is harmonized in this approach, leading to the union of the male and female consorts and the subsequent development by being extracted from the womb. The first two of these explanations present this concept from the point of view of the *basis* of development, whereas the latter does so from the perspective of the *process* of development.

At this point, you may be wondering whether these two approaches of positing oneself as a child are making slightly different points. In the *Chariot to Omniscience,* however, there is an explanation that links all three of these. Therefore, I urge intelligent individuals to examine this interpretation carefully and open the gate to this lucid explanation.

According to the *Great Magical Web,* you should begin by going for refuge and engendering the awakened mind. What happens next is linked with egg birth, which takes place in two stages. First, visualize yourself instantly as the primary male and female consorts and then invite the maṇḍala you are meditating on into the space before you. Next, make offerings, praises, supplications, daily confessions, and so on. Once this is finished, use VAJRA MU to rest evenly in emptiness again. This last point is the unique feature of this approach. Knowing that, the following presentation can be applied in common to both the very extensive approach, as well as to the moderately extensive development stage that purifies womb birth.

In these systems, the skillful means of the development stage are emphasized. Just as a crazed elephant drunk on wine can be subdued either by a hook or with a crowd, there are two approaches at work here. The forms of the celestial palace and the deity purify two elements: the support and the supported. The first of these refers to the external universe and the second to the physical body; the existence of both of these is based on various habitual patterns. The next method puts to rest the mind's tendency to engage outer objects and consists of planting the stake of profound meditative absorption.

This approach allows one to connect with the essence of purification, perfection, and maturation. To elaborate, since it parallels the features of saṃsāra, existence is purified and refined away. Since it parallels the way nirvāṇa is, the result is perfected in the ground. And finally, both of these mature one for the completion stage. This general understanding is of crucial importance.

The extensive mode of development involves generating the five manifestations of enlightenment. In this context, a threefold division is made: 1) the manifestation of enlightenment of the ground, 2) the manifestation of enlightenment on the path, and 3) the manifestation of enlightenment of the fruition. The first of these relates to the basis of purification, the essential nature of saṃsāra. The second concerns the process of purification, where one exerts oneself on the path and develops this in one's own being. Third is the result of purification, the state of having actualized the result that culminates from this process. Although there are three divisions, in reality these are none other than the luminosity of the four emptinesses and their accompanying union. As such, they encompass the main points of all the paths of Secret Mantra.

Ordinary body, speech, and mind, along with the collections (or, said differently, the white and red elements and the energetic-mind, along with their collections) are inherently enlightened. In essence, they are the five wisdoms. This is the manifestation of enlightenment at the time of the ground.

Symbolic wisdom is associated with the path of accumulation and the path of joining, whereas the actualization of true luminosity involves the fourfold emptiness and its accompanying unification that occur on the path of seeing and the path of cultivation. These factors are produced in one's state of being via the development and completion stages. In the former, one meditates on five factors—the moon, sun, and so on. The latter involves the five wisdoms associated with the penetration of the vital points of the white and red essences and the energetic-mind. This process comprises the manifestation of enlightenment on the path.

Once one attains the fruition of this process, the white element is naturally present as vajra body, the red element as vajra speech, and the aware consciousness as vajra mind. Thus, one arises as the embodiment of the awakened mind—dharmakāya wisdom, the luminosity of the final fruition. The dharmakāya, in turn, is inseparable from the sambhogakāya, which embodies the ocean of signs, marks, and positive qualities. This is the unified state beyond training, the manifestation of enlightenment of the fruition.

The bases of purification in this process are the extremely subtle white and red essences, along with the energetic-mind. When these are in an impure state, they form the basis of our ordinary body, speech, and mind. They are also subtle factors that obscure the three appearances and hinder the perfection of true luminosity as it really is. The Vajrayāna path alone is taught to be the antidote to these factors. This is why it is taught that the sole path to journey is that of Secret Mantra.

Once the connection between the basis of purification, the process of purification, and the result of purification is made and thoroughly understood, one will have come to know all of the unique points of the Vajrayāna path.

B. The Three Absorptions

When first starting out, development stage practice is accessed via the three absorptions: the absorption of suchness, the absorption of total illumination, and the causal absorption. The essence of the absorption of suchness is as follows. In and of itself, the mind does not depend on any basis; there is no root from which it grows. It does not exist in any ontological extreme: it is not male, female, or neuter; nor does it have color, structure, or shape. Yet since it is luminous by nature, it is not a blank nothingness either. By calling to mind the wisdom of reality as it truly is, the state of death is purified into the dharmakāya. The belief that things are permanent is purified as well, as is the formless realm. Hence, it is known as the absorption of suchness.

The absorption of total illumination derives its name from the fact that the natural radiance of this great, empty luminosity is an impartial and unified compassion towards all beings. This liberates one from both nihilistic views and the form realm. Furthermore, the inconceivable expressive potential of this pervasive wisdom sets the stage for the intermediate state being perfected into the sambhogakāya.

Out of this, awareness itself then appears in the form of a syllable, such as ĀḤ, HŪṂ, or HRĪḤ, a process known as the "causal method" and "root method." This is the causal absorption, which purifies the consciousness present the moment one's existence is about to enter a new abode. It also purifies the desire realm and matures birth into the nirmāṇakāya.

C. Developing the Supportive and the Supported Maṇḍalas

Having laid the groundwork for the development stage with these three absorptions, one can then go on to develop the support and supported. The exact nature of this process is laid out in the Nyingma School of the Early Translations' vast collection of tantras on the triad of development, completion, and great perfection, such as the *Glorious Secret Essence*. In this approach, the causal or root method leads to the foundational method—the visualization of the celestial palace and throne. This, in turn, leads to the inconceivable method of meditating on the entire supported maṇḍala.

There is agreement, moreover, that meditating on the form of the celestial palace in boundless space allows the impure nature of one's ordinary environment to be blessed as Akaniṣṭha. The factors that make this essential link between the ground, path, and fruition and purity are the thirty-seven factors of enlightenment. The nature of this relationship is taught in the ninth chapter of the *Great Chariot.*

Here, however, we will concern ourselves primarily with the stages of visualizing the supported deity, linking the manner in which the vajra body comes into existence with the development stage. This process purifies the object of purification. The *Heruka Galpo Tantra* explains:

> First, emptiness and the awakened mind,
> Second, the occurrence of the seed,
> Third, the complete form,
> Fourth, setting out the syllable . . .

As implied in this passage, death and the intermediate state are purified by emptiness and the awakened mind. Consciousness, in the form of a disembodied spirit that is about to take rebirth and enter in between the semen and ovum, is purified by the coalescence of the seed syllable. The body then gradually develops, precipitated by the ten energies. This process is purified by the complete form. Once born, the senses awaken to their objects. This, in turn, is purified by the placement of the seed syllable and so forth. The particular explanation given here relates to the symbols of the four manifestations of enlightenment.

In this context, however, the explanation will be made from a gradualist perspective and will fit with the general view of the Collected Tantras. According to the father tantras, development occurs via the ritual of the three vajras, while according to the mother tantras, this occurs via the five manifestations of enlightenment. In both of these traditions, the basis of purification is linked with the purity of the process of purification.

> This second section addresses the three absorptions, an approach unique to the explanatory system of the Nyingma School of the Early Translations. In other systems, nothing occurs aside from developing the intermediate state once the accumulation of wisdom has been gathered. In this tradition, however, it is taught that the core of emptiness

is compassion, and that the momentum ensuing from this union leads one to arise as a divine emanation with a body, face, and arms, and to accomplish the welfare of others via the four kinds of enlightened activity. This is the unmistaken path of the Great Vehicle, the union of the two accumulations.

In the context of one's impure saṃsāric existence, one will not be able to enter the womb unless craving and grasping sustain the karma that propels one to a future rebirth. If this karma is sustained, however, conception will take place. Similarly, when sustained with the momentum of great compassion, one will take hold of the birth of the maṇḍala deities that arise out of the state of luminous emptiness. This accords with the object of purification in the saṃsāric context. It also accords with what occurs in the context of the culminating fruition of this process. At that point, nonconceptual compassion takes on an embodied form out of the dharmakāya and works for the benefit of the infinite number of sentient beings.

So long as you do not lose sight of the elixir of emptiness and compassion, there is no chance that the development stage will end up reinforcing your ordinary state of being. By meditating in accordance with the path of definitive perfection, stability will be attained in the absorption of suchness. With this stability, development and completion will be in union and the genuine completion stage, which the master Buddha Jñānapāda describes as nondual profundity and clarity, will arise in your state of being. Jñānapāda advocated a meditation in which the development stage is sealed with the completion stage. Although it is said that earlier masters did not understand this point, it does accord with the unique way this topic is presented in the Nyingma School of the Early Translations.

When meditating on the three absorptions according to the path of definitive perfection, those who have received empowerment and maintained their samaya vows should first be introduced to the true nature of the view. The next step is to gain conviction in this view by relying upon logical reasoning. One should then settle the mind calmly and naturally in a state of uncontrived simplicity through one of two methods, either by resting subsequent to insight or resting in the immediacy of complete awareness. This allows one to cut the flow of shifting memories and thoughts and settle free from the faults of dullness and agitation. Familiarizing oneself with this state will bring the energetic-mind into the central channel. The visible appearance of the ten signs will reach a state of perfection and, at best, one will even be able to generate the symbolic wisdom that relies upon the three appearances.

Even if this is not the case, you can train the mind by stabilizing the understanding that emptiness is free of conceptual complexities. Then, once you no longer lose sight of this understanding, you will see that saṃsāra appears but does not exist. You can then cultivate an illusory, fixation-free compassion that pervades all of space. By familiarizing yourself with this, when the mind is fixed on emptiness a sense of compassion will effortlessly arise towards all the sentient beings who do not realize this, towards those who are duped by appearances that do not actually exist. Then, even when meditating on compassion, you will not make the mistake of solidifying self and other. Instead, a certainty will arise about emptiness, about the fact that appearances are inter-dependently arisen and illusory; that they have no truly established nature.

Familiarizing yourself with emptiness that has compassion at its core is the key point of the first two absorptions—the absorption of suchness and the absorption of total illumination. For this reason, being bereft of either one of these will leave you powerless to achieve perfect enlightenment. It should, therefore, go without saying what will happen if you have neither. As Saraha wrote, "Without compassion, the view of emptiness will not enable you to find the supreme path. If you meditate only on compassion, however, how will you ever be liberated from saṃsāra?" These two factors are what transform the development stage into the path of the Great Vehicle. Any development stage that does not have these two, in contrast, is no different than that of the non-Buddhists.

This emptiness with compassion at its core expresses itself as ĀḤ, HŪṂ, HRĪḤ and other causal seed syllables. Once you have meditated on such syllables and become familiar with them, you will be able to settle into a meditative state for as long as you wish. When you are able to do this, you can use the occasion to emanate incalculable numbers of syllables, such that they fill the extent of space. Then gather them back into the initial seed syllable and settle into a meditative state. You should continue training in these practices until the eight measures of clarity and stability have been attained. This process is known as "training in the subtle syllable." Being familiar with this process alone will enable you to attain all the mundane spiritual accomplishments and signs of achievement.

If you are not capable of meditating on the three absorptions in accordance with the path of definitive perfection, you can take the approach of devoted training instead. If this is the case, the various aspects of the ritual should be completed at the beginning of every practice session. Do not be content to just mouth the words! Instead, relax from within and settle into a meditative state until the absorption of suchness and the absorption of total illumination are complete. Then, meditate step-by-step on the causal absorption and the other stages of practice. Until your development stage practice is firmly rooted in the primary elements of practice—emptiness and compassion—recitation, projection and absorption, and other such factors should not be made a priority.

Whether you meditate using the approach of devoted training or definitive perfection, you should meditate on the three absorptions as being inseparable from one another whenever the development stage is practiced. Practicing them sporadically is insufficient. To use an example, when one paints a picture on a wall, the wall functions as the basis for the painting because if it is not there, there will be nothing to paint on. But even if there is a wall, if it has not been plastered one will not be able to paint on it. The plaster, for this reason, is the painting's cooperative condition. Even when the painting is complete, the wall, the painting, and the plaster are all still there. In the same way, even as one meditates on the complete maṇḍala circle that arises out of the causal absorption, it is the expression of emptiness and compassion that arises as the deity. As this is the case, these three need to be practiced as a unity.

Still, if you have not purified ordinary appearances into emptiness, how could you possibly meditate on the maṇḍala circle? The fact that all phenomena *are* emptiness, that saṃsāra and nirvāṇa are inseparable, is the very reason we are able to actualize this by meditating on the maṇḍala circle. In other words, emptiness is the basis for the development stage. As it is said, "For the one to whom emptiness is possible, anything is possible." If all phenomena were not empty and ordinary appearances were truly present, development stage meditation would be impossible, as the following quotation points out: "Even though one might empower wheat to be rice, rice won't actually appear."

However, even if all phenomena are realized to be empty in this way, without the momentum of great compassion you will not be able to manifest the rūpakāyas to benefit others. This is similar to the listeners and solitary buddhas, who enter into a state of cessation and do not benefit others with rūpakāya emanations.

Once one understands this point, it will be like the following saying: "All these phenomena are like an illusion and birth is like taking a stroll in a park . . ." Said differently, one will no longer dwell in existence, while through compassion, one will not get caught up in a state of peace either. This is the great, universal path of the offspring of the victorious ones. For all these reasons, making sure the three absorptions are not isolated from one another is a vitally important point.

These days, most of those who have a bit of experience with the development stage harbor anger on their deathbed. Consequently, they end up reborn in the realm of the Lord of Death, a deviation that results in their becoming demons and bringing harm to sentient beings. The reason for this is that such individuals did not habituate themselves to emptiness with compassion at its core. There are many people who have an intellectual understanding of emptiness, are able to visualize clearly in the development stage, and have completed sets of mantra recitation, yet who can still be seen to end up reborn as demons. On the other hand, you will never see a vicious ghoul in possession of the elixir of great compassion!

a. The Ritual of the Three Vajras

Symbolic implements such as the five-pronged vajra purify the mind. By meditating vividly on their form, the object of the purificatory process, the mind, is purified into vajra mind. Similarly, ordinary speech, the object of purification, is perfected into vajra speech. The process of purification in this case consists of transforming these symbolic implements or marking them with syllables such as hūṃ in one's meditation. The next step in the process of purification involves the ritual projection and absorption of light rays, which enacts the twofold benefit, as well as the subsequent transformation into the deity's form, complete with all its adornments and attire. This meditation matures the body, which is the object of purification in this case, into the vajra body. These steps make up the ritual of the three vajras.

These three can also be applied to the process of womb birth. The first stage purifies the merging of the red and white elements and subsequent entrance of the intermediate state consciousness. The second stage purifies the fivefold process of uterine development, which includes the oval shape and other stages that occur after the convergence of semen, ovum, and consciousness. The third stage purifies birth, which occurs once the hitherto scattered elements have coalesced and the body and senses are fully formed.

This process also sets the stage for what happens once the fruition has been attained. An interdependent link is created with certain deeds that are manifested by the tathāgatas. Specifically, this refers to the enlightened deeds of entering the womb of the vajra queen, taking birth, and so on, which are manifested by buddhas once they have taken on a nirmāṇakāya form to tame beings with whatever means are necessary.

b. The Five Manifestations of Enlightenment

In this discussion, we will combine Yoga Tantra's five outer manifestations of enlightenment with the five inner manifestations of enlightenment taught in the Mahāyoga tradition, linking the cause with the way the fruition comes into being. The *Tantra of the Clear Expanse* explains:

> Conception is related to the five manifestations of enlightenment,
> The ten months to the way the ten levels unfold,
> And birth to the natural nirmāṇakāya—
> The spontaneous three kāyas embodied.

As indicated here, the period that begins with the intermediate state and continues to the point where one seeks a physical body relates to the path of accumulation, while actually taking on a physical form in the womb relates to the path of joining. The period from conception on is posited as the path of seeing and the path of cultivation. In essence, the ten months represent the ten levels, which lead to the accomplishment of the natural nirmāṇakāya, the unified state beyond training.

Here, we shall link the definitive process of purification, perfection, and maturation with the various stages of the four types of birth. The first manifestation of enlightenment is the moon disc. This purifies and refines away the following objects of purification: the form aggregate, the element of space, the body and the all-ground consciousness, afflictive ignorance, the semen associated with womb birth, the moisture associated with heat-moisture birth, the male associated with egg birth, the empty aspect of miraculous birth, and so on. In the context of the completion stage, the sixteen joys descend and the first wisdom, discerning realization, manifests as the nature of skillful means. In other words, the mind is perfected into its essence. When this is given form on the path, one meditates that it transforms into a moon disc. In the context of the fruition, this matures into the thirty-two excellent marks and complete enlightenment as mirrorlike wisdom.

The second manifestation of enlightenment is the sun disc. This purifies and refines away the following objects of purification: the aggregate of sensation, the earth element, the afflicted consciousness, greed and pride, the red female element associated with womb birth, the female associated with egg birth, the heat associated with heat-moisture birth, the clarity aspect of miraculous birth, and so on. During the completion stage, the egg and semen are completely refined away, being in essence coemergent bliss-emptiness. This involves a process of ascending stabilization—the nature of knowledge. The twenty elements (form and the rest of the five aggregates each divided in terms of the four elements, making twenty) arise as the twenty emptinesses (the wisdom of the basic space of phenomena and the rest of the five wisdoms linked with each of the four immeasurables, making twenty) and are perfected as awakened mind, the second wisdom. This is then given form on the path by meditating that it transforms into a sun disc. This, in turn, leads to the maturation of the eighty excellent minor marks that occurs during the state of fruition, and to complete enlightenment as the wisdom of equality.

The third manifestation of enlightenment is the seed syllable and symbolic implement. This purifies and refines away the following: the entrance of the intermediate state consciousness (the disembodied perpetuating mind) between the semen and ovum, the aggregate of perception, the fire element, speech, the mental consciousness, afflictive desire, and the intermediate state consciousness that engages in any of the four types of birth. In the context of the completion stage, the semen and ovum reverse course and are purified, after which the karmic energies and daily cycles cease. This perfects them into the third wisdom, that of vajra stability. Giving this form on the path, one meditates that it transforms into the seed syllable and symbolic implements. At the time of the fruition, this matures into the nature of a realization of the distinct character of all phenomena, and leads to complete enlightenment as discerning wisdom.

The fourth manifestation of enlightenment is the blending of the seed syllable and symbolic implement into one taste. This purifies and refines away the following factors: the blending of semen, ovum, and consciousness into one taste, the aggregate of formative factors, the air element, the five active sense consciousnesses, afflictive envy, and (concerning the four types of birth) the merging of the intermediate state consciousness, semen, and ovum associated with womb and egg birth, the merging of consciousness, moisture, and heat that occurs in heat-moisture birth, and the merging of the mere empty clarity of the miraculous birth with the intermediate state consciousness. In the context of the completion stage, the functioning of the semen, ovum, and energies is thoroughly purified. The essence of the causal vajra holder is perfected, as is the fourth wisdom, vajra nature, which involves the comprehension of all that exists and pervades everything that can be known. This is given form on the path by visualizing the essence of this merging being transformed into a sphere or ball of light. At the time of fruition, it matures and is embodied as the activities of all the buddhas merging together into a single taste, and leads to complete enlightenment as all-accomplishing wisdom.

The fifth manifestation of enlightenment is the complete form that ensues from this process. It purifies and refines away the following factors: the completion of the gestation period (which culminates in birth), the aggregate of consciousness, the water element, the aspect of grasping at the reality of the eightfold collection, the mental consciousness, afflictive anger, and the state in which the physical sense fields associated with taking birth in one of the four ways are fully developed. These are refined away and purified into the natural nirmāṇakāya.

The way in which this proceeds and matures into the completion stage is as follows. The semen, ovum, and subtle energetic-mind are perfected into their utterly pure essence. In addition, the resultant vajra holder and the fifth wisdom, the embodiment of the tathāgatas, are perfected in one's being. The latter refers to the fruitional state of complete liberation—the natural buddha wisdom that realizes the way things really are. This is then given form on the path by meditating on the complete form of the deity, along with its adornments and attire. At the time of fruition, it matures into the indivisible nature of the wisdom-expanse, which is free of all obscurations, and leads to complete enlightenment as the wisdom of the basic space of phenomena. A tantra states:

> The moon is mirrorlike wisdom,
> The seven of seven, equality.
> Discernment is said to be the deity's
> Seed syllable and symbolic implements.

All becoming one is perseverance itself,
And perfection, the pure expanse of reality.

Though there are four ways to meditate on the development stage, each linked with the four types of birth, these need to be applied in such a way that they match the individual's predominant habitual patterns and their degree of familiarization with the practice. The lord of victorious ones, Longchenpa, wrote:

Though there are four ways to meditate, you should use
The one that addresses the type of birth that predominates.
To purify habitual patterns, meditate accordingly using them all.
In particular, meditate in harmony with egg birth as a beginner,
And when this is somewhat stable, with womb birth.
Once very stable, meditate in harmony with heat-moisture birth,
And when completely habituated, use this true stability
To develop instantaneously, in harmony with miraculous birth.

II

THE UNDELUDED CONDITION:

THE PATH OF MEDITATION

This section contains two main topics: 1) a detailed explanation that addresses how to train on this path from the ground up according to one's capacity and 2) an outline of the way the results of the path, structured around the four divisions of approach and accomplishment, are linked with the states of the four knowledge holders.

A. Training on the Path According to One's Capacity

The first section contains seven further divisions:

1) Focusing the mind on the deity
2) Correcting flaws that involve change
3) Parting from the deity
4) Bringing the deity onto the path
5) Merging your mind with the deity
6) Connecting the deity with reality
7) Bringing experiences onto the path

1. Focusing the Mind on the Deity

Those with superior mental capacity should refine their ability by practicing the development stage without any sense of clinging or fixation. In this approach, the appearance of the deity and its ornaments are visualized in such a way that they are totally complete, vivid, and distinct from the very beginning. This is the form of great wisdom, the union of development and completion. Beyond being an identifiable entity with a precise nature, it appears clearly yet is devoid of any essence. In other words, clarity and emptiness are indivisible. Like the reflection of the moon in a lake, its very nature is to appear in a distinct manner, down to the pupils of the eyes, while in reality it is empty.

Those with moderate mental capacity should begin their meditation with a sudden recollection of the deity's complete appearance. The next step is to meditate on the clear appearance of the head, and, once this is stable, to then meditate progressively on the right arm, left arm, torso, right and left legs, and finally on the complete form of the deity and its seat. Training in the development stage of illusory clear appearance keeps one from straying into the view of nihilism. When one grows weary of this, the practitioner should recollect purity and refine his or her ability in the essence of this process, the vajralike absorption. This key point keeps one from straying into the belief in permanence.

For beginners with less mental capacity, it may be difficult to visualize in either of these ways. When not yet familiar with this process, one's ability should be refined using a permanent form. Take a consecrated and well-formed representation of the yidam deity, such as a painting or clay statue made by a skilled artisan, and place it before you. Without intentionally meditating, look directly at it from top to bottom without blinking. This is referred to as *the auxiliary practice of setting mindfulness into motion.* At first, the agitated movement of conditioned thought patterns will be experienced. This is the *experience of movement*, which is said to be "like water cascading off a cliff."

At a certain point, though, this will change as the habitual pattern related to the deity's appearance evolves. Once this happens, its appearance will appear vividly as an object in your mind, even when you close your eyes. This is referred to as the *experience of attainment*, which is likened to a thief getting hold of something that is hidden within a container. In other words, at this point one does not actually know the deity's nature as it really is.

Visualizing in this manner will seal your fixation on ordinary appearances. The visualization should not be flat like a painting or protruding and obstructive like a relief. It should be an illusory figure, an empty appearance free of all corporeality, without any flesh, bones, or entrails. You can refine your ability in this process by considering the examples of an immaculate crystal vase and a rainbow, which are completely transparent, brilliant, and luminous. The visualization should be like the reflection in a mirror.

At the beginning, take the form you are using as a support for the visualization and look at it for a long time, meditating only for short periods. As your visualization becomes clearer, you can gradually decrease the amount of time you spend looking at the form and lengthen your periods of meditation.

2. Correcting Flaws That Involve Change

There are seven general flaws that can arise at this point: 1) forgetting the focal point, 2) laziness, 3) doubting one's ability to succeed, 4) dullness, 5) agitation, 6) overexertion (not being satisfied even though the deity appears clearly), and 7) underexertion (resting indifferently even though the visualization is unclear). There are also twelve flaws that involve changes in the visualization: 1) haziness, 2) vagueness, 3) shadowy darkness, 4) changes in size, 5) changes in appearance, 6) changes in shape, 7) changes in number, 8) changes in position, 9) appearing only as color, 10) appearing only as shape, 11) gradual disappearance, and 12) incomplete appearance.

The antidotes to these flaws are as follows. To remedy forgetfulness, stabilize mindfulness. If you succumb to laziness, cultivate faith and diligence. When in doubt, focus on basic space, and stay in a bright, cool place if you feel dull. In the case of agitation, generate a sense of disillusionment and direct your gaze downwards. If you overexert yourself, relax your mind, and if the problem is underexertion, be diligent. Similarly, if your visualization happens to be hazy, vague, or shady, hold a crystal in front of your eyes. Then look at the meditation support and examine its shape. Once you've done that, visualize it in your mind.

If, on the other hand, the size of the body, its appearance, posture, or shape are fluctuating, there are various things you can do. You can meditate that the deity's body is huge and solid, that deer are frolicking on its arms, legs, fingers, and toes and that pigeons are flying in and out of its nostrils. In particular, with peaceful deities these problems can be eliminated by visualizing the deity as having a nature endowed with nine traits. On this point, the *Awesome Flash of Lightning* states:

> Each of their supreme forms
> Possesses nine traits.
> They are soft, well-proportioned,
> Firm, supple, and youthful;
> Clear, radiant, attractive,
> And blazing with intense presence.

Wrathful figures should be visualized as having the nine expressions of the dance. As stated in the *Heruka Galpo Tantra*:

> Captivating, heroic, and terrifying;
> Laughing, ferocious, and fearful;
> Compassionate, intimidating, and tranquil;
> Assume these nine expressions of dance.

Continuing, the following passage from the *Guru of the Magical Web* addresses the problem of fluctuations in the number of deities:

> Even the many projections and absorptions of the divine assembly
> Are the great miraculous display of one's very own mind.

As stated here, you can refine your ability in this process by recalling how the forms in the retinue arise from the miraculous display of the sole main deity. On the other hand, if only color appears, then visualize the shape. If only shape appears, change it into various colors. When the visualization gradually fades away, meditate that the face and hands are completely solid and, if it is incomplete, focus on the visualization of whatever happens to be missing.

This topic is broken down into seven categories, the first of which is easy to understand. In the context of the second, however, we find twelve flaws that involve changes in the visualization. The first of these is *haziness*, referring to when the deity's appearance can barely be visualized and its complexion, face, hands, and other features are unclear. The next, *vagueness*, involves an ill-defined sense of the colors of the visualization. When this occurs, the white, red, blue, and other colors of the visualization are not as intense and overwhelming as they should be, like the clear, brilliant light of a thousand luminous suns. Instead, they are only vaguely white and vaguely red. It might also be that when you fix your mind on the visualized appearance of the deity, a *shadowy darkness* obstructs your mental perspective. Or, even if this doesn't happen, the appearance is hazy and trembling like a shadow or vague impression, in which case the thickness of the arms and legs and the width of the face and eyes do not appear distinctly.

Another problem that can occur involves *changes in the size* of the deity. You might visualize something the size of a small seed, for example, but when it appears it is the size of your thumb. It might also refer to the form of a peaceful or wrathful deity being out of proportion, as if it were based on an imprecise drawing. When *changes in appearance* take place, the nine expressions of the dance, the adornments of the peaceful deities, and other such factors are not as they should be in the visualization. Another problem occurs when the deity undergoes *changes in shape*, such as when you are visualizing a peaceful deity whose face is the shape of a mustard seed, but whose appearance ends up more like the shape of a magnetizing female deity. *Changes in number* occur when three faces become four or when many main deities appear rather than few. *Changes in position* involve shifts between the lotus, half-lotus, and other postures.

It may be that *only color* appears; in other words, differentiations in white, red, and the other colors are present, yet thickness and other characteristics relating to the shape of the visualization are unclear. It can also be the case that *only shape* appears, not color. When a *gradual disappearance* occurs, the visualization becomes progressively less and less clear even though you are not in the dissolution phase. *Incomplete appearance* occurs when you are able to visualize each of the heads, hands, main and subsidiary deities, and so on, but are unable to visualize them as a whole.

The nine traits of peaceful deities remedy these problems. The deity's form, face, arms, and so forth should be *soft*, not hard like bone or wood. They should be *well-proportioned*, with the thickness of their bodies gradually tapering at the waist. Their flesh should not be loose, but *firm*. They should be *supple* as well, in the sense that their joints and so forth are flexible. Their bodies should be healthy and their skin delicate, thus *youthful*. Their colors should be distinct and *clear* and they should be *radiant*, in terms of the boundless light they project. Their forms should also be majestic, beautified with the signs of superior beings, and, hence, *attractive*. Finally, they should have an *intense presence* that overwhelms everything with its splendor.

Wrathful deities have nine qualities as well. Their expression of desire should be *captivating*, their expression of anger *heroic*, and their expression of ignorance *terrifying*. These are their three physical expressions. They should be *laughing* out loud with expressions like "ha ha" and "hee hee." They should shout *ferocious* things like "Capture! Strike!" They should also be *fearsome*, with a voice like the roaring of a thousand rolls of thunder and a thousand bursts of lightning occur-

> ring in a single moment. These are their three verbal expressions. They should also be *compassionate*, taking ignorant beings and realms under their care; *intimidating*, as they subdue barbaric sentient beings with their wrath; and *peaceful*, in the sense that they experience everything as having the same taste within reality. These are the nine expressions of the dance.

3. Parting from the Deity

The third topic concerns what is referred to as "parting from the deity." In the intervals between these meditations, alternate periods of deity meditation with nonconceptual contemplation. This will relieve any sense of weariness you may have with the practice. Then once again meditate only on the deity, visualizing it in a flawless manner separate from nonconceptuality.

4. Bringing the Deity onto the Path

The fourth topic addresses how to bring the deity onto the path, in other words, how to refine your ability once you have become adept in these practices. Visualize the deity standing up, sitting, and lying down. Envision it standing on the crown of its head, on its back, face down, far away, close by, inside a mountain, in the depths of the ocean, massive like Mount Sumeru, and tiny like a speck of dust. If you are able to meditate in this way, you will have reached the "riverlike" *experience of familiarity*; you will have brought the deity onto the path.

5. Merging Your Mind with the Deity

The fifth topic is termed "merging your mind with the deity." To eliminate any dualistic fixation you may have on a meditator and a meditation, train by blending your mind indivisibly with the form of the deity. Once you are able to stay with the complete and perfect form of the deity for as long as you wish and remain uninterrupted by thoughts, you will have reached the mountainlike *experience of stability*.

Even beyond this, there will come a point when you are able to visualize the deity in great detail, down to the pores of its body and the pupils of its eyes; when you are not influenced by any circumstance whatsoever and can meditate day and night on any maṇḍala you choose. With this level of complete mastery, your ability will be perfected.

There are eight measures of clarity and stability that can be used to gauge whether or not this has occurred. The four measures of clarity are lucidity, clarity, vibrancy, and vividness. The four measures of stability are immutability, steadfastness, complete steadfastness, and complete malleability. Once these eight measures of clarity and stability have been attained, you will have reached the stage known as the *experience of perfection*. You will have merged appearances with the maṇḍala of the deity.

The third and fourth topics are easy to understand. In the fifth, we find the eight measures of clarity and stability. The first of these is *lucidity*, which refers to the appearance of whichever deity you meditate on being clear and distinct, down to the pupils in its eyes. The next measure is *clarity*, a state in which awareness has a sense of vitality—an experience of being clear, empty, and vividly awake, rather than dull and lacking clear awareness. If the deity you meditate on is just a dead, solid appearance and not the rainbowlike form it should be, every detail needs to be embraced by the wisdom of omniscience, down to the pores of its body and the strands of its hair. Once they are, hundreds of qualities related to the clear sense faculties will arise and be brilliantly present, thus *vibrant*. The form of the deity should also be intensely *vivid*. In other words, you should not have to think about it, inferring its presence and appearance. Instead, it should arise before your mind in a direct way, with striking clarity. These are the *four measures of clarity*.

Next are the *four measures of stability*. The first of these is *immutability*, which means that your meditation cannot be swayed by general flaws like forgetfulness and laziness. The second involves being *steadfast* in the face of the flaws that involve changes in the visualization, such as when it becomes hazy or vague. Once your visualization no longer occurs for only short periods of time, but can be maintained in a meditative state day and night without being disturbed by even the most subtle thoughts, it will be *totally steadfast*. Finally, when you meditate on factors such as the deity's complexion, face and hands, movements, and the projection and absorption of light rays, and everything comes out just as it's supposed to, your practice has become *completely malleable*.

Generally speaking, the ability to remain clear and composed when you practice deity meditation is a positive quality. Nevertheless, regardless of whether the deity's form is somewhat unclear when you meditate or brilliantly clear even when you do not, it is a mistake to become attached to the visualization. Therefore, once you have familiarized yourself with the clear appearance of the visualization, you must train in the dissolution stage.

These days, most people do not practice the dissolution stage except as a brief conclusion to their session. They say all sorts of things, like "you should never lose sight of the three maṇḍalas, so don't do the dissolution stage." This only shows that not only have they not even partially understood the unique key points of development and completion, they don't even see the conceptual fixation they have towards the sublime deity as a mistake! As far as the teachings go, this is an obvious sign of ignorance. For this very reason the dissolution stage is taught.

The dissolution stage purifies the habitual patterns associated with death and establishes a causal link with the dharmakāya. On the path of the completion stage the illusory body dissolves into luminosity. Not only does the dissolution stage mature the practitioner for this stage of practice, but also for the act of penetrating the vital points of the vajra body and bringing the channels, energies, and essences into the central channel. Generally speaking, it is this alone that gives rise to all the enlightened qualities of the Vajrayāna path.

Whether you have developed the symbolic or the true luminosity in your own state of being, there are ten signs that appear once the elements have successively dissolved, while out of the natural dissolution stage the luminosity of the three appearances arises. Once this occurs, all ordinary confused appearances recede into the expanse and the three appearances dissolve into luminosity. This is an occasion that sees only the arising of reality, wisdom free of conceptual complexity.

As this is the case, certain individuals should stress the dissolution stage more than the development stage. This holds for those who wish to apply themselves to virtuous pursuits at night during the states of deep sleep and dreams, and likewise for those who are inclined towards daytime practices that bring the energetic-mind into the central channel. Those who wish to practice the unique completion stage practices that actualize the illusory body and luminosity should also stress the dissolution stage, as should those who want to arise in the divine form of the unified path of training once they have cast their ordinary body aside. This also applies to individuals who desire the culmination of this process, the actualization of the unified state beyond training. This state is brought about by dissolving the mental body, which is grounded in the habitual patterns of ignorance, into luminosity. Finally, there are also those who end up not being liberated in this lifetime and who wish to arise in the unified form of the sambhogakāya by resting in the luminosity of the first intermediate state, the realization of the dharmakāya. These individuals as well should emphasize the dissolution phase more than the development stage.

Alternatively, there may be those whose only wish is to accomplish minor activities like subduing spirits and granting protection. To this end, such individuals focus solely on the visualized appearance of the yidam deity and the projection and absorption of light rays. Such individuals may feel content with their visualizations and the feelings of pride they engender, but this approach is no different than that of the non-Buddhists. In the end, they will experience the consequences of their negative acts.

"That may be the case," some might object, "but what's the point of mixing up our terminology with that of the New Schools, using terms like 'illusory body' and 'luminosity.'"

What an embarrassment to say such things! These are Nyingma followers who have not even seen certain classes of Tantra, such as the *Tantra of the Perfect Secret* and the *Heruka Galpo Tantra.* Such people know nothing about the general texts associated with the practices of the three inner tantras!

Nevertheless, it *is* said that the unique feature of the Nyingma School of the Early Translations is the assertion that the stronghold of realization is seized from within the expanse of the vajra peak, the pinnacle of all vehicles. In making such a claim, what is meant is that you should abandon all forms of mental busyness, even those of the development stage and the other ten natures. In other words, you should rest in the naked openness of empty awareness, as taught by Drime Özer in the *Treasury of Precious Reality*. Follow in the footsteps of this perfect buddha and I will rejoice!

6. Connecting the Deity with Reality

You should not be satisfied with just merging your mind with the deity. To connect the deity with its true nature you must realize that it is your own mind, with its eightfold collection of consciousnesses, that arises as the form and wisdom of the deity. In its innate state, awareness itself is the awakened mind, the fruitional form of the deity. Once manifold, these are matured into a single taste via the union of the development and completion stages—the great form of wisdom.

a. The Four Stakes That Bind the Life-Force

If this point is not grasped, however, the development stage will do nothing more than form habitual patterns reinforcing your ordinary state of being. You will turn your back on the path of liberation and your attainment will amount to nothing more than becoming an evil spirit or demon like Rudra! This is why the four stakes that bind the life-force are taught to be of such vital importance. The thirty-ninth chapter of the *Tantra of the Perfect Secret* explains:

> Whether wisdom or mundane, if the four stakes
> That bind the life-force are not planted,
> Practice will never be fruitful, like running in place.
> The way to capture the life-force of all glorious ones
> Is to understand one point and attain the life-force of all.
> Just as Rāhula swallows the sun out of the sky
> And, without having to catch its reflection in a thousand ponds,
> Attains the life-force of them all,
> The four stakes that bind the life-force are essential.

The stake of absorption allows the intense clinging we have towards our ordinary body to be perfected into the form of a deity. This occurs by focusing one-pointedly on a divine form, such as the support you are using for the visualization, and then familiarizing yourself with it. The tantra states:

> As the stake of absorption, focus the mind one-pointedly
> On the form on a skull cup and do not wander.
> Master the three objects and meet
> The Great Glorious One face to face.
> Otherwise, the heruka will not be experienced.
> Without the stake of constant absorption
> One will never see the enlightened form.

The three objects are mastered in the following way. First, the deity is clearly present as an object of thought, then clearly present as an object that can be seen, and finally clearly present as an object that can be touched. This deity is mind matured into the divine form, the meeting of which is termed "perfect visualization." The *Advice of the Great Glorious One* states:

> All the forms of wisdom deities
> Are first clear as an object of mind.
> The strength of their actual appearance will then develop,
> And then, through the strength of completely purifying mind itself,
> Their nature will appear as an object of the senses.
> Finally, the two truths inseparable,
> The complete pliancy of body and mind will be attained
> And the deity will become manifest, clear as a tangible object.
> Once you have mastered the three objects,
> You will conquer the manifest appearance of the impure body!

For *the stake of the essence mantra,* focus one-pointedly as the root mantra either circles the spiritual life-force or spins back and forth. Then, as you count the mantra, the exhalation, inhalation, and resting of the breath are purified into their essence, enlightened speech. The same tantra states:

> As the stake of the essence mantra, recite the mantra
> Of the main deity of the whole assembly
> As the root mantra encircles the spiritual life-force HŪṂ.
> Visualize projecting and absorbing, and count the life-force mantra.
> At that time, glory, prosperity, and prophecy will manifest.
> The potential power will be perfected and deities will gather.
> Without perfecting approach via the stake of the essential life-force,
> The deities and oath-bound will not be attracted.

Third is *the stake of unchanging realization.* No matter how you practice, whether with the Great Glorious One or any other peaceful or wrathful deity, you must realize that the deity is none other than your own mind. With this realization, the deity will mature into its very essence, becoming of one taste with reality; the two will become a great equality. The tantra explains:

As the stake of unchanging realization, the Great Glorious One
And the whole range of peaceful and wrathful deities
Are none other than one's own mind.
Even Rudra is the mind and is nowhere else.
In being empty, mind itself is dharmakāya.
In being clear and distinct, it is sambhogakāya.
And appearing naturally in a variety of ways, it is nirmāṇakāya.
Appearances are the male consort and emptiness the female;
The union of appearance and emptiness is wisdom's form.
The limitless thoughts and memories as well
Are completely perfect, the retinue of the Glorious One.
They are inconceivable and enlightened right from the start,
As they never move from this very nature.
Without the stake of unchanging realization,
Accomplishing the Great Glorious One
Will not bring supreme accomplishments,
Only the ordinary, and one will end up like Rudra.

Fourth is *the stake of projection and absorption*. This great miraculous display involves mastering each of the four types of enlightened activity. It is as essential as white borax is for the task of alchemy. The tantra explains further:

In the stake of projection and absorption
Visualization is used to transform.
Knowing this, all desires will be fulfilled.
Through visualizing projection and absorption,
The mind's potential is brought to perfection
And whatever one imagines will appear.
By the power of the blessings of mantra and mudrā,
All activities, beneficial and harmful, will be accomplished,
Whether pacifying, enriching, magnetizing, or wrathful,
Just as making prayers and offerings to a single jewel
Creates the circumstances for the fulfillment of every wish.
If the nail of the various projections and absorptions is lacking,
A single focus will not accomplish one's goal.
But if you know how to shift between projection and absorption,
Then even the lowest tedrang spirit
Will have unhindered activity and accomplish all deeds,
For everything is the mind's miraculous creation!

Once the main points of these instructions on the four stakes have been internalized, enlightened form will be directly perceived and you will rob its life-force away. Accomplish true speech and you will seize the life-force of enlightened speech. And once reality itself is mastered, you will grasp the life-force of the awakened mind. Your own three gates will merge with the enlightened body, speech, and mind of the peaceful and wrathful sugatas, the manifold becoming one taste. Do this and you will attain the thousandfold life-force of all saṃsāra and nirvāṇa. You will refine the innate potential of wisdom and master the various forms of enlightened activity.

The fifth topic is clearly explained. The sixth topic concerns connecting the deity with reality, which is also referred to as "enhancing the development stage" and "connecting through the activity of the proximate cause." Practicing the essential points of the development stage meditation as outlined above entails engaging in yogic practices that involve specific time periods and numbers. This allows one to transcend worldly paths and connect directly with the path of seeing, the supreme spiritual accomplishment of the great seal. This is what is meant by the term "transcending with conduct."

In the *Excellent Chariot* it is said that however sublime a path such as the development stage may be, it will not bring liberation on its own; other factors such as enhancement practices are still necessary. Thus, though you may have mastered the eight measures of clarity and stability on the path of the development stage, if you do not utilize the key instructions on the four stakes that bind the life-force to enhance this through conduct, it will be next to impossible to attain the result of this process, the state of a knowledge holder.

Therefore, in the context of connecting the deity with reality, you should meditate on the path of definitive perfection. Familiarize yourself with the various stages, from the great emptiness of the absorption of suchness up to the complete maṇḍala circle in its elaborate form, and gain mastery over the eight measures of clarity and stability. This is called "the path with definite periods and numbers for practice." As the saying goes, "One will gain mastery and attain the supreme class within six, fourteen, or sixteen months." Thus, with transformative rituals, it is simply impossible not to attain the level of a knowledge holder within six months.

Even should this not be possible, it is said that those who take devoted training as their path also need to have a clear objective for the teachings they engage in. This type of practitioner first develops a correct understanding of key points concerning development and completion and then, from the outset, links their practice with approach and accomplishment by relying upon the key instructions of the four stakes that bind the life-force. In this way, the various qualities take birth in one's being according to the mental aptitude of the individual.

Anything other than this, however, is tantamount to turning one's back on the main points of development and completion. Just calling one's practice "approach and accomplishment" and staying in retreat for years will produce nothing but hardship. Completing hundreds of millions of mantras will not even bring the warmth of the ordinary qualities that mark one's progress on the path! In other words, if the essential points of the path are not taken into account, perseverance will amount to nothing more than chasing a mirage.

In the context of the stake of absorption on the deity, there is mention of "mastering the three objects." The text reads, "First, clearly present as an object of thought, then clearly present as an object that can be seen, and finally clearly present as an object that can be touched." This can be stated differently by saying, "First, clearly present as an object of the mind, then clearly present as an object of the senses, and finally, clearly present as an object of the body."

At the beginning, you will have yet to gain familiarity with the appearance of the deity. At this point, you are the deity only in a conceptual or verbal sense. The deity, in other words, is clear from the perspective of the analytic mind and one must entertain thoughts about it being a particular way. This is termed "clearly present as an object of thought" and "clearly present as an object of the mind."

When you then familiarize yourself with the deity's appearance and gain some stability in this process, you will no longer have to seal your meditation with the thoughts you entertained in the previous stage. Instead, it will be as if the deity is visible to a fully functioning eye faculty. Without losing sight of the elixir of thought-free calm abiding, the appearances of your visualization will be distinct, down to the pupils of the deity's eyes. This is what is meant by the phrases "clearly present as an object that can be seen" and "clearly present as an object of the senses."

At the end of this process the development stage will be mastered. Once you have attained the state of a matured knowledge holder, you will no longer experience ordinary, impure appearances; they will have merged with the maṇḍala of the deity. At this point, the illusory body, the unified form of the deity, will be actualized. This is referred to with the phrases "clearly present as an object that can be touched" and "clearly present as an object of the body."

The instructions on the four stakes that bind the life-force are key points that will allow you to master the thousandfold life-force of saṃsāra and nirvāṇa. These essential points inextricably link the ordinary body, speech, mind, and activities that we experience in the context of saṃsāra with the enlightened body, speech, mind, and activities associated with buddhahood, binding their life-force as a stake would. Once familiar with these points, you will gain complete mastery over saṃsāra and nirvāṇa and your impure body, speech, and mind will be purified, transforming into enlightened body, speech, and mind. From that very moment, you will carry out the works of a buddha via the four types of inconceivable enlightened activities—pacifying, enriching, magnetizing, and wrathful. Hence, the four stakes that bind the life-force contain the essential key points of the development stage path.

Paths devoid of these principles, it is said, are like "running in place," which means that such activities produce only fatigue. The truth of the matter is that these paths result in nothing more than wearing the practitioner out. Not only that, although we classify the deities we meditate on as being either wisdom or mundane, this division is actually made on the basis of whether or not emptiness has been realized. In other words, as long as you possess the stake of the unchanging realization of reality, even visualizing yourself in the form of a worldly demon will have the power to bring you the supreme spiritual accomplishment.

On the other hand, those without the stake of unchanging realization believe themselves and the deity to be different. Such individuals will not be granted supreme spiritual accomplishment even if they meditate on a transcendent yidam deity. What they are doing is training their minds to be angry and impassioned. Even in the short term they will end up with intractable minds, like cruel savages who engage in sacrificial rituals and other heartless practices. What these people are actually doing is practicing with powerful worldly spirits, under whose sway they will fall. Though they might call this "Secret Mantra," in truth it is the so-called "demon Dharma" that the *Kālacakra Tantra*

> warns against. With this approach, you will stray off course and end up as a demon or a ghost.

7. Bringing Experiences onto the Path

The seventh topic contains two parts: the ten things to understand and the six fundamental samaya vows. On the first of these, it is said that Secret Mantra should be practiced in the manner of the ten things to be known, starting with an illusion and a mirage. Hence, it is taught that Secret Mantra should be practiced with a tenfold understanding. This applies in all contexts, whether one is meditating on the maṇḍala of deities in a meditative state or in postmeditation. This tenfold understanding is as follows: all sādhanas are like an illusion; all names and words have no substance, like a mirage that deceives a wild animal; all activities are like a dream; all things lack any true nature, like the reflection in a mirror; all lands and places are like a city of spirits; all sounds are devoid of an essence, like an echo; all divine forms are like the reflection of the moon in water—they appear, but have no true existence; the various meditative absorptions are like bubbles surfacing on a lake; the entire range of projections and absorptions is manifold, like optical illusions; and all miraculous displays appear in various ways but have no characteristics of their own, like magical emanations.

The second topic concerns six fundamental samaya vows. Never cease longing for the master who teaches you the key instructions. Try to obtain favorable circumstances for meditation and abandon those that are unfavorable. Do not let your meditative absorption fade, no matter what you do. Do not abandon your yidam deity. Finally, keep the nature of your meditation and conduct secret from those who are not suitable to hear about them.

> The seventh topic in this section addresses how to bring the object of purification onto the path, which is easy to understand.

B. The Results of the Path Linked with the Four Knowledge Holders

1. Approach

This second section explains the levels of realization associated with the four knowledge holders according to the unique path, locating these four levels within the cask of the four divisions of approach and accomplishment. All that was just explained pertains to the practice of approach, where one fixes the mind on the subtle absorption, the single seal, and the other elements involved in visualizing the three objects. Meditating in this way causes the qualities associated with the paths of accumulation and joining to manifest. From the interdependent link associated with the applications of mindfulness and so forth, the subtle energies of the five elements will enter the central channel as an experience of this knowledge. There are certain signs that mark the occurrence of this process, including the appearance of smoke, mirages, fireflies, and a cloudless sky. These can all be understood to be signs that the appearance of meditative experiences is beginning to evolve.

There are also certain omens that appear in dreams. Repeatedly being naked is a sign that one's habitual patterns are being purified. Ascending a staircase into the sky is a sign of attainment. Riding a snow lion or elephant marks the mastery of a spiritual level. There are also signs associated with the granting of a prophecy; an image of the deity may smile, for example. In brief, the *Vajra Array* teaches that there are an inconceivable number of signs that mark one's progress on the path. Taking delight in these as signs of your own superiority, however, should be seen as the work of demons, so you should do your best to remain free from hoping for anything positive.

Similarly, when meditating on the stage of outer heat, one will see minute particles, letters, symbolic implements, subtle divine figures, and other signs. Objects and colors associated with fire, water, wind, and other such factors will also be perceived. At the stage of inner heat, the movements of the breath will become imperceptible as a result of meditating on the deity. At the stage of secret heat, one's entire range of experience will be understood to be illusory. Without having to make a concerted effort or rely upon causes and conditions, all phenomena will be realized to be enlightened within basic space. As a result, one's entire range of experience will appear vividly as wisdom.

There are many signs that occur during this process. The outer signs are the appearance of lights, sounds, and smells. Images may smile, butter lamps may burn on their own, and skull cups may hover in midair. One may also enjoy good health and a feeling of enthusiasm. Inner signs include a heightened sense of compassion, less attachment, an unbiased attitude, greater respect for one's samaya vows, and affection for one's guru and Dharma friends. There may also be an absence of hope for positive results, no sense of trepidation towards saṃsāra, and no fear of demons. As before, you should avoid feeling elated if any of these should occur.

In mastering the summit stage, various signs occur that mark the merging of mind and appearances. The five afflictions, for instance, no longer arise in relation to external objects, nor are the five outer elements able to harm one's body.

At the stage of acceptance, the whole range of appearances becomes malleable and certain signs occur that mark one's control over mind and appearances. Gold can be produced from sand, for example, and water from dry earth and trees from charcoal. At this point, one's body will not necessarily change from its ordinary state, but the mind will mature into the form of the deity.

This stage is referred to as the "matured knowledge holder." *Vast Illusion* explains:

> Just like wax and the embossment on a seal,
> The great seal is on the verge of being attained—
> None other than the perfect, powerful form.

In this passage, the phrase "embossment on a seal" is a metaphor for the body, while "wax" refers to the mind. The meaning here concerns the accomplishment of the great seal. This passage is pointing out that if one passes away at this stage without attaining the supreme state, the great seal will be attained in the intermediate state, like a clay statue coming out of its mold. The reason for this is that the body that results from the ripening of karma will have been cast aside and the mind will have already matured into the form of the deity. In *Stages of the Path*, it is written:

> When practicing approach for sixteen months,
> The vajra body will have yet to be attained.
> Due to little strength, inferior conditions and aspirations,
> The residual body, caused by concepts, remains.
> With awareness, one proceeds to the state of the vajra holder.

On the other hand, once the powerful state of absorption associated with the level of the supreme state has been attained, one will have full control over the life-process. A tantra states:

Once the state of a knowledge holder
With power over longevity is attained,
One will gain mastery and attain the supreme class
Within six, twelve, or sixteen months.

2. Close Approach

The path of joining is taught to take place during the practice of close approach. A tantra states:

The offerings perfected, including the retinue,
Exert yourself as in the system of approach.

At this stage, regardless of how one meditates, from the single class of the great secret up to the complex seal, the clarity and stability of the visualization merge with reality, the nature of great bliss. Practicing in this way causes the qualities of the seven factors of enlightenment to manifest in actuality. As the mind will have reached the path of joining, the five forms of clairvoyance, the four miraculous powers, and the other factors associated with this stage will be attained. One will also be able to hear the Dharma directly from nirmāṇakāya buddhas. Furthermore, as the true nature of objects will have been actualized, the great, supreme state will be brought to a state of culmination and the defiled body will be transformed into a vajra body. Because this form is free from birth and death, it is referred to as the "knowledge holder with power over longevity." *Stages of the Path* states:

With the attainments of accomplishing the eight collections,
The nature is seen, engaged, and perfected,
And the defilements of the body, realms,
And birthplace come to an end.
Becoming a vajra body, the class of life,
All that one sees is nirvāṇa.
Without discarding the body,
The level of buddhahood is attained.
All fears vanish and miracles are mastered.

This stage of accomplishment is similar to the great master Padmasambhava's attainment at Maratika Cave, where Mandarava acted as his practice companion and he attained a state free from birth and death through the practice of the proximate cause.

3. Accomplishment

The practice of accomplishment is taught to perfect the path of cultivation. On this topic, a tantra states:

> With accomplishment, exert yourself on the path of cultivation—
> The rainbowlike form of the deity, the great seal.

In terms of its characteristics, the essence of this meditative state is free from delusion and, thus, comparable to the buddhas. There are differences, however, when it comes to the state of postmeditation. At this stage, one's ability in relation to the equality of reality is still being refined. On the basis of the body maṇḍala, various miraculous powers are attained while in a state of immovable meditative concentration. As a result, the nature of the body maṇḍala appears in a rainbowlike form and the mental impurities associated with the nine levels are purified. Furthermore, the eightfold noble path is thoroughly perfected within the form of luminosity, wisdom free from subtle concepts. Through this, one is able to receive both mental and symbolic teachings from the sambhogakāya. A tantra states:

> One's body becomes the seal of the victorious ones,
> The deity manifest through cultivation.
> Adorned with marks and signs
> One is the knowledge holder of the great seal.

There are various subdivisions in this category. Those on the second to fifth levels are known as "vajra knowledge holders." Since their realization is vajralike, it destroys the obscurations of each individual level. Those on the sixth level focus on practicing the perfection of knowledge and turning the wheel of the Dharma. Hence, they are referred to as "wheel knowledge holders." Those on the seventh level are understood in the same way, since, through their skillful means, they work efficiently like a wheel. Those on the eighth level possess a jewel-like nonconceptual wisdom and have mastered their own completely pure potential. Therefore, they are known as "jewel knowledge holders." Those on the ninth level are referred to as "lotus knowledge holders," as they are free from attachment and able to cultivate pure lands and work for the welfare of others. Those on the tenth level have perfected their enlightened activity, via which they carry out the welfare of sentient beings. Hence, they are known as "sword knowledge holders." *Stages of the Path* states:

> The second form of enjoyment, the class of the seal,
> Consists of the knowledge holders
> Of the vajra, wheel, jewel, lotus, and sword.

An example of this level of accomplishment is the great master Padmasambhava's attainment at Yangleshö in Nepal. There he relied upon the maṇḍala of Glorious Viśuddha Heruka and demonstrated how one progresses to the level of a knowledge holder of the great seal. This is also where he mastered the four types of enlightened activity.

4. Great Accomplishment

Fourth is the practice of great accomplishment, which concerns the completion of the path beyond training. On this topic, it is said:

> Once the signs become stable,
> Demonstrate great accomplishment.

At this stage, the previous paths have been completely traversed and the emphasis is on group practice, which enables the gathering, along with a hundred thousand, to connect with the enlightened state. In this maṇḍala, those of the spontaneous class are, for the most part, equal to the buddhas in terms of the supreme qualities they possess. Nevertheless, in the Mantra tradition, there is still an instantaneous progression that takes place through the individual phases of this stage, whereby the training process is brought to perfection. Once this has come to pass, the state of buddhahood beyond training is attained and the dharmakāya is met face to face. In other words, abandonment and realization will have reached a state of culmination. This is how the lord of victorious ones Padmasambhava explains the spontaneously present knowledge holder. *Stages of the Path* explains further:

In perfecting the power of the previous classes,
As explained, impurities are refined away
And the threefold knowledge of buddhahood unfolds.
The spontaneously present class is attained.

It may be thought that holding the spontaneously present class to refer explicitly to the level of buddhahood is problematic. This, however, is not the case. The underlying intent of using the four classes of knowledge holder found in the Mantra tradition is to present the five paths of the Sūtra tradition. This is justified by the overarching principle that the inner meaning of the tantras is explained via the six limits and four modes. In this way, great accomplishment, as it is explained in the context of progressing through the four divisions of approach and accomplishment, is also said to be the objective of practice, in which there is nothing to eliminate or achieve. The fact that this is the implicit meaning here eliminates any such contradictions.

The spontaneously present knowledge holder *is* classified as the level of buddhahood. Nevertheless, there are still further levels to be attained as the nature of this stage reaches full strength. The supreme level of lotuslike nonattachment occurs once one remains untainted by any negative shortcomings, regardless of how nonreferential knowledge is employed in analysis. This also applies to the level of the great accumulation of the wheel of syllables and the various inconceivable enlightened qualities, such as the thirty-two excellent signs and eighty unique marks. Finally, there is also the thirteenth level of the vajra holder, where one enjoys the eternal wheel of adornment, the tathāgata's enlightened body, speech, and mind.

The *Dense Array of Ornaments* states:

Unless they have awakened
In the supreme realm of Akaniṣṭha,
The perfect buddhas do not perform
Their enlightened deeds in the desire realm.

As implied above, the individual levels of the Mantra tradition are traversed in a single moment of experience, through which enlightenment is manifested in Akaniṣṭha and an infinite number of enlightened activities, such as the twelve deeds of unobstructed skillful means, are carried out. These classifications, made in light of the causal links that are automatically created, have been explained as they actually are. A tantra states:

> As the culminating, spontaneous
> Accomplishment, one acts as a regent—
> Genuinely turning the secret wheel,
> Teaching the appropriate Dharma to all,
> And manifesting the twelve deeds as well.

An example of this level of attainment is the great master Padmasambhava in his current state, where he will remain until the very end of saṃsāra. Present at the level of a spontaneously present knowledge holder, Padmasambhava is indivisible from all the buddhas. He teaches the Dharma to a pure retinue in the Akaniṣṭha realm of Lotus Light and never tires of working compassionately for the welfare of sentient beings.

With these, the great master himself positioned the knowledge holder with power over longevity and that of the great seal. Hence, no delineation was made on this topic by most of those who followed in his wake. What I have just explained here, however, accords with my own realization, which I owe to the second buddha, whose light rays of compassion caused the lotus bud of my mind to bloom.

Some hold that the great seal covers the first to seventh levels, while the state of spontaneous presence refers to the three pure levels. This, however, is in error, as evidenced by the quotation just cited from *Stages of the Path.* On this topic, the Omniscient One wrote, "The position held by some masters that the state of the great seal covers the first to seventh levels and that the state of spontaneous presence refers to the three pure levels appears to be an incorrect understanding. The reason for this is that the progression through the four types of knowledge holder encompasses the state of a beginner all the way up to the state of buddhahood."

Individuals who have already familiarized themselves with the two accumulations to a great extent and have attained great strength in terms of their knowledge and meditative absorption may traverse these paths in a more direct fashion. Such individuals are carried instantaneously from the path of joining through the paths of seeing and cultivation. Through this, they proceed to the ultimate path. There are also some with exceedingly powerful minds who move straight from the path of joining to the state of buddhahood. A tantra states:

Some perfect the five true kāyas in sixteen,
From the class of mastery itself,
While others progress from the state of the great seal
To the unexcelled state of Samantabhadra.

With this in mind, one might begin to wonder whether or not the second buddha, master Padmasambhava, attained realization gradually, as the examples above seem to indicate. That, however, would be a misunderstanding. As texts such as the *Enlightenment of Vairocana* and the *Secret Sphere of the Moon* point out:

In the joyful realm known as Akaniṣṭha
Buddhas become fully enlightened
And then manifest enlightenment here.

This was also the case with Buddha Śākyamuni. Although he became enlightened and perfected his own abandonment and realization an incalculable number of ages ago, he nevertheless manifested the twelve deeds in this realm.

The second section explains how the paths and levels of the knowledge holder are traversed, structuring the discussion around the four divisions of approach and accomplishment. Generally speaking, these four practices can be applied in various contexts. They can be applied in the context of a single ritual, for example, or with the times and numbers related to practice; any of these are fine. In this context, however, they are taught in relation to the stages of the path.

On the path of accumulation, one is introduced to and directed towards the deity of the empowerment. Subsequently, by not doing anything that goes against the samaya vows, which are the life-force of empowerment, the yidam deity is approached as being inseparable from one's own mind. Once the four practices of the path of accumulation are complete, there are enhancement practices that are utilized on the path of joining. Adhering to such practices will actualize the signs that mark the stages of heat, summit, and acceptance. Subsequently, the great supreme state will be actualized as well, the state of a matured knowledge holder. This is "approach."

On the path of seeing, true luminosity will arise directly in one's state of being. Consequently, the fire of wisdom will refine away the elements and the impure body. At this point, one will have come even closer to the yidam deity, having discovered a state that transcends birth and death. This is "close approach."

Subsequently, the path of cultivation will see the actualization of the knowledge holder of the great seal, which is similar in form to the yidam deity. This is "accomplishment," meaning that one's own and others' benefit is accomplished simultaneously.

On the path of liberation, the efforts one makes on the path for one's own benefit come to an end. During the postmeditation of this stage, the enlightened activities that one engages in for the benefit of others are no different than those of the tathāgatas. Hence, there is "great accomplishment."

In the context of the path of accumulation, the subtle energies of the five elements enter the central channel, eliciting five ordinary signs. When the earth energy enters the central channel, signs such as smoke appear; when water energy enters, mirages appear; when the fire energy enters, fireflies appear; when wind energy enters, candle flames appear; and when space energy enters, space appears. These five are signs that appear directly to the senses. At this point, whatever you look at will appear to be wafting and hazy like smoke, shimmering like a mirage, flashing like a firefly, orange like a burning candle, or like sections of a cloudless sky. These occur only in the context of the primary meditative equipoise.

The explanation of the stages of heat, summit, and acceptance on the path of joining is easy to understand. However, in the context of the stage of the supreme state, which correlates to the matured knowledge holder, there is a difficult passage that begins with the statement, "Like wax and the embossment on a seal." The word *embossment* here refers to the design on the face of stamp, while *wax* refers to the material that is used to make a seal. However, for all intents and purposes, this example is similar to that of a clay statue being removed from its mold. The meaning here is that although the mind may have matured into the form of the deity, one has yet to leave behind the physical body, which is the maturation of past karma.

Further below, the phrase "the supreme class of mastery" appears. This refers to the fact that at this stage one attains a body of light as a support, and is equal in fortune to the gods of the form realm. In this sense, it is similar to the Almighty—the king, or "master," of these pure heavens. Alternately, it also makes sense to explain the perfectly enlightened yidam deity as being the "Almighty."

In the case of the knowledge holder with power over longevity, the cause is defined as knowledge. This refers to the view, seeing the inseparable nature of saṃsāra and nirvāṇa. The condition is defined as entrance, meaning the absorption. Hence, one who has perfected the four practices of the path of accumulation can reach the path of seeing by utilizing various enhancement practices that involve group practice on the path of joining.

At this point in the process, the three defilements dissipate and the unborn and undying vajra body is attained. The three defilements are those of the body, realms, and birthplace. The first of these entails an inability to control the processes of death and illness. The second refers to the inability to use states of meditative concentration to take rebirth willfully in the desire realm. The third involves the inability to control the process of taking one of the four types of rebirth.

The four miracles are those of verbal expression, fitting instructions, displays, and manifesting phenomena. Though there are two different types presented in the *Condensed Realization*, this categorization is very easy to explain. The miracle of verbal expression relates to the enlightened mind, in this case referring to knowing the minds of others via one's own psychic powers. Miraculous displays are able to transform the perception of others, instilling faith in one who has none, for example. The miracle of fitting instructions pertains to enlightened speech, referring to the teaching of whichever of the three vehicles of Dharma is the most suitable to tame disciples. Finally, the miracle of manifesting phenomena involves the ability to do things such as shake the earth in six directions and manifest eighteen great omens when teaching the Dharma.

The path of cultivation is associated with the knowledge holder of the great seal. In this context, the phrase "impurities associated with the nine levels" occurs. This refers to the nine ordinary levels on the path of cultivation, from the second level up.

The spontaneously present knowledge holder is linked with the path of liberation, where we find the phrase "the threefold knowledge of buddhahood." This is synonymous with the three types of understanding taught in the *Sūtra of Vast Display,* where it is said that our teacher attained three types of understanding when he manifested enlightenment. The first of these is the knowledge of previous lives, which spans an inconceivable length of time. The second type of understanding is the knowledge of death and rebirth, which is knowledge of the details of every single sentient being's time of death and future life. Hence, one has an inconceivable knowledge of death and rebirth. Finally, there is an understanding of the exhaustion of defilements. This is the precise knowledge of whether or not the defilements have been exhausted, both in terms of oneself as well as others.

The listeners, solitary buddhas, and bodhisattvas do have a semblance of these three types of understanding. Nevertheless, in a perfect buddha these three kinds of understanding have reached a state of culmination and are completely perfect. Thus, there is nothing else quite like them.

The unique signs and marks can be found in the tantric commentaries. In the naturally manifested realm of Akaniṣṭha, various realms, celestial palaces, central figures, retinues, and so forth appear as the miraculous display of a single wisdom. In this context, the sixteen beings of the minor class and their female consorts form the retinue. These are the signs. The presence of five deities in the crown of each male consort comprises the marks. Together, these are the *inner signs and marks.*

III

The Pure Fruition:

Attaining the Unified State

A. The Essence of Fruition: A General Presentation

By practicing in this manner, the profound meditative absorption of emptiness will refine one's pure wisdom, while visualizing the deity with the instrumental meditative absorption will purify the impurities that lead one to become involved with ordinary states of existence. By realizing that the deity is the natural manifestation of wisdom, not something to be experienced as an external object, the habitual patterns associated with conceptual processes will disappear. Furthermore, the transformation of the all-ground will lead to the wisdom of the basic space of phenomena. In a similar way, as *Gateway to the Three Kāyas* points out, "The all-ground consciousness disappearing into basic space constitutes mirrorlike wisdom." Likewise, the mental consciousness disappearing into basic space constitutes the wisdom of equality, the afflicted mind disappearing into basic space constitutes discerning wisdom, and, finally, the five sense consciousnesses disappearing into basic space constitutes all-accomplishing wisdom.

At this point, a number of changes take place. On an external level, appearances transform into buddha realms. Internally, the aggregates transform into the form of the deity and, on a secret level, the eight collections transform into wisdom. This is what is referred to as having become "enlightened in every way." As written in the *Seventy Stanzas on Refuge:*

> Because one awakes from the sleep of ignorance
> And expands the mind, encompassing all that can be known,
> Buddhahood blossoms, just like the petals of a lotus.

According to the approach of the *Great Magical Web*, five kāyas are perfected simultaneously once the lotus-endowed level of nonattachment and that of the great accumulation of the wheel of syllables have been actualized. Here I will give just a brief overview of these five.

1. Vajrakāya

The unchanging vajrakāya is addressed in the *Net of Wisdom*:

> The purity of basic space is the vajrakāya—
> Unchanging, indestructible, and beyond thought.

To explain, the sole path tread by all the buddhas is that of natural luminosity, primordial basic space. In reality, the culmination of this process is unchanging, while its vajra nature is permanent and unconditioned—hence, the term "vajrakāya." Considering how it is both naturally pure, being inherently free of impurity, and also utterly pure, in the sense of being free from all forms of incidental impurity, the vajrakāya is also referred to as "buddhahood with twofold purity."

2. Abhisambodhikāya

Concerning the abhisambodhikāya. The same text states:

> The abhisambodhikāya
> Is said to be pure, as it is free of impurity,
> Consummate, since the qualities have blossomed,
> And unified, having merged indivisibly.

Once the brilliant clarity of the mind's nature has reached a point of culmination, it is included as part of this twofold purity. In terms of its apparent aspect, all the unique enlightened qualities of buddhahood are present. This includes the ten strengths, the four types of fearlessness, the eighteen distinct qualities of buddhahood, great compassion, the thirty-seven factors of enlightenment, and so forth. In brief, this covers all the inconceivable qualities of knowledge, love, and ability. It is from this perspective that the term "abhisambodhikāya" is employed. This kāya is the basis for the arising of all the unique qualities of buddhahood.

3. Dharmakāya

The third of the five kāyas is the peaceful dharmakāya. The dharmakāya is not held to be a blank emptiness, since it is not merely the wisdom of awareness. When viewed from the perspective of being reality itself, the dharmakāya is vajrakāya as explained above, while from the perspective of its manifold appearance and distinct essence it is the abhisambodhikāya, which was covered in the preceding section. So how is the dharmakāya identified in the present context? It is not permanent because it is beyond being something that can be observed or thought about. Yet neither is it nothing, since it also happens to be the wisdom of discerning self-awareness. It is not both of these, nor is it neither, because neither permanence nor nothingness is established. Hence, it is of the nature of basic space, without center or edge like the sky. In this expanse, extremely subtle wisdom is merged into one taste. And though it resembles a new moon in being unmanifest, its cognizant aspect, meaning the inner clarity of wisdom, is unceasing.

The dharmakāya functions as the essence of the unfolding of wisdom, the clarity that is directed outwards from the meditative state. As such, it functions as the cause for the rūpakāyas, the embodied forms that appear to the victor's offspring that abide on the levels and to the masses of sentient beings. This includes the forms that appear to their eyes, the enlightened speech that they hear, smelling the scent of the noble ones' discipline, experiencing the taste of Dharma, the blissful sensation of meditative concentration, and the knowledge associated with the conceptual analysis that evaluates phenomena. For this reason, it is referred to as "wisdom that is inwardly directed, but not dull." The *Guru of the Magical Web* states:

> The dharmakāya is the nonreferential basis for arising;
> It is an inwardly clear, extremely subtle wisdom.

These three kāyas, the inwardly luminous basic space, are extremely difficult to fathom.

4. Sambhogakāya

Concerning the fourth division, sambhogakāya, *Stages of the Path* states:

The appearance of awareness to oneself,
Spontaneously perfect, arises as manifold rays of light,
Realms, celestial palaces, thrones, and ornaments.

As indicated here, enlightened forms endowed with the fivefold certainty appear out of this inner clarity, the basic space of reality. Like the clear appearances that occur when sunlight hits crystal, they appear naturally as the embodiment of the ocean of the signs and marks. These are the appearances of buddhahood itself, the regents who are the teachers of the five buddha families. They manifest like empty forms and enjoy the continuous wheel of eternity. As they are wholly unique, even those who have mastered the tenth level do not see them, the reason being that they have yet to abandon the obscurations in their entirety and have yet to attain the mental perspective that beholds the entire range of qualities associated with how things really are and how they appear. The *Supreme Continuum* states:

Not something that can be spoken of, it is subsumed by the ultimate.
Not an object to conceptualize, it transcends every example.
As there is nothing higher, it falls in neither existence nor peace.
Even the noble ones cannot fathom the domain of the victorious ones.

The celestial palace and other elements associated with the perfect place appear to oneself and come into existence based on this ground luminosity. This can be likened to the pure appearances that arise in the dream state. While they *do* appear to those who have eliminated the whole range of obscurations, they should not be viewed as real and solid entities that exist in some other place. This is similar to the fact that various empty forms may appear to a yogi whose energies have entered the central channel, yet others who are in the same place at the same time will still not be able to see these forms.

Once the light of a crystal has receded inwards, it remains present within the basis for the appearance of this spectrum of light. In the same way, the three kāyas of this inner clarity are distinctly present within the basic space of subtle wisdom. The following example makes this easy to understand. When the sun is present as a condition, a spectrum of light will project outwards from a crystal. Similarly, as the elements that appear to oneself emerge in an objective manner, the outward quality of wisdom blazes forth as forms endowed with all the signs and marks of buddhahood.

5. Nirmāṇakāya

The fifth division is the nirmāṇakāya, which can manifest as anything whatsoever. Here we have what is referred to as "sacred teachers, captains who lead the offspring of the victorious ones, noble ones, and other such beings to the isle of peace." These teachers are reflections of the sambhogakāya that manifest in the perception of supreme disciples.

Though they appear to be similar to the great sambhogakāya of basic space, which consists of elements that appear to oneself, this is not what they actually are. To use an example, the difference between these two is like the difference between the reflection in a mirror and the real thing. As its reflection, what appears does resemble the sambhogakāya with all its signs and marks. However, these pure realms, retinues, and other such factors appear to others and are included within the appearances of the tenth level. For this reason, the *Tantra of the Sun and Moon's Union* classifies them as "half-nirmāṇakāya, half-sambhogakāya."

Because they are natural emanations of that which appears to oneself, they are known as "natural nirmāṇakāya pure realms." These realms are called The Unsurpassed, Complete Joy, The Glorious, The Blissful (also known as Lotus Mound), and Accomplishment of Supreme Activity. In these five realms, Vairocana and the other buddhas of the five families teach their pure retinues. On the tenth level, they teach them the nature of the five buddha families, the five dharmas, and the five transformations, empowering them with great light. This is the very perfection of the great deeds of the buddhas. The *Illusion of Manifest Enlightenment* states:

> Having mastered the pure levels
> And from the complete perfection of the five teachers,
> The five supreme teachings, and the five wisdoms,
> One proceeds to the essence of perfect enlightenment.

From this state one arises as a "nirmāṇakāya that tames beings." The form of the nirmāṇakāya comes about from the seeds of the wholesome karmic momentum that beings have, appearing in a manner similar to the way in which the moon casts its reflection in water. In the same way that the moon has the power to cast a reflection, the moonlike sambhogakāya has the power to project emanations that manifest in the perception of those in need of guidance. And just as the water acts as the causal link that enables the reflection of the moon to occur, those in need of guidance have merit that allows for the appearance of these emanations. When these two are brought together, the emanated reflections appear to tame beings in whatever way is required, just as the reflection of the moon in water comes about effortlessly.

According to the karma of each individual being, these emanations may take the form of the higher realms that manifest upwards, animals that manifest laterally, or hell beings and spirits that manifest downwards. They work for the welfare of the six classes of beings, who experience all manner of suffering, in accordance with the perception of each class of existence. To this end, they carry out the welfare of others by emanating as awareness beings, the six sages. Some are tamed by the enlightened body, such as the twelve deeds performed by the body of great merit. Others are tamed by enlightened speech—the various vehicles that transcend truly-existent sounds and words. Still more are tamed by the enlightened mind, the six forms of clairvoyance, such as the completely-perfect activities of Samantabhadra. Yet more are tamed by the inconceivable enlightened activities carried out in every way, both direct and indirect. As the *Avataṃsaka Sūtra* states:

> Ah, noble child, the emanations of the tathāgata are boundless. They carry out the welfare of beings, using whatever forms, colors, and names are best suited to tame them.

Of these, the one that manifests the twelve enlightened deeds is known as the "supreme nirmāṇakāya." The other forms that tame others with their compassion are known as "manifold nirmāṇakāyas." Those that are born in this manner are emanations in physical bodies that directly benefit beings. Such emanations have worked for the welfare of others by emanating, for example, as the giant fish that appeared in a time of famine, as the creature that emanated during an epidemic, and as the horse Ājāneyabalaha that went to the land of demonesses.

"Created nirmāṇakāyas" appear as physical objects, such as paintings, carvings, lotuses, wish-fulfilling trees, parks, gardens, celestial palaces, jewels, ships, bridges, and lanterns. In brief, all things that are given to benefit sentient beings are blessed emanations. All of these arise out of basic space and dissolve back into it. The way in which this takes place is able to withstand the most intense scrutiny.

The Omniscient One explains further:

When there are none to be tamed, that which tames recedes
into space;
Sambhogakāya's own display fades back into dharmakāya.
Just as the reflection of the moon recedes into the sky when
there is no water to hold it,
Just as the moon vanishes into space when the time has arrived,
And just as the new moon neither waxes nor wanes,
When there are beings to tame, they gradually appear as before.
This is the spontaneously present fruition.

As shown here, when there is no water to hold the reflection of the moon, it naturally fades back into its space. In a similar way, when there are no beings to be tamed, the moonlike reflection of the nirmāṇakāya—the buddha that appears in their perception—simply dissolves into a state of peace within the sambhogakāya's own display. However, although this example is used, it is certainly not the case that one thing arises from something else and then dissolves back into it.

Similarly, the sambhogakāya as well dissolves back into the inner luminosity of the basic space of the dharmakāya. This process, referred to as "wisdom gathering back into space," is likened to the new moon remaining in a state of internal clarity. The followers of the Madhyamaka tradition explain this occurrence as a meditative equipoise within the state of supreme cessation, which is caused by resting peacefully in the basic space of phenomena. They also hold that beneficial works are performed in the perception of others based on one's previous aspirations. The *Supreme Continuum*, on the other hand, holds that although the wisdom of meditative equipoise does not fluctuate, an inconceivable amount of benefit is brought to sentient beings via the postmeditation state. It explains:

Wisdom is held to be nonconceptuality
And its subsequent attainment.

Since the content of this first section is explained extensively in the main treatise, it is fairly easy to understand. Furthermore, since giving a detailed explanation would take too long, I have not done so. I also feel that there are not any difficult points that need clarification.

B. The Unique Presentation of Mantra

In terms of the wondrous state of twofold purity, in which abandonment and realization have reached a state of culmination, it is said that there is no difference between the buddhahood of Sūtra and Mantra. This is the position of my teacher, the omniscient lord of speech, Longchenpa. However, when the qualities of basic space are evaluated with the profound realization and activities of the illusory wisdom of realized beings, inconceivable points can be realized in a precise manner, for it is the very nature of their knowledge to do so with whatever it engages.

One such individual who was unparalleled in explaining such topics was Yungtön Dorje Pal. In the tradition of the Zur masters, those who practiced the Great Glorious One, he composed a treatise that distinguishes the Sūtra notion of buddhahood from that of Mantra. It is well known that when it came to this text, even unrivalled masters of exposition were humbled. Nevertheless, after thorough consideration, it does seem possible to offer an analysis of this subject based on this master's tantric treatise.

With regard to the dharmakāya, he taught that there are three distinctions that can be made: a distinction in terms of essence, a distinction in terms of characteristics, and a distinction in terms of blessings. First we have the distinction in terms of essence. The dharmakāya of the Causal Vehicle of Characteristics is emptiness, the absence of conceptual projections. The dharmakāya of the Mantra Vehicle, on the other hand, entails the union of appearance and emptiness, as stated in the *Vast Illusion*:

> The animate and inanimate universe
> Appears, yet has no essence.

Concerning the second difference, it is explained that the dharmakāya of the Causal Vehicle falls into the extreme of emptiness, while the dharmakāya of the Mantra tradition is the indivisibility of appearance and emptiness. As such, it does not fall into any extreme. On the third difference, he explains that, through the blessings of the dharmakāya of the Causal Vehicle, only the two form kāyas occur, whereas in the Mantra tradition, the blessings of indivisible appearance-emptiness are such that the five kāyas and any other form can arise.

Upon examination, however, I do not see any valid reason to make a differentiation in terms of the dharmakāya's essence. The reason for this is that when it comes to the extremely subtle wisdom that is inwardly directed yet not dull, appearance and emptiness are not identified as such. Furthermore, the passage from the *Vast Illusion* that is cited in this context actually fits well with the division made in terms of the characteristics of the dharmakāya.

The second section deals with the differences between the two form kāyas in these traditions, of which there are three. Concerning the first, in the Causal Vehicle of Characteristics, the two form kāyas come into existence due to causes and conditions, whereas in the Mantra Vehicle this is not the case. Again, the *Vast Illusion* states:

> Because they do not depend on causes and conditions . . .

The next section has two subdivisions, one concerning differences in terms of the sambhogakāya and one concerning differences in terms of the nirmāṇakāya. There are two differences when it comes to the sambhogakāya, the first of which concerns a difference in that which is enjoyed. The Vehicle of Characteristics holds that positive factors are enjoyed, while negative factors are not. In the Mantra Vehicle, on the other hand, both are enjoyed. There is also a distinction made based on the methods for enjoying these factors. The Vehicle of Characteristics has no methods for utilizing negative factors, whereas the Mantra Vehicle has methods to utilize both positive and negative factors.

There are also two differences in terms of the nirmāṇakāya. The first of these concerns their object, the beings in need of guidance. The nirmāṇakāya of the Vehicle of Characteristics is only able to tame disciples with a wholesome character, not those who are negative. The nirmāṇakāya of the Mantra Vehicle, on the other hand, makes no such distinctions. The second difference is in terms of the methods that are used to tame disciples. Again, the nirmāṇakāya of the Vehicle of Characteristics does not have any methods for subduing disciples of a negative bent, whereas the nirmāṇakāya of the Mantra Vehicle has methods for subduing both positive and negative disciples. Hence, the text concludes, the Mantra Vehicle can also be understood to be superior in terms of the indivisible vajrakāya and the abhisambodhikāya.

> This section explains the unique points of the Mantric system on the topic of buddhahood. There are three traditions for distinguishing the buddhahood of the Sūtra and Mantra Vehicles. The first holds that,

aside from being of varying lengths, the two paths of Sūtra and Mantra are essentially the same, insofar as both lead to the state of buddhahood as their result. The second asserts that without practicing the path of the Secret Mantra Vajrayāna, one will lack the ability to actualize the state of perfect and complete enlightenment. The third holds that while it is possible to progress on the Sūtra path to the eleventh level of this tradition, the level of universal illumination, that which is understood as buddhahood on the Sūtra path cannot be equated with the genuine state of the unified vajra holder, the embodiment of the ocean of kāyas and wisdoms that is taught in the Mantra tradition. In other words, this tradition distinguishes the buddhahood of Sūtra from that of Mantra.

When carefully examined, the latter two positions come down to the same point. With the first position, furthermore, one must accept that the state of buddhahood—the eleventh level of universal illumination, the path beyond training—is the ultimate state to be attained on the Sūtra path. In contrast, if this path does not lead to the fruition it is said to produce, the path and its result will have parted ways, just like the paths to liberation in non-Buddhist schools. This would be an intolerable denigration of the Vehicle of Characteristics.

According to the latter positions, one would have to accept that once the state of buddhahood associated with the Sūtra path has been attained, it is still necessary to enter the path of Mantra to attain the state of the unified vajra holder. On the other hand, one may hold that the buddhahood of the Sūtra path is the culmination of its own path and does not apply to the path of Mantra. The problem with this, however, is that one ends up with two ultimate vehicles and the path of Mantra cannot even be included in the three vehicles.

Both positions have been held by numerous wise and accomplished individuals. In particular, scriptural support for the differentiation of buddhahood in Sūtra and Mantra can be found in both the *Magical Web* and the *Recitation of the Names of Mañjuśrī*. This explanation was stressed by the Indian master Buddhajñānapāda as well. In light of the fact that there are also numerous other instances of scriptural support, this should not be viewed as a groundless or merely provisional position on this topic.

Concluding Verses and Colophon

Like a firm step to the basic space of the supreme and unchanging great bliss,
Adorned with the golden jewelry of the detailed instructions on the meaning of the tantras,
This collection of good advice will hasten the journey to Akaniṣṭha,
Shouldering, as it does, the responsibility for the words and meanings in the most supreme vehicle of all.

Embodiment of all buddhas, Lord of Uḍḍiyana, Mahāpaṇḍita Vimalamitra,
Omniscient Lord of Dharma, and the very life-force of the Ancient Translation School, bodhisattvas Zurchen and Zurchung—
As most of the teaching traditions of these masters are barely alive in these dark times,
They have been illuminated by the light blazing from the sun of Rangjung Dorje Khyentse.

This treasury of wish-fulfilling jewels distills the essential key instructions
Of the collected tantras and sādhanas, completely and without error.
Those who tread these steps and are led to the five kāyas
Are undeniably fortunate guests indeed.

The peaceful river of this pristine collection of merit,
Accompanied by a succession of waves of the three excellences,
Brings about the knowing dedication of Mañjukumāra.
Through this, may all reach the level of Samantabhadra!

Chaksam Rigdzin, the supreme reincarnation Yeshe Lhundrup Palzangpo, is someone who has attained the sublime mind's eye that beholds in a vast manner the subjects that the tathāgatas teach so well. Still, he remains without conceit, regarding the teachings and those who uphold them with great care and reverence. With great persistence he asked that I compose this text, *Ladder to Akaniṣṭha: Instructions on the Development Stage and Deity Yoga*, accompanying his request with a red cloth embroidered with gold and a pair of multicolored scarves.

With this request, the lotus bud of my mind was opened in a single instant by the great miraculous light rays of love and wisdom that shone upon me from the glorious Padmasambhava and his spiritual partner. As a result, an understanding of all phenomena arose naturally and I was able to remain fearless in the face of the genuine truth. I, Rangjung Dorje Jigme Lingpa, a practitioner of the Great Perfection who is also known as Longchen Namke Naljor, then composed this text at Tsering Jong. It was put into writing in the midst of the forest of enlightenment at the center known as Padma Ösel Thekchok Ling, a beautiful place for spiritual practice, in the temple guarded by the tathāgatas of the five families. At the time I wrote this explanation, I was thirty-nine years old. It was completed on a Thursday in the lunar month of the dancer, in the Year of the Pig, 1767, at which time the house of the lion was rising.

Virtue! Virtue! Virtue!

If the good fortune of hearing just a single word of the excellent teachings
Contained in the Omniscient One's lineage transcends the realm of thought,
Then these definitive ideas, based as they are on explanation, debate, and composition,
Appear, I feel, due to the strength of many eons of collecting merit.

Thus, though I myself have not found the slightest bit of certainty
Through study, contemplation, and meditation,
I have written this to familiarize myself with these teachings
And to benefit a few fortunate individuals with good character.

Learned scholars who have studied widely,
Yogis experienced in meditation,
And those fortunate individuals with the key instructions of the lineage,
Please examine this approach and clear away any impurities with your love.

I thus exhort all such learned individuals, whose delineation of a hundred texts

Can clarify the explanations of the Omniscient One's lineage
By cutting through the faults that pollute them with the impurities
Of ignorance, misunderstanding, and partial understanding.

If there is anything here of a clear explanation, I dedicate
The accumulation of merit to the continuation of the Three
Jewels—
To those who clarify the essential teachings of the Capable One
And continually uphold, explain, and practice them.

At the request of Lhundrup Dorje of Palri, one with clear intelligence both inborn and learned, I, the careless vagabond Apu, wrote down whatever came to mind. May this bring great virtue!
SARVA MAṄGALAṂ!

THE MELODY OF BRAHMA REVELING IN THE THREE REALMS

Key Points for Meditating on the Four Stakes That Bind the Life-Force

by **Patrul Chökyi Wangpo**

Unchanging, all-pervasive, and ever-present
In the delight of the supreme secret—
Homage to Vajrasattva,
Great bliss and lord of the family.

One, through another, arrives without hardship
At the state of complete liberation, like iron refined.
This wondrous method brings liberation in an instant
And belongs to the highest vehicle, Vajrayāna, alone.

The vajra path of unity is skillful means
And knowledge; development and completion.
Whoever speaks of these two stages
Should bind the life-force of the first with four stakes.

To explain:

The supreme secret—the enlightened mind of all victorious ones—
Has a vajra nature, the delight of great bliss.
It is present in all saṃsāra and nirvāṇa, with no fluctuation or
change.
Homage is paid to this lord of the family, Vajrasattva.

This wondrous method, the ritual of the great secret, constitutes
a path
Capable of freeing the fortunate into the state of complete
liberation in an instant.

Among development, completion, and their union, these three,
The entire path of the development stage is condensed in the
four stakes that bind the life-force.

To explain further, in this passage first homage is paid to Vajrasattva. The meaning of what then follows is this: *One*, an individual with good fortune, *through another*, the path of the Vajrayāna, *arrives without* difficulty or *hardship at the state of* buddhahood, *complete liberation, like iron refined* into gold. Without taking a long time, *this wondrous method brings liberation in an instant*—in a single life and a single body—*and belongs to the* very *highest vehicle* of all, the Secret Mantra *Vajrayāna, alone.*

When condensed, all paths of this vehicle are included in *the vajra path of unity*. This *is* the unity of *skillful means and knowledge*, the unity of the *development* stage and the *completion* stage, respectively. Of these two stages, the four stakes of the life-force are factors that bind the life-force of the entire range of skillful means found in the development stage. As such, there is not a single aspect of the development stage path that they do not encompass. Hence, if you do not understand this topic, you will not understand the development stage. For this very reason, I will now give a brief and accessible explanation of this approach.

The vajra path allows us to purify our ordinary body, [speech], mind, and actions, and actualize enlightened body, speech, mind, and activities. This path can be condensed into four divisions: deity, mantra, reality itself, and projection and absorption. To elaborate, meditative absorption is the factor that purifies the ordinary body and matures it into the enlightened form of the victorious ones. This constitutes the vajra path. The factor that purifies the obscurations of ordinary speech is recitation, through which one attains the enlightened speech of the victorious ones. Unchanging realization liberates the mind itself; it is the secret factor that establishes the enlightened mind. And finally, projection and absorption transmute ordinary activity and establish it as supreme enlightened activity. These four aspects are all contained within the four stakes.

All the various paths associated with the development stage perform three functions—they purify, perfect, and mature. In terms of cyclic existence, development stage practice corresponds with the nature of saṃsāra, which allows it to refine away and *purify* saṃsāra and its attendant habitual patterns. On a higher level, it also corresponds to the nature of nirvāṇa, through which it brings the deeds of the buddhas onto the path, thus *perfecting* the fruition within the ground. In terms of the path, the development stage also conforms to the vital points of the completion stage, through which it *matures* one for the second stage of the path.

The four stakes that bind the life-force condense the skillful methods of development stage practice. Respectively, they are: 1) the stake of absorption in the deity, 2) the stake of mantra recitation, 3) the stake of reality, and 4) the stake of the enlightened activity of projection and absorption.

The Stake of Absorption

Begin by laying a foundation for practice with the three absorptions. In a state of simplicity, settle evenly in the basic space of great emptiness. This is the *vajralike absorption of suchness*. Next, cultivate a sense of illusory compassion towards all the beings that do not have this realization. This constitutes the *illusory absorption of total illumination*. Finally, as the expression of these two, meditate on the seed syllable of the deity you are practicing. This is the *causal absorption*, the *heroic gait*.

Having laid the foundation with these three, next visualize the external universe as a celestial palace and its inhabitants as deities. As you do, link this with the process of purifying the habitual patterns of whichever of the four types of birth is most relevant. Visualize your body as the illusory form of the deity. In appearance, it should be complete and perfect, distinct down to the pupils of its eyes. It should also be empty, however, without even a shred of concrete existence. Visualize this great union of appearance and emptiness with vivid clarity. You should also complete the various aspects of the practice, such as the bestowal of the empowerments of the five wisdoms and the seals of enlightened body, speech, and mind.

In terms of saṃsāra, this process will *purify* and refine away the habitual patterns related to the body, as they relate to the four types of birth. In terms of buddhahood, the fruition will be *perfected* in the ground. The fruition, here, is the inconceivable secret of enlightened form, which is beyond having a face, hands, or marks, yet can appear in any form whatsoever, in whatever way is needed to tame beings. In terms of the path, the web of pure channels will be refined into the deity. This, in turn, will *mature* one for the practices of the completion stage, in which the vital points of the vajra body are penetrated.

The Stake of the Essence Mantra

At the heart center of each of the assembly of deities you are meditating on visualize a wisdom being that resembles the deity it inhabits, though bereft of ornamentation and implements. Then, at the heart center of each of these wisdom beings visualize absorption beings, the spiritual life-force present in the form of syllables. Starting in front and then encircling these syllables is the mantra chain of activity, the essence mantra that is being recited for each individual deity.

Recite the mantra while focusing one-pointedly on this visualization. You can do so until you have accumulated a certain number of recitations, such as a hundred thousand for each syllable, for a fixed length of time, like a month, or until certain signs of accomplishment occur, such as seeing the face of the deity. In particular, you should practice the vajra recitation assiduously, with the knowledge that the exhalation, inhalation, and resting of the breath are mantra.

From a saṃsāric perspective, this process will *purify* the nature of the sounds we use to communicate, the habitual patterns related to the ordinary speech of beings. In the pure context of buddhahood, the fruition will be *perfected* in the ground. The fruition, here, refers to the inconceivable secret of enlightened speech, which transcends sounds, words, and expressions, yet appears in a whole range of forms, such as the infinite number of vehicles. In the interim, in terms of practice, this process will purify the nature of ordinary speech and the subtle energies into the essence mantra. This, in turn, will *mature* one to practice the completion stage practices in which one relies on the energies, as taught in the father tantras.

The Stake of Unchanging Realization

The stake of unchanging realization is to be suffused with the view of reality. In this way, all sights and sounds, the environment and its inhabitants, are visualized as being spontaneously present as deities, mantra, and the celestial palace. It is not that these are conditioned phenomena, constructions emanated by the conceptual mind, however. Rather, they are the natural expression of the great emptiness and pure equality of ultimate reality, in which all that appears and exists is the manifest ground.

Within this maṇḍala there is not even the slightest fixation on self and other, samaya being and wisdom being, practice and goal, or pure and impure as being separate entities. Saṃsāra and nirvāṇa are inherently enlightened within the nondual expanse of this great equality. In other words, within this maṇḍala there is no fixation whatsoever on a so-called "self" and "deity" that are different from one another.

The true nature of your own being is one of complete purity. Within this divine nature you have been inseparable from the great wisdom mind of the deity from the very beginning. In truth, therefore, here you are training in equality, in the maṇḍala of vajra space.

Let me put this approach into verse:

> One with the nature of nondual great bliss
> Is the spacelike expanse of Vajrasattva.
> Space cannot be shown,
> As showing is purely conventional.
> Realize this point and saṃsāra and nirvāṇa will be nondual.
> Enlightened from the start, existence will be left just a name.
> In this unborn expanse is the vajra mind of all the victorious ones—
> The pure basic space of reality, free from meeting and parting.
> Appearance is the deity; apart from the deity there is nothing to see.
> Sounds as well are mantra; aside from mantra there is no sound.
> Yet deity and mantra are not real, but dharmakāya—
> A state of pure equality, free of fixation on self and other.
> Empty or not empty, how could it be?
> A path beyond conceptual mind, it is the king of vehicles.
> Never lose sight of this under any circumstance,
> Lest the visualized deity become a cause of bondage.

In terms of saṃsāra, this process will *purify* the negative mind and its habitual patterns that are present as self-aware, natural clarity. In the context of buddhahood, the fruition will be *perfected* in the ground, this fruition being the inconceivable secret of the enlightened mind, reality free from the complexities of thought and perception, as well as all the various forms this inconceivable clairvoyance can take. In the interim, in the context of practice, it will *mature* one for the completion stage meditations on bliss, clarity, and nonthought, where one relies on bodhicitta, in both its ultimate and relative forms, to familiarize oneself with the reality of nondual appearance-emptiness.

THE STAKE OF PROJECTION AND ABSORPTION

The stake of visualizing the projection and absorption of light rays entails engaging in the specific methods for putting the four types of enlightened activity into practice, both in terms of the supreme and mundane spiritual accomplishments. Here, the entire universe and all of its inhabitants, visualized as the divine maṇḍala, do not waver from enlightened mind, the realization of reality itself. Enlightened speech, the indomitable melody of the essence mantra, becomes the sixty melodious qualities. Enlightened form is also present, manifest as a display of the nine traits of peaceful deities and the nine expressions of the dance of wrathful deities.

From the mantra garland at the heart center of the deity an infinite number of light rays radiate outwards—brilliant white, shining yellow, dazzling red, and dark green. In a display similar to the heaven where beings delight in their own emanations, this is offered to the victorious ones of the three times and ten directions and their offspring, who are present as the maṇḍala circle. These are offered without making any distinction between the one being offered to and the one doing the offering. The recipients are then sated with the taste of the great wisdom of bliss-emptiness.

Though in one's own perception (as the manifest aspect of wisdom) not even the name "saṃsāra" can be observed, in the perception of others (the appearances of the ordinary mind) concrete entities, objects, and bodies exist. The entire range of these nonexistent, illusory appearances comprises the innumerable places and beings found within the six realms. The projected light of this skillful means connects with all of these, instantaneously purifying all forms of confused fixation and ignorance. All ordinary bodies awaken into divine forms, all ordinary speech awakens into the essence mantra, and all ordinary mental states awaken into the unchanging realization of the dharmakāya. Once this happens, not even the name "existence" remains. This understanding emphasizes the supreme spiritual accomplishment and is referred to as "the practice of spontaneously accomplishing the twofold benefit."

On a temporary level, these light rays have a different function. The white light carries out pacifying activity, the yellow light performs enriching activity, the red light accomplishes magnetizing activity, and the green light performs wrathful activity. The visualized projection and absorption and the ability to direct one's enlightened activity bring, among other things, the eight mundane spiritual accomplishments.

In a saṃsāric context, this process will *purify* and refine away all ordinary forms of physical, verbal, and mental activity, such as defeating enemies, caring for loved ones, business, agriculture, and so on. In the pure context of buddhahood, it will *perfect* the fruition in the ground, meaning all forms of inconceivable activity related to enlightened body, speech, and mind. In the interim, in the context of practice, this will *mature* one for the completion stage, in which one trains on the path that purifies intentional efforts to accomplish the twofold benefit spontaneously. At this stage, there is an ordinary path that entails a reference point and relies upon physical, verbal, and mental activities, as well as the practice of luminosity, which involves the direct realization of nonreferential wisdom. Through this, all that appears and exists will be purified into bodies of light.

As is said:

> Ground, path, and fruition are not different,
> But a union—this is the path of the buddhas.
> From the very beginning they are not manifold,
> But the perfect result, of a single taste.

The meaning here is as follows:

> The view—unchanging realization—is the ground,
> While meditation is the path, meaning
> Deity and mantra, and, implicitly, conduct.
> Enlightened activity, supreme and mundane, is fruition.
> These are the so-called "primordial path of unity."

As shown here, the stake of unchanging realization is the view. Hence, it is also the ground. Meditation consists of the stake of deity absorption and the stake of the essence mantra. This implicitly refers to conduct as well. Hence, these are the path. The stake of visualizing projection and absorption brings the supreme and mundane spiritual accomplishments and enacts enlightened activity in the present. This, therefore, is the fruition.

In this way, the four stakes that bind the life-force, or view, meditation, conduct, and fruition, as well as ground, path, and fruition, should not be seen as being different or separate from one another, nor should they be viewed as alternating or progressive stages. Instead, they should be seen as an indivisible unity that, from the very beginning, has known neither one nor many.

As the great purity and equality of reality itself, this unchanging realization is the enlightenment of space and wisdom. Its own display is the union of development and completion, which appears naturally as the relative maṇḍala of vajra space. Within this state, one trains by transforming empty sounds, the natural sound of mantra, and by manifesting the enlightened activity of projection and absorption.

Great wisdom, the enlightened body, speech, and mind of the buddhas, is free from deliberate effort and conceptual complexities. At the same time, it accomplishes the twofold benefit spontaneously. This fruition, which is here in this very moment, is what is known as the Secret Mantra Vajra Vehicle, the Vehicle of Fruition.

By realizing the view of the ground—that the cycle of wisdom is the equality of saṃsāra and nirvāṇa—one gains mastery over the life-force of both existence and peace. Through the path of meditation, the cycle of deity and mantra, one masters the life-force of both development and completion. Finally, by engaging in the spontaneous accomplishment of the twofold benefit, mastery is gained over the life-force of the inconceivable, great skillful means. To give an example, when Rāhula swallows the moon out of the sky, he naturally takes hold of all its reflections as well. In the same way, just by knowing these instructions on the four stakes that bind the life-force, one will be able to practice all the inconceivable key points and intents of both Sūtra and Tantra simultaneously.

Key Points for the Stake of Unchanging Realization

There are various key points that relate specifically to each of the four stakes. First are the eighteen key points that concern the stake of unchanging realization:

- Knowing the equality of saṃsāra and nirvāṇa is the key point that utterly purifies acceptance and rejection.
- Knowing the emptiness of one-taste is the key point that destroys clinging to reality and attachment to true existence.
- Knowing appearance and emptiness to be a unity is the key point that perfects the two accumulations simultaneously.
- Embracing the view is the key point that prevents development and completion from parting.

- Not wavering from the state of realization is the key point of meditation arriving at the view.
- Being freed from clinging to the sublime deity is the key point that prevents errors in the development stage.
- Perfecting all that appears and exists as the manifest ground is the key point that eliminates dualistic fixation on self and other.
- Realizing that primordial liberation is perfected in the ground is the key point that eliminates the faults of the five poisons.
- Arriving at the realization of the dharmakāya is the key point that perfects the three kāyas in one's own state of being.
- Knowing the ground and the fruition to be of one taste is the key point of not needing to practice or make conscious effort on the paths and levels.
- Meditation arriving at the fruition is the key point of not searching for enlightenment elsewhere.
- Fruition arriving at the ground is the key point that liberates fixation and attachment to the idea that there is something to attain.
- Oneness in the expanse of reality is the key point that purifies clinging to the samaya being and wisdom being.
- Realizing the sovereign lord of the one hundred families is the key point of practicing one deity and accomplishing them all.
- Achieving the supreme accomplishment is the key point that spontaneously accomplishes the twofold benefit.
- Being beyond good and evil, and acceptance and rejection, is the key point of not depending on ritual purity or righteous conduct.
- Knowing nonaction to be primordially completed is the key point of not needing the gradual arrangement of ritual.
- Purifying attachment to philosophical systems is the key point of having reached the peak of all vehicles.

These are the eighteen major key points. As there are even more than this, however, these are the "life-force of the life-force." Since they bind even the life-force of the other three life-forces, they are utterly indispensable and, therefore, placed first.

Key Points for the Stake of Absorption

There are six key points that relate to the stake of the development stage deity:

- Visualizing appearances as the deity is the key point that prevents one from straying into a one-sided emptiness.
- Taking the relative as the path is the key point that unites the two truths.
- Purifying the solidification of objects is the key point of abandoning clinging to things as being ordinary and truly existent.
- Perfecting the aspects of the ritual is the key point for perfecting the great accumulation of merit.
- Visualizing the features of the enlightened body is the key point that becomes the proximate cause of the form kāyas.
- Being in harmony with the actual nature of the fruition is the key point that spontaneously accomplishes the three kāyas.

Key Points for the Stake of the Essence Mantra

Next are the ten key points that concern the stake of the essence mantra:

- Taking vajra speech as the path is the key point that purifies the obscurations of speech.
- Meditating on the series of three beings is the key point for simultaneously liberating body, speech, and mind.
- Focusing on the visualized mantra chain is the key point for abandoning ordinary thoughts.
- The recitation that is like a moon with a garland of stars is the key point for resting in the natural flow of meditative concentration.
- The recitation that is like a spinning firebrand is the key point for producing the wisdom of empty bliss.
- The recitation that is like a broken beehive is the key point for liberating voices and sounds as mantra.
- Counting the essential life-force is the key point for receiving the blessings of the deity.
- Developing the strength of speech is the key point for making all that one says be of benefit to others.
- Accomplishing the true speech of knowledge mantras is the key point for accomplishing whatever aspirations one makes.
- Mastering the speech of the victorious ones is the key point for having gods and spirits, as well as all that appears and exists, follow one's command.

Key Points for the Stake of Projection and Absorption

The last six key points concern enlightened activity, the stake of projection and absorption:

- Accomplishing the supreme spiritual accomplishment is the key point for the automatic occurrence of the mundane accomplishments.
- Being able to direct the visualization is the key point for not being dependent on other activity practices.
- Perfecting enlightened activity is the key point of effortlessly benefiting others.
- Spontaneously accomplishing the benefit of others is the key point for accomplishing the deeds of the buddhas.
- Being inspired by the impetus of engendering the awakened mind is the key point for not straying into the Lesser Vehicle.
- Ripening and liberating those in need of guidance is the key point for upholding the lineage.

As outlined here, these four fundamental practices contain forty key points which subsume the entire range of key points that pertain to the path of the Secret Mantra Vajra Vehicle. Without them, any path is sure to be nothing but a lifeless corpse. This is why they are called "stakes that bind the life-force." They are also stakes that bind all aspects of duality into the oneness of nondual wisdom. If one were to explain the meaning of all these in detail, there is a great deal that could be said. For the time being, however, this much will suffice.

> "Do not keep these secret instructions hidden," a vajra friend said,
> "For they condense the key points of the path of Secret Mantra."
> With this request I set forth my own thoughts on this subject.
> Indeed, it accords with the scriptures of direct and indirect statements,
> But in truth, neither does it contradict the intent of the
> oceanlike collection of tantras.
>
> These are the secret words of Abu Shri.
> If any harm should come from this,
> I apologize to the deity and protectors.
> May the gatherings of virtue be of one taste
> With the ocean of omniscience.

ADDENDUM

The Fortress, Precipice, and Life-Force

Capturing the *fortress* of the view, freeing oneself from the *precipice* of meditation, and establishing the stronghold of the *life-force* of activity are known as the "yogic practice of mantra." These can be explained in general as well as individually. From a general point of view, these three principles condense the view, meditation, and conduct of the intent of all the infinite Great Vehicle sūtras and the collected tantras of the Mantra tradition.

This can be understood as follows. The view consists of the eighteen kinds of emptiness. In this view, one must be like a *fortress*, in the sense of being free from doubt. Meditation concerns the thirty-seven factors of enlightenment, which should have crossed over the *precipice* of dullness and agitation. Conduct involves the six perfections and plants the *life-force* of being free from self-centeredness. This is how the masters of the past explained this topic.

To continue, the view is not a way of being. This means that designations by the subjective mind are purified and have no existence within the inconceivable expanse of reality. Once this has come to pass, it is known as "capturing the great fortress of emptiness beyond conceptual mind."

What we call "meditation" entails resting continuously and evenly in this view once it has been realized. However, since one has crossed over the precipice of dullness and agitation, as well as that of clarity and obscuration, it is an effortless state of nonmeditation. For those who practice this way, appearances and mind are not two different things. In contrast, objective appearances arise as meditation (or, said differently, all that appears and exists arises as scripture). When that happens, it is said that meditation is not a way of nonbeing.

Mastering the view and meditation naturally liberates any sense that there are some things to accept and others to reject. This is known as "conduct devoid of both being and nonbeing," the great maintenance in which there is nothing to maintain. In other words, one has established the stronghold of the life-force—the single sphere of the dharmakāya. This fruition is the collapse of rejection and attainment, one has arrived at the essential character of the awakened mind, free from hope and fear.

These three, the fortress, precipice, and life-force, can be understood to provide the framework for the practice of a single yogi, from the time that he or she attains the empowerments that mature and instructions that liberate, up to the point where the levels and paths have been completely traversed. Furthermore, it is also said that the *fortress* of the development stage involves visualizing oneself in deity yoga, while the *life-force* of the completion stage is the unity of appearance and emptiness, the unconditioned nature of reality. Clearing away the *precipices* of both, such as dullness, agitation, and inferior mindsets, is known as the "activity of Samantabhadra."

The Three Visualizations

In the context of the activity ritual, it is held that one should visualize three objects. The outer object, the signs of the apparent aspect, is visualized as Rudra. The inner object, the symbolic weapon, is visualized as the Supreme Son. The secret object is the continuity of realization, which is visualized in the form of the divine appearance. Visualizing oneself as the Great Glorious One is done for the purpose of irreversibility. The visualization of the kīla dagger as the Supreme Son is done for the sake of invincibility. Visualizing the symbolic object as the actual enemy is done for the purpose of hostility.

In the heart center of the individual who is the focal point of the practice is the essence of blood, which is roughly the size of a sparrow's head. In its center, visualize a white ĀḤ syllable as a support for their life, merit, and vitality. This is then gathered into the three HŪṂ syllables at the tip of the kīla dagger and absorbed into one's own spiritual life-force. This is the transmission of life.

Together with the white ĀḤ syllable is the support for the afflicted mind and conciousness, visualized as a NRI or TRI syllable. When this is stabbed with the kīla dagger, the individual faints and falls unconscious. All of his or her thoughts dissolve into reality itself and the seed syllable then transforms into a sphere of light. This is the transmission of purification.

The sphere itself then dissolves into the three HŪṂ syllables on the tip of the kīla dagger. Next, it is ejected with three exclamations of PHAT and dissolved into the heart of the heruka. It then travels through the body and becomes a son in the space of the mother. This is the transmission of place.

THE FIVE MANIFESTATIONS OF ENLIGHTENMENT

According to the New Schools, the five manifestations of enlightenment are: 1) enlightenment as the lotus and moon disc seat, 2) enlightenment as the syllables of enlightened speech, 3) enlightenment as the symbolic implements of enlightened mind, 4) enlightenment as the complete enlightened form, and 5) enlightenment as the wisdom being.

In the Nyingma tradition, the first manifestation of enlightenment is the moon disc, the second is the sun disc, the third is the seed and the symbolic implement, the fourth is the transformation of these two into a sphere of light, and the fifth is the appearance of the complete form.

Composed by Chökyi Wangpo

HUSKS OF UNITY

A Clarification of the Development Stage Rituals

by **Getse Mahāpaṇḍita Tsewang Chokdrup**

Homage to the guru!

Buddha nature, the essence of reality itself,
Is fully expressed in the form of the deity
That seals the entire range of ordinary phenomena.
This method of development is the path of Vajradhara.

Appearing, yet free of clinging to reality,
Like a magical illusion, it lacks fundamental existence.
Beholding this wisdom is to see
The union of the two truths of mantra.

In the Secret Mantra tradition of Anuttarayoga, one attains the supreme and mundane accomplishments by relying upon the sublime deity. For those who wish to pursue this practice, there are some very important points to be aware of. Here, I will present a few such key points, explaining them mainly to facilitate an understanding of their relevance in terms of practice. For those inclined towards a more detailed approach, extensive explanations of this system can be found in the scriptures of the Transmitted Teachings and the Treasures, as well as in the works composed by masters of the past. It should go without saying, however, that this topic cannot be understood with just a brief explanation.

In this system, the basis for purification is buddha nature—buddhahood itself, complete with the powers and all its other qualities. Though this is the natural possession of all sentient beings and has been present in their minds from the very beginning, it is temporarily encapsulated in defilement. It is from this perspective that our buddha nature is termed "capacity" and "potential."

The object of purification is all that obscures this buddha nature. When the expression of this essence is not recognized for what it is, consciousness begins to operate in a dualistic manner, apprehending in terms of perceiver and perceived. Overpowered by delusion, the mind then imputes the existence of all saṃsāric phenomena, though in truth they do not exist. This is the process that obscures our buddha nature.

Generally speaking, the process of purification can involve a great variety of factors. In the context of this unique path, however, this process involves the skillful means of the development and completion stages that conform to both the ground and the fruition. In this context, I will emphasize the first of these two stages.

The result of purification is the purification of all temporary defilements. It also involves the actualization of all the qualities of the dharmakāya, the naturally pure essence, as they abide in the ground. This result comes about through the strength of having meditated on the path.

The principles of ground, path, and fruition are well known in both the causal and fruitional aspects of the Great Vehicle. Nevertheless, if you are not aware of these principles and how they relate to the fruitional path, an understanding of the development stage and the other aspects of this path will not take root. For this reason, it is important to be aware of these principles.

This being the case, you might wonder whether or not the principles of ground, path, and fruition are going to be taught in detail here. In this context, however, they will not be explained, as we shall focus instead on clarifying the core meaning of the development stage, predominantly in terms of the object of purification and the process of purification. The characteristics of the development stage were taught by the venerable Künga Nyingpo, who wrote:

> Its unique rituals are the complete development stage rituals taught in the tantras. Its unique result is the capacity to develop the power of mantra. Its unique essence is the nature of emptiness and blissful melting. Its unique function is the completion of purification, perfection, and maturation. To impute conceptually a divine form that possesses these four aspects constitutes the development stage yoga.

There are three main topics in this discussion: 1) the preliminaries, 2) the main practice, and 3) the concluding activities.

I

The Preliminaries

This section is divided into two parts: 1) the general preliminaries and 2) the unique preliminaries.

A. The General Preliminaries

Generally speaking, any person who practices Mantra must already be engaged in the attitude and conduct associated with the Great Vehicle. It is, therefore, an indispensable prerequisite for the attainment of unsurpassable enlightenment to have the correct motivation and conduct. This entails always assuming the great responsibility involved in working for the benefit of others in whatever you do, as well as never losing sight of this motivation. You should act out of a deeply rooted love, with the sincere recognition that all sentient beings are your own kind parents. Your compassion should be so intense that it blazes like the fire at the end of a great eon. Unless this has come to pass, your wishes and actions will oppose one another and you will never be able to attain the state you desire, even if you strive earnestly to attain the state of complete enlightenment. In fact, as such a person, you will be suited neither for the Great Vehicle nor the Lesser Vehicle.

Therefore, engendering the awakened mind by taking the bodhisattva vow is indeed an excellent part of the practice, regardless of the support you use. Through the capacity of the enlightened potential, the mind of a person with love, compassion, and the awakened mind will be matured as he or she obtains empowerment and enters the maṇḍala of any common, specific, or extraordinary yidam deity within the great maṇḍala of Secret Mantra. Such a person will then be upholding the three vows.

For this reason, the most important point to consider is the necessity of laying a foundation for correctly maintaining the main and subsidiary samaya vows. Then, you must understand how to give rise to renunciation and then take refuge, which is the cornerstone of all the vehicles. The next step is to engender the root of the Great Vehicle—the awakened mind.

1. Renunciation

At present, you have obtained a rare and precious human body with all its freedoms and riches. Nevertheless, though you may have it now, there is no way to know when impermanence will suddenly strike and you will die. Think this over well. You should also know with certainty that the connection between actions and their results is infallible.

With this certainty, contemplate deeply the suffering of saṃsāra. No matter where you are born in saṃsāra, whether high or low, there is no freedom from suffering. Even what may momentarily seem like happiness can suddenly change and vanish, like the sun behind clouds. Joy and sorrow, victory and defeat . . . all such experiences are transitory. You can see with your own eyes that not even a single one of them is lasting and stable. Think this over carefully.

You should train in this process until your attitude actually changes, until you no longer experience even a momentary wish for the happiness and wealth of saṃsāra. Instead, you should come to think that nothing is worthwhile and useful aside from the Dharma. Whether you chant a liturgy for this topic or not, it is important to apply this mind training to your own being when you first begin.

2. Refuge

The next section concerns the significance and practice of taking refuge. According to the Great Vehicle, the root of taking refuge is the unique attitude of wishing to liberate all sentient beings. All of these beings have, at one time or another, been your very own mother. As though tossed into a pit of fire, they are now tormented by the sufferings of saṃsāra.

As for the objects of refuge, you should stop looking to Brahma, Śiva, Viṣṇu, and all the other seemingly powerful guides in the world as a source of refuge. This also holds for their teachings—the perverted paths of those who have fallen into the abyss of permanence and nihilism—as well as the non-Buddhists who follow them. Finally, neither should you seek refuge with the various groups of barbarians or the local spirits of the place where you live. This includes deities, nāgas, and the spirits of your ancestors.

From a general point of view, the object of refuge is the Three Jewels. You should also be aware, however, that there are unique objects of refuge specific to the Secret Mantra tradition, in which the general Three Jewels are also included. The first such object of refuge is the guru, the essence of all Three Jewels. Second is the yidam deity, the jewel of the buddha, and third, the ḍākinīs and Dharma protectors, the jewel of the saṅgha.

The guru is the essential embodiment of all of the jewels: his or her empty yet apparent form, manifesting in the shape of the chief yidam deity of the maṇḍala, is the buddha; the secret mantras that express meaning are the Dharma; and the ḍākas and ḍākinīs that make up his or her retinue constitute the saṅgha. Thus, the Three Jewels are all included in a single great maṇḍala.

Alternatively, the same purpose will be accomplished by knowing that a single object can suffice as the object of refuge. In this case, devotion is directed towards the guru, the wish-fulfilling jewel who embodies all the Three Jewels and Three Roots. As stated in the *Tantra of the Emergence of Cakrasaṃvara*:

> The guru is the Buddha,
> The guru is the Dharma,
> And the guru is the saṅgha—
> The guru is the glorious Vajradhara.

Next is the actual practice of taking refuge. In the sky before you imagine your root guru sitting on an open and vast throne supported by lions, in the form of Vajradhara and surrounded by the lineage gurus. In front of him is your own supreme yidam deity, surrounded by the host of deities from the maṇḍalas of the four and six major classes of Tantra. To his right are the precious buddhas, in the form of the buddhas of the three times, such as the thousand of this excellent eon. Behind him are texts spontaneously resounding with the sound of the Sanskrit alphabet, the *āli kāli*, embodying the sacred Dharma. To his left is the saṅgha of the Great Vehicle, the noble assembly of bodhisattvas. This includes the eight great close sons, who are surrounded by the sixteen beings of this excellent eon, together with those on the Great Vehicle's paths of accumulation and joining. This also includes the noble assembly of the Lesser Vehicle, the listeners and solitary buddhas. Assemblies of ḍākas, ḍākinīs, Dharma protectors, and guardians surround them, amassed like thick cloudbanks. Imagine all of these beings seated before you—they are the great guides who will now lead you. With their limitless qualities of knowledge, love, and power, they look upon you with great love and affection.

Next, imagine that you are accompanied by every sentient being on the face of the earth. Headed by your parents and the demons that do you harm, everyone joins their palms in prayer. Then, with intense devotion you all think the following: "From now until we reach the very heart of enlightenment, we rely on and make offerings to you. Aside from you, we have no other refuge, no one else in whom we can place our hope." At the same time, recite the refuge verses from the scripture you are using, either three times or until you feel content. Next, you and all sentient beings dissolve into the objects of refuge. These, in turn, dissolve into the central guru, Vajradhara. Finally, with the visualization completely pacified, rest as long as you can in a nonconceptual state. This is the ultimate refuge, the natural state.

Taking refuge in this way lays the foundation for all types of training and supports the entire range of vows. Once you have taken refuge, you will be part of the Buddhist community. It also has the power to protect you from all fears and to bring an inconceivable amount of merit.

As for the refuge precepts, once you have taken refuge in the guru, you should take everything he or she says to be valid. Having taken refuge in the Buddha, you should not venerate worldly gods. Once you have taken refuge in the Dharma, you should cease causing harm to sentient beings. Finally, once you take refuge in the saṅgha, you should not associate with those who do not believe in the words of the Conqueror. In a general sense, you should take refuge six times every day. You should also have confidence in the Three Jewels and respectfully venerate statues, scriptures, and other sacred objects, make offerings to them, and avoid disrespectful behavior.

3. The Awakened Mind

Next is the significance and meditation of engendering the awakened mind. From the very beginning, all sentient beings have an utterly pure nature and the potential for enlightenment. Nevertheless, as an expression of their failure to recognize this nature, they form dualistic concepts of subject and object, and wander in a state of constant confusion as a result. These beings, all of whom have been our own mothers in the past, long to be happy, yet their actions bring only suffering. Like madmen, what they wish for and what they do are in complete opposition.

With intense compassion, think to yourself, "I must free all these beings from their torment and establish them in a state of constant, unsurpassable happiness—the state of perfect enlightenment. To begin with, however, I must attain this state myself." This is the awakened mind of aspiration. The awakened mind of application, on the other hand, is to think, "To this end, I will train in the unique methods of the profound and swift path, the development and completion stages of the yidam deity." Finally, think to yourself, "With these two superior intentions of aspiration and application, I have engendered the sacred and stainless awakened mind." As you think all this, recite the verses for engendering the awakened mind three times in a heartfelt manner, using whatever scripture you happen to be using.

Engendering the awakened mind produces limitless benefits. You will become a child of the victorious ones as soon as this mind-set is formed, for example, and whatever wholesome actions you set out to accomplish will be conducive to liberation. All your negative karma will be instantaneously exhausted as well, and even the most miniscule virtue that you create will develop into an unlimited amount of merit. Thus, you will have stepped onto the path of freedom. The *Sūtra of the Tathāgata's Secret* states:

> If the merit of the awakened mind
> Were to have a form,
> It would fill all of space,
> And even then could not be contained.

All the precepts associated with the awakened mind can be included in two factors: constantly wishing for the welfare of others and always longing for the enlightened state. On the other hand, if these are given up, you will have severed the very root of the awakened mind, both in terms of aspiration and application. Through this, the root of the Great Vehicle will be cut as well. Therefore, since you will never find any other method for attaining the state of complete enlightenment, you should concentrate intensely on this practice. This is why mental vows are said to be the central factor for a bodhisattva. As before, you should apply the ideas and meditations outlined above to all the relevant verses for engendering the awakened mind.

B. The Unique Preliminaries

The unique preliminaries consist of: 1) clearing away adverse conditions and 2) gathering positive conditions.

1. Clearing Away Adverse Conditions

This section has two parts: 1) expelling obstructing forces and 2) establishing the boundary.

a. Expelling Obstructing Forces

The nature of this meditation is as follows. Start out by turning your attention to the natural state, in which all phenomena abide as emptiness. Then, as the expression of this state, visualize yourself instantaneously in the form of the glorious heruka Hayagrīva or any other suitable yidam deity, like a bubble emerging on the surface of water. Next, focus on the torma for the obstructing forces and utter the three syllables. The syllable OṂ purifies all impure defilements and removes imperfections and defects. The syllable ĀḤ multiplies the substance so that it increases and expands infinitely. The syllable HŪṂ endows it with perfect color, smell, and taste, so that it appears as the essence of all that is desirable. Finally, the syllable HOḤ removes its defiling stains and transmutes it into the nectar of undefiled wisdom.

Next, visualize light radiating from your heart center. This light summons all demonic forces before you, who then listen to your command. Chant the command liturgy from the scripture you are using, offer the torma, and send them off to their respective dwellings. As for those who will not listen to your order and set out to make obstacles, visualize innumerable flaming weapons and small wrathful emanations emerging from the seed syllable in your heart center and elsewhere, shooting like stars in all directions. As numerous as dust particles in sunlight, these emanations crush the bodies and minds of these forces into minute particles and incinerate them to the point where not even their names remain.

b. Establishing the Boundary

Establishing the boundary is analogous to locking your door after you have kicked out a thief. As the weapons that were visualized earlier gather back in, they merge and melt together, giving the entire ground the appearance of molten metal. This vajra ground encompasses all directions and is encircled by a tall wall, which surrounds this spacious land like a range of iron mountains. The wall consists of alternating layers of upright and horizontal vajras. It is crowned by a vajra dome, which is high in the middle and slopes down at the sides. This dome resembles a skull and is attached to the fence like a lid. At the point where the dome and fence meet, a vajra grate forms a covering canopy. The entire exterior of the fence and dome is covered by a vajra lattice, which is attached to crossed vajra cords. The top of the dome is ornamented by a half-vajra. Vajra garlands bind the exterior of the fence's midsection. The spaces between the larger vajras are filled by smaller vajras, such that they appear to be melded together. All of these vajras are blue. From above, a rain of small wrathful emanations and various weapons pours down.

Surrounding all this is a dome of blazing fire, which itself is surrounded by a dome of vajra rivers with wild, stormy waves. Further out is another dome, a violent black vajra tempest that cuts anything it touches like a razor. These domes mark the boundaries of the surrounding protection circle and prevent any demons and negative forces from approaching. On the inside, you, your possessions, and retinue are protected.

While visualizing this, chant the verses for establishing the boundary line and protection circle from whichever text you are using. Then, to conclude, bring to mind the wisdom that is free from any focal point, in which there is no one to protect, no one doing the protecting, and no act of protection. This will transform all that you have visualized into the protection circle of reality itself—the supreme form of protection.

2. Gathering Positive Conditions

This section has two parts: 1) the descent of blessings and 2) consecrating the offering articles.

a. THE DESCENT OF BLESSINGS

In this context, the descent of blessings occurs by invoking the compassion of the Three Roots with fervent devotion. Visualize all their blessings and spiritual accomplishments in various forms. Their enlightened bodies appear as divine forms, their enlightened speech as seed syllables, and their enlightened minds as symbolic implements. Like snow falling on a lake, all these dissolve into you, your dwelling place, and all the ritual articles, blessing them in the process. As you imagine this, recite the verses for the descent of blessings.

b. CONSECRATING THE OFFERING ARTICLES

The nature of the meditation for consecrating the offering articles is as follows. As you visualize yourself as the deity, emanate the syllables RAṂ, YAṂ, and KHAṂ from your heart center. Fire appears from the RAṂ syllable and burns away all the impure faults and defects of the offering articles. From the YAṂ syllable, wind arises and scatters all the bonds of believing things to be real. Finally, from the KHAṂ syllable, water streams forth, washing away and purifying all the impurities of your negative habitual patterns. In essence, this purity is spacelike emptiness, devoid of true existence.

While resting in that recognition, visualize an infinitely large cloud of offerings radiating outwards, filling the entirety of space. This includes flowers and other common offerings, and also the five outer and five inner offerings. All of these appear inside a vast, open jeweled vessel, which itself arises from a BHRUṂ syllable. Within this vessel, an OṂ syllable gives rise to the outer offerings—flowers of divine substances—as well as the inner offerings—self-arisen substances like the flowers of the five sense faculties. Every possible desirable thing is present there. An infinite number of goddesses then radiate out from each group of offerings, each carrying their own individual offerings.

The next meditation relates to the unique offerings of nectar, torma, and rakta. The first of these is the offering of nectar. Visualize a vast, open, self-existing skull cup that contains the five meats and five nectars. Human flesh and excrement are in the middle, cow meat and semen in the east, dog meat and brain to the south, horse meat and ova in the west, and elephant meat and urine in the north. Next, successively visualize the ten male and female buddhas of the five families arising from the syllables HRĪḤ, BAṂ, HŪṂ, LAṂ, TRĀṂ, MAṂ, OṂ, MUṂ, ĀḤ, and TĀṂ. A stream of red and white bodhicitta then flows down from the place where they unite. At the conclusion of this process, the deities melt into light and dissolve into the nectar. The nectar, in turn, becomes the essence of the five wisdoms, perfect in color, smell, taste, capacity, and power.

Next is the torma offering. Start out by visualizing a jeweled torma vessel as big as the entire earth. Visualize the torma within it, a mass of desirable things and nectar that fills up the entire expanse of space with all that brings pleasure.

As for the offering of rakta, visualize a vast, open vessel made of a fresh skull with the hair still on it. Then imagine that all the concepts of craving and attachment related to the three realms coalesce within it. Though they take the form of blood, their essence is that of unattached great bliss. Out of this ocean of blood, clouds of every possible kind of desirable object emanate, filling all of space.

In certain abbreviated practice manuals, you will not find these preliminary practices, from refuge and the awakened mind up to the practices just discussed. There are even some that contain nothing but refuge and bodhicitta. For this reason, you must make time for these elements.

II
The Main Practice

This section consists of two topics: 1) the practice of the meditation state and 2) the subsequent practices.

A. The Practice of the Meditation State

The first topic has three further divisions: 1) enlightened body, the practice of the deity; 2) enlightened speech, the practice of recitation; and 3) enlightened mind, the practice of luminosity.

1. Enlightened Body: The Practice of the Deity

There are five subdivisions in this section: 1) the framework of the three absorptions, 2) visualizing the maṇḍalas of the support and the supported, 3) invoking the wisdom beings and requesting them to remain, 4) the activities of homage, offering, and praise, and 5) focusing on the deity's appearance, the primary focal point.

a. The Framework of the Three Absorptions

i. The Absorption of Suchness

In the absorption of suchness, the object of purification is the death process. The first stage of death involves a series of outer and inner dissolutions. Once this process is complete, the three phases of appearance, increase, and attainment occur, each of which dissolves into the subsequent stage. In the last phase, full attainment dissolves into luminosity. If this moment goes unrecognized, the death state involves a turning away from this momentary appearance of luminosity, the clear, empty, and thoroughly nonconceptual dharmakāya.

The process of purification is the absorption of suchness, which refers to witnessing the nature of reality itself. In this very moment, the innate, natural state of the ordinary mind is one of simplicity. When you rest directly in this nature of mind, without trying to alter it in any way, you will see that the entire range of apparent phenomena do not go anywhere, nor are they present anywhere. They are not conceptualized and there is no grasping at them as being real.

As for the way it is, having never existed, it is not nonexistent. Yet since it has never been nonexistent either, neither does it exist. Thus, it is *emptiness*. In no way is it a permanent phenomenon, nor is it completely nonexistent. It cannot be ascertained as an object of knowledge or put into words, and so it possesses *no characteristics*. Finally, because its essence does not fall within the realm of the compounded, its identity is *without desire*. In this way, it possesses the characteristics of the three gates to complete liberation.

The result of purification is the dharmakāya, the wisdom of the buddhas that is utterly free from mental fabrication. Thus, both the object of purification and the result of purification are similar to the absorption itself. When training in this way, in terms of saṃsāra, the habitual patterns of the death state are purified and refined away, as is one's fixation on actual entities. The latent potential associated with dharmakāya is nourished as well, whereby the fruition of nirvāṇa is perfected. Until that takes place, it lays the foundation for the birth of luminosity in one's mind and matures one for the higher paths.

ii. The Absorption of Total Illumination

In the absorption of total illumination, the object of purification is the disembodied consciousness that arises the moment one fails to recognize the luminous dharmakāya during death. This refers to the mental body of the intermediate state that develops from the energetic-mind in this state. This form of consciousness has the complete range of faculties and an appearance that is flickering and momentary, like a dream.

The process of purification involves training in a detached and illusory compassion, one that includes all sentient beings of the six realms without any sense of bias or partiality. Here, reflect on the fact that saṃsāra and nirvāṇa are not two different things when it comes to their true nature, suchness. Still, although they never part from this state, beings cling to illusory appearances as though they were real and end up wandering helplessly in the realms of saṃsāra as a result. Reflecting on this, you should then think, "I must free all these beings from suffering!"

The result of purification involves the emanation of the illusory wisdom body of the sambhogakāya, clear and complete, with all its marks and signs. The illusory absorption of total illumination accords with both saṃsāra and nirvāṇa. By training in this absorption, the stains of saṃsāra are purified and refined away. These are the habitual patterns of the intermediate state and any ideas one may have about a one-sided emptiness. In terms of nirvāṇa, the seed that allows for an actualization of the sambhogakāya is nurtured. Until that takes place, it matures one for the completion stage by laying a foundation for developing great compassion, which is the cause for arising from luminosity in the form of the wisdom deity.

iii. The Causal Absorption

In the causal absorption, the object of purification is the energetic-mind of the intermediate state that is on the verge of being reborn. This occurs once the mental body of a sentient being in the intermediate state becomes directed towards its future rebirth and generates attachment to one of the four types of birth.

The process of purification involves meditating on the self-aware unity of emptiness and great compassion—the syllable of the root life-force of any deity, such as HRĪḤ or HŪṂ. Apparent and yet without intrinsic nature, such syllables are the support for the awakened mind. The essence of this great subtle life-force is both vividly clear and utterly unchanging, yet it is capable of arising in any form.

The result of purification is the coarse form emanated by the sambhogakāya, which arises in this manner for those in need of guidance. This absorption corresponds to the factors that cause rebirth to take place, the energetic-mind of the intermediate state as it is on the verge of entering a new birthplace. It also corresponds to the way in which nirmāṇakāya buddhas manifest various emanations in the perception of those who need guidance.

Due to this correspondence, training in the causal absorption by meditating on the seed syllables that generate the whole range of maṇḍalas enacts a process of purification, perfection, and maturation. In terms of saṃsāra, the habitual tendency to enter a new birthplace is refined away and purified, as is the idea that appearance and emptiness are two different things. In terms of nirvāṇa, this nourishes the seed of liberation, leading to the actualization of the nirmāṇakāya, whereby the fruition is perfected. In between these two stages, one is matured for the completion stage by laying the foundation for the ability to arise out of bliss, energy, and mind in the form of the wisdom deity.

These three absorptions are the basis for accomplishing the entire range of development stage practices. As such, they are indispensable, regardless of whether one's practice manual is elaborate or condensed.

All deity meditations are preceded by the mantra OṂ SVABHĀVA ŚUDDHAḤ SARVADHARMĀḤ SVABHĀVA ŚUDDHO 'HAṂ. In reciting this mantra one is saying, "Just as all phenomena are naturally pure, so too am I pure by nature," which captures the meaning of the absorption of suchness.

In certain contexts, the mantra OṂ MAHĀ ŚŪNYATĀ JÑĀNA VAJRA SVABHĀVĀTMAKO 'HAṂ is recited. This mantra condenses the meaning of all three absorptions. Its meaning is, "I am the very embodiment of the nature of vajra wisdom and great emptiness." In this mantra, the phrase "great emptiness" refers to the absorption of suchness, while the remainder illustrates the latter two absorptions. The term "vajra wisdom" points to the union of emptiness and great bliss or, alternately, to the union of emptiness and compassion. What one needs to understand here is that the significance of both the absorption of total illumination and the causal absorption is contained in the statement, "I am the very embodiment of the nature of vajra wisdom."

b. Visualizing the Supportive and Supported Maṇḍalas

This second section has two parts: 1) visualizing the supportive palace and 2) visualizing the supported deity.

i. The Supportive Palace

The first topic has three further divisions: 1) visualizing the layered elements that form the foundation, 2) visualizing the celestial palace where the deities dwell, and 3) visualizing their seats.

1) THE LAYERED ELEMENTS

With the first of these divisions, the object of purification consists of the impure karmic appearances of one's own mind. This includes the maṇḍalas of the four elements, along with the central mountain, all of which appear to the relative, confused consciousness.

The process of purification involves the following visualization. Within the extremely vast and spacious protection circle that was visualized previously, imagine the syllable of the causal absorption resting in space. Then, gradually visualize the seeds of the five elements and the central mountain appearing from this syllable. The syllable E becomes the source of phenomena. It is deep blue and of infinite dimensions, with its tip pointed downwards and its corners facing up in a wide opening. On top of that, the syllable YAṂ transforms into the wind maṇḍala. It has the shape of a crossed vajra and is surrounded by a ring of dark green light rays that resemble smoke. Above that, the fire maṇḍala arises from the syllable RAṂ, its appearance a red triangle encircled by a garland of fire. Higher up is the water maṇḍala, which appears from the transformation of the syllable BAṂ. This maṇḍala is white and swirls in a circular motion, surrounded by white light. On top of that is the syllable LAṂ, which becomes the earth maṇḍala. It is golden, square, and surrounded by yellow light. Finally, the syllable SUṂ becomes the central mountain, which is made of four kinds of jewels and has four terraces.

The result of purification is ultimate wisdom, also known as undeluded natural perception, the basic space of phenomena, great liberation, and the bhaga of the Vajra Queen along with its symbolic form, and the utterly pure expanse of space of the five female buddhas.

2) THE CELESTIAL PALACE

The second section concerns the celestial palace where the deities dwell, which is located on top of the elements. The object of purification in this stage is conceptual attachment that fixates on houses and the other places where beings live as if they exist in their own right.

For the process of purification a five-colored letter BHRŪṂ appears from the syllable of the causal absorption and descends onto the central mountain. It then melts into light and produces the celestial palace (at this point, it is not mandatory to visualize the layered elements, with their respective maṇḍalas, and the inner contents of the protection circle, such as the vajra fence and dome, beyond what has already been done). On top of the central mountain visualize an even vajra ground. On its perimeter is a vajra fence that resembles iron mountains, blazing with innumerable masses of five-colored fire. Inside the vajra fence are the eight great charnel grounds, arranged in a circle on the vajra ground. A jeweled lotus with a thousand petals sits in the center. On its anthers rests a clear and radiant sun disc, equal in size to the anthers. This in turn supports a crossed vajra with a blue square at its center.

This is where the celestial palace is located. It is square in shape and has walls that are constructed of five kinds of jewels. These walls are five in number and gradually layered from within, beginning with the color that corresponds to the particular family of the main deity. A ledge of red jewels surrounds the external foundation of the celestial palace, which protrudes at the base. Upon it are sixteen offering goddesses, all of whom are facing towards the celestial palace and holding their respective offerings.

At the upper end of the walls runs a yellow border, adorned by jewel tassels that hang down like lotus flowers. On top of that run the beams, which are supported by posts. These are also known as pillar stabilizers. On top of these hang lattices and tassels made of jewels, which extend from the mouths of the dragons at the end of the rafters in the ceiling. The roof rests on the rafters and extends out to the edge of the external foundation. Beneath, on the inside of the roof, is a line of rainspouts made of white jewels, each of which looks like an anointing vase turned upside down. The garlands between them are fastened directly beneath the low end of the rafters. On the roof, right above them, is the railing, which consists of three or four levels of white jewel planks.

Inside the celestial palace there are eight pillars that support four interlocked beams, upon which twenty-eight rafters rest. Except for a skylight in the center, the ceiling is made of flat panels made of white jewel planks resting on top of the pillars. Jewels are scattered all over the roof. The so-called "central chamber" refers to an arrangement of pillars or wooden posts constructed around four window openings. They support the upper roof, on top of which, at the peak, is a jewel-crested vajra.

In each of the four directions there are four entrances with vestibules, each of which is in the exact center of one of the walls. Their upper part has two protruding corners, while their lower part connects with the external foundation. Each has four pillars, upon which are four interlocked beams that support the eight-leveled architraves.

These levels are the horse ankle, lotus, casket, lattice, cluster ornament, garlands, rainspout, and roof. The horse ankle consists of a row of yellow vajras standing upright on a blue background. The lotus is a row of lotus petals made of red jewels. The casket is a smooth casket made of various jewels and inserted between the pillars and the beams. The lattice is a network of white jewels. The cluster ornament is a webbed hanging. The garland is made of jewel lattices and tassels. The rainspouts and roof were described above. On top of the roof there is a golden wheel supported on either side by a golden deer, one male and one female. The wheel is surmounted by a beautiful white jeweled parasol.

This covers the general appearance of the celestial palace. In some wrathful maṇḍalas, however, the structure of the blazing charnel ground palace is taught, which functions to tame those of a more intractable nature. In that context, you should visualize that the palace walls are made of conjoined dry, fresh, and old skulls. The pillars and beams are made up of the eight great gods and the eight great nāgas, respectively. The ceiling consists of the twenty-eight lunar mansions, while the skylight is made up of the eight planets, the sun, and the moon. The lattices and tassels are made of snakes and skulls. The architraves are ornamented with fingers, skulls, the five sense organs, and garlands of the sun and moon. The ledge is made of backbones. The roof consists of the hollow skull of Mahādeva and is ornamented with a heart at its top. The banners and canopies are made of human skin. Inside and out, the whole area is filled with charnel grounds and swirling oceans of blood. Terrifying fires and fierce storms rage everywhere.

When training in this manner, if you do not recall the purity of each individual element of the visualization, your meditation will do nothing more than produce an ordinary state of mind. The recollection of purity is, therefore, what illustrates (or gives form to) the perfectly pure properties of buddhahood, its qualities and inconceivable compassion and activity (which are inconceivable because they are hard to fathom, or not understood at all). In the perception of those who, being of a lesser capacity, fail to realize the natural state in an accurate manner, the features of the celestial palace and the deity's form transform their training into the genuine path. That is why you must keep the symbols and their meaning in mind. If, on the other hand, you fail to understand this point, your meditation will be constricted by the habitual patterns of your ordinary state of mind. As a result, you will not be able to rise above saṃsāra and will end up like a worldly god or Rudra.

As for the purity of the celestial palace, the four corners symbolize that the basic space of phenomena is utterly without inequality. The four gates symbolize that the four immeasurables lead to the palace of great bliss. The eight graded architraves indicate that, once the eight vehicles have been journeyed, one arrives at this vehicle of nonduality. The four resultant architraves represent the four means of magnetizing. The eight or four streamers on each of these symbolize the perfect qualities of the philosophical systems of the eight or four vehicles. The uninterrupted spinning of the wheel of the Dharma is shown in the wheels and other such factors. The external foundation represents the four foundations of mindfulness. The four pillars that constitute the architraves symbolize the four authentic eliminations. The four gate openings represent the four bases of miraculous power. The five-layered walls symbolize the five capacities. The hangings, the streamers at the top border, the rainspouts, the ledge, and the dome symbolize the five strengths. The ornaments of the jewel lattices and tassels, the flower garlands, the silk streamers, the mirror, the moon, and the tail fan symbolize the seven factors of enlightenment. The eight pillars symbolize the eightfold noble path. The pillar capitals symbolize the eight emancipations. The four beams symbolize the four types of fearlessness. The twenty-eight internal rafters symbolize the eighteen types of emptiness and the ten perfections. The upper flat panels symbolize inconceivable qualities. The four supporting posts symbolize the four correct discriminations. The crowning ornament symbolizes that all maṇḍalas of the enlightened ones coalesce in the expanse of self-aware wisdom. The parasol symbolizes that all beings are protected with great compassion, while the flag symbolizes great compassion itself.

The light that radiates in all directions represents the eternal wheel of adornment belonging to enlightened body, speech, and mind. The radiance of unobscured lucidity free from inside and out represents the totality of wisdom manifestations. The crossed vajra that forms the ground symbolizes the wisdom of emptiness. The twelve enclosures symbolize the complete purity of the twelve links of interdependent origination. The sun seat represents the natural luminosity of reality itself. The lotus garlands show that reality is unstained by any faults. The eight charnel grounds represent the innate purity of the eight collections of consciousness and illustrate the eight examples of illusion. The vajra fence symbolizes nonconceptual wisdom. The masses of flames indicate that the fire of wisdom consumes demons and disturbing emotions.

Although it is important to be mindful of the purity of each symbol as well as what they represent, as a beginner you may not be able to recall all these factors in a single practice session. If this is the case, you can approximate the recollection of purity by thinking to yourself that all the features of the celestial palace represent the inconceivable qualities of the abandonment and realization of the buddhas. The result of purification is the delight of the supreme secret, which is also known as the palace of great liberation, the great city of nirvāṇa, the true Akaniṣṭha, the way things truly are, and the utterly pure and naturally appearing palace.

To continue, the successively piled elements together with the central mountain symbolize the five root cakras and the central channel. The basis of the maṇḍala, the lotus, sun, and crossed vajra, symbolize the energy and essences at the center of the root cakras. The mind that mingles with all these—the factors of clarity, emptiness, and bliss—is represented by the celestial palace. By meditating in this manner, the channels, essences, and energies will become pliable and controlled. This, in turn, lays the foundation for the birth of the wisdom that occurs in the completion stage, maturing one for the higher paths.

3) THE SEAT

The third section concerns visualizing the deity's seat. In this context, the object of purification is the habitual tendency associated with the birthplace of sentient beings, such as semen and ovum or heat and moisture. The process of purification involves visualizing a red lotus seat in the middle of the celestial palace. In the next step, imagine a red sun disc and a full moon disc, equal in size to the center of the lotus and stacked on top of it. This pertains to the main deity. You should also be aware of the seats and other features associated with the other deities in the retinue. In this context, wrathful deities have their own specific seat, which consists of Rudra, a corpse, an animal, and so forth. The result of purification is the ability of a nirmāṇakāya buddha to remain unstained by faults and defects, regardless of its birthplace. This result also entails the naturally pure luminosity of the enlightened mind and the perfection of wisdom, the union of means and knowledge.

A particularly wonderful feature of this approach is that the factors visualized here correspond to elements of the higher paths. The lotus symbolizes the root cakras, while the sun represents the "small A" in the practice of yogic heat and the moon corresponds to the HAṂ syllable at the top of the head. These factors mature the practitioner by laying the foundation for the attainment of unchanging bliss, which occurs based on the blissful melting of blazing and dripping.

ii. The Supported Deity

The third topic concerns visualizing the supported deity, which has two parts: 1) the development rituals and 2) the characteristics of the deity.

1) The Development Rituals

There are three varieties of development ritual: the extended ritual of the five manifestations of enlightenment, the moderate ritual of the four manifestations of enlightenment, and the condensed threefold ritual. Among these three, the condensed ritual is the most common in the treasures of the Early Translation School.

According to this system, the object of purification is the entrance of the intermediate state consciousness in between the parents' ovum and semen and the subsequent stages of physical development. Here the sun disc seat corresponds to the mother's ovum and the moon to the father's semen. The seed syllable of the causal absorption descending onto the seat corresponds to the moment when the consciousness of the intermediate state enters the coalesced red and white elements in the mother's womb.

When the seed syllable transforms into the deity's symbolic implement, the inseparable blending of semen, ovum, and mind that takes place once consciousness has entered in between the red and white elements is purified. The subsequent projection and absorption of light rays purifies the gradual development of the aggregates, elements and sense fields formed by the four elements of the body in the womb. The transformation of the symbolic implement into the full form of the deity purifies the habitual patterns of beings in the womb, from the time their body is fully formed until they are born.

This manner of visualization is also capable of purifying the habitual patterns of other modes of birth. In terms of egg birth, the seed syllable of the deity purifies the disembodied consciousness, while the transformation of this syllable into the symbolic implement purifies the entrance of this consciousness in between the semen and ovum in the womb. Finally, as the symbolic implement itself melts into a sphere of light at the conclusion of the projection and absorption of light rays, the habitual patterns associated with egg birth are purified.

This can also be applied to birth from heat and moisture. In this context, the sun seat purifies heat, the moon seat purifies moisture and the seed syllable and symbolic implement purify the energetic-mind of the intermediate state. The projection and absorption of light rays and the full formation of the deity's body purify the development of the body in the midst of heat and moisture.

In terms of miraculous birth, the divine seat purifies the birthplace, while the seed and symbolic implement purify the energetic-mind of the intermediate state. The projection and absorption of light rays purify the perpetuation that occurs through the power of craving and grasping a birthplace and a new body. The full development of the deity's body purifies the body instantaneously coming into existence.

The process of purification can be summarized as follows: First, in the ritual of the syllable of enlightened speech, the causal seed syllable rests in space and then descends onto the deity's seat. Next, in the ritual of the symbolic implement of enlightened mind, limitless light radiates out from the symbolic implement, which is marked by the letter of the essential seed syllable. This light invites all buddhas to gather in the sky before oneself. The symbolic implement and its seed syllable then dissolve into light. Finally, these two transform into the resultant vajra holder, the form of one's particular yidam deity with all its marks and signs vivid and complete. This comprises the ritual of the complete enlightened form. The result of purification for this stage entails certain enlightened deeds that occur once one has arisen as a nirmāṇakāya that tames beings, here referring to the point of entering the womb up until birth.

This also relates to the higher paths. The joined sun and moon on the lotus seat represent the union that takes place through the blazing and dripping of blissful heat in the knots of the root cakras in the central channel. The seed and symbolic implement symbolize the energetic-mind dissolving into the central channel. The transformation enacted by the projection and absorption of light rays symbolizes the empty bliss that arises from blissful melting. The complete formation of the enlightened body illustrates how one can accomplish the form of the wisdom deity from naturally-coemergent empty bliss. Thus, these elements also mature one for the completion stage.

In abbreviated practice manuals, only the seat may be included and not the celestial palace. There are also a great number of concise development stage practices where the entire visualization takes place instantaneously just by a moment of recollection. Thus, as each of these may appear in a particular context without being subject to any final scheme, one should understand that it is not always necessary to perform an elaborate visualization of the celestial palace and the other elements of the visualization.

2) The Characteristics of the Deity

The second section concerns the characteristics of the visualized deity. At this point, nothing definitive can be presented concerning the object of meditation aside from what appears in the practice manual of the deity that is being practiced. However, when it comes to recollecting purity, which relates to the nature of the deities that are being meditated upon, the following principles can be said to apply universally.

a) Peaceful Deities

A deity with a single face symbolizes the single sphere of dharmakāya, while three faces symbolize the three gates to complete liberation (or the three kāyas). Two arms symbolize the skillful means of great compassion and the knowledge of emptiness. Four arms symbolize the four kinds of wisdom. Alternatively, they can also symbolize love, compassion, empathetic joy, and equanimity. Six arms symbolize the five wisdoms and self-existing wisdom. Sitting in the cross-legged vajra posture symbolizes the equality of existence and peace, or the lack of abiding in such extremes. Since the deity is beautified with the elegance of the nine traits of peaceful deities, it is attractive with nothing unpleasant to the eye.

The nine features just mentioned are as follows. Peaceful deities have slender and soft bodies, symbolizing pure birth. All parts of their body are pliable and well proportioned, symbolizing the purification of disease. As the basis for dying has been purified, their bodies are not loose, but firm, and also supple and upright. Furthermore, they are soft and youthful and have an attractive appearance because the basis for aging has been purified. These are the essential qualities; when counting "firm" and "supple" separately, there are five in total.

Since they are adorned with the flowers of excellent signs and the fruits of illustrative marks, the deities' bodies are pure and have a clear complexion. Having perfected the sphere of totality, their bodies are radiant. They are also attractive, being both dignified and beautiful.

Finally, as their radiance overpowers those to be tamed, they have an overwhelming presence. These are the four physical features. Thus, in total there are nine aspects.

As a sign of being free from the torments of disturbing emotions, the deity wears a white silk scarf, an upper garment embroidered with gold, and a checkered skirt tied with a multicolored cord. Symbolizing the perfection of all virtuous phenomena, their long hair is tied in a topknot. Ornaments of jewels and flowers illustrate the superiority of not abandoning sense pleasures as the adornment of wisdom.

Their jewelry illustrates the seven factors on the path of enlightenment. To elaborate, their jewel necklace represents mindfulness, while their crown illustrates the discrimination of phenomena and their bracelets signify diligence. Their earrings stand for pliancy and their armbands represent concentration. The shorter necklace stands for equanimity and, finally, the flower garland illustrates joy. Their six bone ornaments symbolize the complete purification of anger. Symbolizing the perfections, the necklace represents generosity, the bracelets and anklets symbolize discipline, the earrings stand for patience, the ring on their head symbolizes diligence, the belt represents meditative concentration, and the offering string symbolizes transcendent wisdom.

The essence of the deity is as follows. When considering the activity of great compassion that acts for the welfare of beings at a relative level, one meditates on the form of the male consort. This is the manifest aspect of the most excellent and immutable wisdom, the skillful means of great bliss. Apart from its empty essence, there is not a single thing that truly exists, not even an atom. This holds true for all phenomena, both those associated with the pure peace of nirvāṇa, as well as the entire universe, its inhabitants, and all forms, sounds, smells, tastes, and everything else associated with saṃsāra. All these illusory phenomena, therefore, do not obstruct each other; anything whatsoever can arise. Emptiness is the very basis for the appearance of phenomena. This includes birth and death, waxing and waning, movement and change, causes and results . . . all that seemingly exists. For this reason, ultimate emptiness is referred to as the female consort, meaning the empty aspect of the basic space of wisdom. Contemplating these divine forms ensures that this practice becomes a genuine path.

Furthermore, emptiness is seen based on appearance, while appearances arise unhindered from the expressive potential of emptiness, which itself manifests as causality. Since the truth of this is undeniable, the two truths are in union; they do not conflict with the principle of interdependent origination. You cannot attain the perfect result of nirvāṇa by utilizing just one of these while abandoning the other. Therefore, the way to bring this onto the path is to meditate on male and female deities in union, symbolizing the indivisible union of skillful means and knowledge.

The naked body of the female consort illustrates freedom from the obscuration of conceptual symbols. As an illustration of unchanging great bliss endowed with the sixteen joys, she appears in the form of a youthful, sixteen-year-old girl. Her hair hangs loose, showing the unlimited way that wisdom expands impartially out of basic space. She is adorned with five bone ornaments. Of these, the ring at the top of her head symbolizes the wisdom of the basic space of phenomena, while her bone necklace represents the wisdom of equality. Her earrings stand for discerning wisdom, her bracelets for mirrorlike wisdom, and her belt for all-accomplishing wisdom. Illustrating the unity of calm abiding and insight, her secret space is joined in union.

To mention briefly the purity of the symbolic implements, the five-pronged vajra symbolizes the five wisdoms, while the curved knife illustrates cutting through concepts. The skull cup represents sustaining the bliss of nonconceptual wisdom. It is filled with blood to illustrate how one should make use of great wisdom to conquer the four demons and bring saṃsāra under one's control. The sword of knowledge symbolizes cutting the root of birth and death. The khaṭvāṅga represents cutting the roots of the three poisons.

b) Wrathful Deities

The second section presents a general description of the purity of wrathful deities. Their three eyes symbolize the vision of the three times. They bare four long fangs to illustrate that the four types of birth are severed at the root. They display a wrathful presence to tame all violent beings. These deities also display the nine expressions of the dance, which embody the five families and four consorts. Displaying these nine expressions, they are captivating, heroic, terrifying, laughing, ferocious, fearsome, compassionate, intimidating, and peaceful. Their upper garment is made of elephant skin, showing how the ten powers of knowledge conquer ignorance, while their tiger skin skirt signifies the way anger is conquered through bold and wrathful acts of subjugation. Their ornamental silk streamers symbolize the enlightened mind overcoming desire. Their crown of five dry skulls embodies the five buddhas, symbolizing that pride is conquered. Their necklaces are composed of garlands of fifty-one fresh human heads, which indicates the complete purity of the fifty-one mental states that ensues once jealousy has been overcome. Their bodies are adorned with six ornaments that embody the six perfections. They stand in the center of a mass of fire of the five wisdoms and amidst streams of five-colored light, symbolizing that the knowledge that realizes egolessness burns away the three levels of existence.

The manifestation of the retinue is simply an emanation created by the central buddha that accords with the capacity of those in need of guidance. As such, the main deity and retinue are indivisible. Furthermore, the entire celestial palace and all its deities do not have any independent existence. Rather, they appear exclusively as the magical display of the unceasing wisdom of the main deity, the miraculous manifestation of blissful aware emptiness. In fact, like a rainbow appearing in the clear sky or stars and planets reflected in a still lake, all these visualizations appear yet lack true existence. For this reason, it is important to rest in the recognition that the nature of all these features is one of interdependent origination.

It is necessary to visualize the colors, symbolic implements, and other symbolic features of each individual deity while remembering their significance, the purity that each represents. Beginners, however, may not be able to link the development stage with the nature of mind. Consequently, this may not be possible and the clear appearance of the deity may last for only a short moment.

If this is the case, it is extremely important to rest in one-pointed devotion once this moment has passed. Think to yourself how the entire visualization is a wonderful method that consists of symbols that represent the wisdom of the dharmakāya, the inconceivable qualities, limitless compassion, and enlightened activity of all the buddhas. Your practice will then bear a resemblance to the actual recollection of purity.

This meditation purifies all the following aspects of life. In the context of the basis, one is first born as an infant, then grows up and begins to be plagued by feelings of desire. Next, one follows after these desires and gets married. One's physical, verbal, and mental abilities gradually develop as well, ensuring proficiency in the vocation of the particular social class to which one belongs. All this is purified by meditating in this way.

As the result of purification, one takes birth as a nirmāṇakāya buddha and, in the pursuit of enlightenment, receives ordination and performs austerities. One then goes even further and arrives at the very heart of enlightenment, taming all demons. As a result, one develops meditative concentration and attains the wisdom of omniscience.

In the context of the higher paths, the aim is to attain the divine form of the wisdom of empty bliss. To this end, blissful energetic-mind arises as the divine form. Then, with an earnest desire for the supreme accomplishment, one relies on either a karma mudrā or wisdom mudrā. In so doing, one will gradually gain familiarity with coemergent wisdom. This, in turn, enacts a process of maturation by laying the foundation for the swift attainment of the supreme accomplishment.

c) The Blessing

In terms of the blessing, the objects of purification are the habitual patterns present once a child has grown up and fully developed its physical, verbal, and mental abilities. The process of purification involves visualizing oneself as the samaya maṇḍala. In other words, the vajra body is present as a vividly-clear white oṃ syllable, which rests on a wheel at the top of the deities' heads, inside the skull mansion of the brain. Vajra speech is represented by a vividly-clear red āḥ syllable. This syllable is found at the throat center, resting on a red lotus with eight petals. Vajra mind is symbolized as a vividly-clear blue hūṃ syllable, which rests in the heart center on a sun and moon disc seat. There are also certain practices where one meditates on the three deities associated with enlightened body, speech, and mind, as well as the syllables they are marked with.

When these elements are not present, however, it is sufficient to visualize the three syllables alone. These very letters are the symbolic form of wisdom, while the three vajras embody the six wisdoms. Thus, even if the face, hands, and other aspects of the divine form are not visualized, these elements and their symbolic forms will still be present. The result of purification is the mastery that one gains over the inconceivable secret of the three vajras—the enlightened body, speech, and mind of all the buddhas.

c. Invocation and Request

The third section explains the invocation of wisdom beings and the request for them to remain. Here, the object of purification is the habitual tendency of immature beings to have the same intelligence and ability as in their own past existences. The process of purification involves invoking the natural wisdom maṇḍala and requesting it to remain.

Concerning the first of these, as you visualize yourself as the samaya being, imagine a HŪṂ syllable at your heart center. In essence, this syllable consists of faith and devotion. Its features are white and glittering, red and shining, and sharp and swift. Thus, its appearance is threefold, while in terms of its empty aspect, it is one. Visualize light shining forth from this syllable in the form of hooks, pervading the entire range of the spontaneously present pure lands of the victorious ones. Next, imagine that this causes the perfect nature of the dharmakāya of all tathāgatas in the ten directions and four times to arise as rūpakāyas that are similar in appearance to the visualized samaya being. As they are summoned before you, recite the relevant invocation verse and imagine the natural wisdom maṇḍala merging indivisibly with the maṇḍala of the samaya being, becoming of one taste like water poured into water. Finally, request them to remain.

To give a brief explanation of the mantra DZAḤ HŪṂ BAṂ HŌḤ, the syllable DZAḤ summons the wisdom beings to the samaya beings. HŪṂ makes them dissolve indivisibly, while BAṂ binds them so they do not depart until one's wishes have been fulfilled. Finally, with the syllable HŌḤ, they remain joyfully present.

The result of purification is the realization of nonduality, the indivisibility of all the tathāgatas and wisdom that occurs at the time of enlightenment.

d. Homage, Offering, and Praise

The fourth section concerns making offerings and praising the nondual maṇḍala. The object of purification here is the habit of immature beings to strive for the enjoyment of pleasant objects and the attainment of wealth and prestige. The process of purification involves paying homage, making offerings, and offering praises.

i. Homage

Paying homage entails the merging of the maṇḍala of samaya beings in one's meditative absorption with the maṇḍala of the natural wisdom beings, like water poured into water, and the subsequent recognition that these two are an indivisible maṇḍala within the state of nondual basic space and wisdom. As a respectful gesture, envision the activities of homage and so forth taking place in the same way that the gods in the Heaven of Delightful Emanations are pleased by their own magically created enjoyments. Visualizing yourself as the main deity, imagine replicas of yourself emanating out from your heart center, like one candle being lit from another. Next, visualize them paying homage while you recite the relevant verses from the text you are using. The purpose of paying homage is to experience the indivisibility of the host of maṇḍala deities you are paying homage to and your own awareness. As a mere symbol of this, you can gather the accumulations by paying homage to the extraordinary qualities of the deities with a deeply respectful attitude.

ii. OFFERING

There are four different types of offering: outer offerings, inner offerings, secret offerings, and the offering of reality itself. First are the common outer and inner offerings.

1) THE OUTER OFFERING

Visualizing yourself as the main deity, imagine innumerable offering goddesses streaming forth from your heart center and making offerings in the manner of deities offering to other deities. The offerings they make surpass the imagination, completely filling every single place and realm of experience with outer and inner offerings. As you recite the verses of offering found in your text, visualize the offering goddesses holding their offerings and giving them to the senses of each of the deities. Clear, cool, and delicious water is offered to drink; clean water is offered to cool and rinse the hands and feet; multicolored flowers grown on meadows and in ponds are offered to the head; natural and produced pleasant-smelling incense is offered to the nose; jewels, oil lamps, and other illuminating sources of light are offered to the eyes; cool water scented with sandalwood and saffron is offered to the heart; delicious and healthy food is offered to the tongue; and various types of music played by cymbals, horns, drums, sitars, and other instruments are offered to the ears. To conclude, imagine the goddesses themselves dissolving into the sense faculties they are offering to.

1) The Inner Offering

Second is the inner offering of medicine, torma, and rakta.

a) Medicine

The offering of medicine involves offering the original purity of uncontrived, naturally-existing nectar, which is the essence of all phenomena in saṃsāra and nirvāṇa. This is symbolized by either the outer, inner, and secret aspect of the eight primary medicinal ingredients or the four outer and four inner primary medicinal ingredients related to each of the five primary nectars. Each of these eight divisions can be further divided into one hundred twenty-five medicinal subcategories so that there are one thousand in total. The sacred substance that is made from such ingredients appears from the realization that all phenomena are equality, beyond acceptance or rejection. In form, it is nectar that dispels the demon of dualistic thinking.

At this point, you will already have consecrated the nectar as the essence of the five wisdoms and five buddha families. Next, continue on with this notion and recite the verses for the offering of medicine from your scripture while maintaining the appropriate visualization. At the same time, stir the ocean of nectar with the sun and moon sphere of the thumb and ring finger and then scatter the nectar. Visualize these drops dissolving into the mouths of the deities, such that the entire host of deities is sated with the taste of great bliss.

b) Torma

Next is the torma offering. On a torma plate as vast and open as the basic space of phenomena, imagine a torma made of wonderful, sacred substances. Its appearance is that of food and drink—a mass of all the most pleasurable and desirable objects that please the senses. In essence, it consists of wisdom nectar. While you recite the verses for the torma offering, visualize it being offered to the deities. With great delight, they consume the torma, taking it in through a tube of light that emerges from their vajra-shaped tongues. This all takes place within the expanse of luminosity; the foods that are enjoyed are actually the five sense objects, while drinks are the consciousnesses.

c) Rakta

For the offering of rakta, imagine that attachment and clinging—the root of suffering—coalesce in the form of blood and dissolve into the expanse of great bliss devoid of attachment. This is then offered to the maṇḍala deities as a great sacred substance that liberates saṃsāra into basic, unborn space. The definitive meaning, however, is that the course of the sun is arrested at the peak of the secret space, whereby the continuity of saṃsāra is cut. With this intent and mind-set, imagine that saṃsāra itself is offered as an ocean of blood and consumed rapidly by the deities, to the point where nothing remains.

3) The Secret Offering

The third section pertains to the secret offerings and has two parts. The first of these is the offering of union. Subjective appearances relate to the masculine principle of skillful means. In contrast, the object, emptiness, relates to knowledge, the feminine principle. The indivisible unity of these two is the great primordial union of everything.

In the present context, the taste of great bliss that appears from this union satisfies the entire maṇḍala. This is symbolized by the male and female consorts being joined together as individual couples in union. Single female deities are also joined in union with the symbolic form of the lord of the family, the concealed masculine principle, which takes the form of a khaṭvāṅga. Through this union, an extraordinary blissful melting occurs in which a descending flow and an ascending stabilization are gradually perfected. Once the mind settles on the wisdom of great bliss, all the deities give rise to the pride of being inseparable from this passion.

Second is the offering of liberation. That which is to be liberated here is the belief in a self—the concepts associated with apprehended phenomena and apprehending thoughts. Insofar as this belief propels one into saṃsāra and prevents the realization of nondual wisdom, it is the enemy. Liberation is performed with a sharp weapon, the wisdom devoid of dualistic thoughts. It liberates dualistic fixation and desirous thoughts into unborn space. This is the meaning of the great primordial universal liberation.

Generate great compassion from within that state so that you can protect all sentient beings within the ten fields from the unbearable suffering that results from the negative karma they accumulate. In essence, the self and that which is to be liberated do not have even a shred of true existence, just like a trick or an optical illusion. With this realization, you will free them and purify all your thoughts into the basic space of phenomena. Imagine that you perform this offering within the state of the single flavor of saṃsāra and nirvāṇa.

4) The Offering of Reality

The fourth type of offering is the offering of reality itself. All that appears and exists, the entire range of phenomena found in saṃsāra and nirvāṇa, is naturally and innately pure, spontaneously present as the great maṇḍala of the victorious ones. As this is the case, do not focus on the recipient of the offerings, the person making the offerings, or the offering itself. Instead, recall the meaning of the Great Perfection, the fact that these three, in terms of their true nature, do not have the slightest bit of concrete existence. The most superior offering is precisely this—the Great Seal, freedom from the concepts of subject, object, and action.

The actual verses for the offerings of union, liberation, and suchness may not always be included in the practice text. In a number of abbreviated texts these three are shortened down to just one line each, so you need to know the meaning of these practices.

iii. Praise

The third section addresses the topic of praise. Having completed the offerings, proceed by recalling the superior qualities of the maṇḍala deities and give rise to a most inspired frame of mind. The basic space of phenomena is free of all complexities and pervades all knowable phenomena throughout the three times. It manifests as great bliss in all aspects of saṃsāra and nirvāṇa.

While never straying from the dharmakāya—the unimpeded and unattached wisdom that understands all existing phenomena precisely as they are—the play of the two rūpakāyas still works for the benefit of the limitless beings in need of guidance. These forms manifest in various peaceful, passionate, and wrathful expressions and are perfectly adorned with the marks and signs of enlightenment. Their melodious and majestic speech is endowed with sixty aspects, while their nonconceptual minds are free from complexity and always delighted with great bliss. Possessing inconceivable qualities of abandonment and realization, their effortless and spontaneous activity tames others with whatever means are the most appropriate. Recalling these symbolic and actual forms of superiority, keep your attention on the relevant verses and offer praise with the understanding that those who are praised and the one praising are identical.

As the result of training in these activities, you will effortlessly receive limitless offerings once you attain enlightenment. Further, you will become an unsurpassed recipient for the offerings and praises of all of saṃsāra and nirvāṇa.

e. Training in the Deity's Appearance

The fifth section addresses the practice of focusing on the appearance of the main deity in the visualization. This training contains four elements: clear appearance, stable pride, the recollection of purity, and training in bliss, clarity, and nonthought.

i. Clear Appearance

Clear appearance involves visualizing the entire form of the deity in an instant and then holding the visualization in mind. Alternatively, you can also start by visualizing each element of the deity's form and ornamentation individually, moving from the jeweled crown on their head to the lotus they are seated on. When you are able to visualize each element, they can all be visualized together. Next, let your mind rest one-pointedly on the visualization, which should be like a reflection in a pure, clear, and pristine pond that is undisturbed by the breeze. Once you have begun this training and are focusing on the individual elements of the deity's form, you do not have to follow a fixed order or number of sessions. Instead, you should train according to your own capacity.

ii. Stable Pride

The pride you need to develop here involves thinking that you yourself are the very deity you are meditating on, a buddha in whom all faults are exhausted and all qualities are complete. When this vivid sense of pride is embraced by a detached frame of mind, the genuine unity of development and completion will have been reached. Its object of purification is the presence of ordinary, impure manifestations, along with the tendency to grasp these impurities as being the self. The process of purification involves training in clear appearance and the recollection of purity, which later transform into pure appearance and pure pride, respectively, through the skillful method of training in the pride of the deity.

iii. Recollection of Purity

The points that were previously explained in the context of visualizing the deity should be applied to the meditations here as well. The main thing to understand is that the qualities of the buddhas are naturally and spontaneously present within the mind's innate nature. Therefore, since these qualities are primordially pure as the deity and its essence, you should understand that the deity in your own meditative practice is pure as well, being in essence those very same qualities.

Naturally, you need to keep these purities in mind as you recite the liturgy. In the context of meditating on the appearance of the deity, you must train in these pure aspects with strong interest and develop a stable appreciation of each individual purity. At that time, when you rest in the meditative concentration of the development stage, you should connect this with the clear appearance and stable pride mentioned above.

iv. Bliss, Clarity, and Nonthought

It is very important that your development stage practice be clear, pure, and stable as just taught. Further, it should also be free from any form of conceptual fixation, any sense that these factors truly exist. Instead, your practice must be embraced with the knowledge that its very essence is empty while its nature is to appear in a way that is utterly unidentifiable, like the moon's reflection in a pond or a rainbow.

If you seal the development stage with the completion stage, it becomes a wonderfully skillful method for letting all maṇḍalas arise as the dharmakāya. It transforms the accumulation of merit of the mentally imputed development stage into the absolute, unconditioned accumulation of wisdom. In this way, it unites the two accumulations, the two kāyas, the two truths, and skillful means and knowledge. For this very reason, you should be aware that this is one of the hallmarks of the profound and short path of Mantra.

If you do not know this and approach the development stage in isolation, as something that truly exists in its own right, then it does not matter how stable your visualization and pride may be. Not only will it not be a path that leads to awakening, it will be a terrible impediment that ties you to saṃsāra. If you apprehend a peaceful deity as existing in its own right, you will be reborn as a god in the form realm, while meditating on a wrathful deity in this way will bring you a rebirth as a karmic ghost or powerful demon like Rudra. In the annals of the Secret Mantra tradition there are stories of this actually happening.

To conclude, it is important to train in the development stage while incorporating these elements of clarity, purity, and stability. You should do so for as long as possible, without becoming weary and fatigued. However, when fatigue does set in, you should begin the recitation.

2. Enlightened Speech: The Practice of Recitation

This section explains the significance of the practice of recitation, enlightened speech. There are seven parts: 1) an overview of the practice, 2) its specific function, 3) the essence of recitation, 4) the types of recitation, 5) the way to perform recitation, 6) the number of recitations, and 7) the subsequent activities.

a. Overview

In mantra recitation the object of purification is mistaken utterance, the expression of names, words, and syllables within the impure context of saṃsāra. This also includes the habitual patterns associated with fixating on these factors. The process of purification involves the continuity of sustained repetition and the recitation of mantra sounds, primarily via verbal recitation. As the result of purification, an interdependent link will be created that will allow you to work for the welfare of sentient beings once enlightened, here referring to the enlightened activities of vajra speech, such as turning the wheel of Dharma for those in need of guidance.

b. The Function of Recitation

The particular function of mantra recitation is to purify mental impurities and develop the power of speech. It also functions to invoke the wisdom deities. For example, a person will naturally come nearer to you once you call out his or her name. In a similar manner, even though the wisdom deities do not actually come closer when you call them and recede when you do not, repeatedly reciting their names is a conducive cause for vajra speech and functions as an antidote to the obscurations in this capacity. As such, it will gradually bring you closer to the wisdom deity. A vajra song says:

> The enlightened ones, the awakened beings,
> The ḍākinīs, and your own queen—
> To bring them right before you
> Invoke them with mantra.

c. The Essence of Recitation

If you practice with enthusiasm, showing interest in wisdom knowledge mantras by meditating on the features of the ordinary syllables that resemble these mantras and reciting them in a sustained and repetitive manner, an unfailing bond will be formed with the vajra speech of the buddhas. On a temporal level, you will be able to carry out pacifying, enriching, magnetizing, and wrathful activities. Ultimately, this will function as the direct cause for attaining the vajra speech of the buddhas. Continuous repetition is what is meant by the Sanskrit term *jap*; this is the essence of recitation.

d. Types of Recitation

There are four different styles of recitation: 1) the arranged recitation, which is similar to a moon with a garland of stars, 2) the palanquin recitation that resembles a spinning firebrand, 3) the recitation of projection and absorption, which is likened to a king's messenger, and 4) the recitation that is like a broken beehive.

i. The Arranged Recitation, Like a Moon with a Garland of Stars

The first section addresses the basis for recitation. As you visualize yourself as the appropriate yidam deity with clarity, purity, and stability, imagine your jewel heart to be made of light and shaped like an immaculate, translucent dome. Within it is the wisdom being, resting on a sun and moon disc seat and similar in appearance to the samaya being. In certain contexts, considering the significance of the emanation itself as well as the basis from which it emanates, the wisdom being is visualized as a sambhogakāya form in the heart center of the nirmāṇakāya samaya being. Amitābha may be visualized in the heart center of Avalokiteśvara, for example, or Vajravarāhī in the heart center of Yeshe Tsogyal. Whichever is the case, you must visualize the symbolic implement of the appropriate class within the clear, luminous, and stainless sphere of light at the heart center of the wisdom being.

If we use the general vajra to illustrate this process, one begins by visualizing either a nine- or five-pronged vajra, whatever happens to be described in the liturgy. The symbolic implement stands upright and has a sun and moon disc seat at its center. Alternately, this seat can also be in accordance with the general approach of visualizing a moon disc seat alone for peaceful deities, or a solitary sun seat if the deity is wrathful. The seat itself should be approximately the size of a split pea. Upon it is the absorption being, the root spiritual life-force, which refers to HRĪḤ, HŪṂ, or whatever the seed syllable of the yidam deity happens to be. It should have the same color as the deity and be bright and dazzling like a candle flame. It should also be standing upright and face the same direction as the deity. The three beings are constructed by visualizing in this manner.

In some cases, only the seed and mantra chain in the heart center of the samaya being are visualized, while the wisdom being and symbolic implement do not appear. For this reason, be aware that there is no way to be completely certain about this aside from following the approach of the individual scripture you are using. That said, the mantra you are reciting should be visualized as a garland of clear, glowing syllables that are extremely fine, as if written with a hair. This garland should circle around the root life-force, starting in front.

You may visualize the syllables of the mantra in any script, whatever happens to be the easiest. There is no need to transform the syllables into Sanskrit. Generally speaking, the teachings of the Victorious One are based on their meaning. In particular, it is the very nature of the Buddha's compassion to reach whoever has devotion, and to do so without delay. This is not a tradition in which one simply adheres to words, syllables, and other mere sounds. In contrast, just knowing the meaning of what you are visualizing is sufficient in and of itself.

As for the way the mantra is arranged and spins, it is important that you perform this as explained in the actual liturgy of each individual deity. For mantras that spin in a clockwise direction, the syllables face outward. They should be arranged from left to right, as though they are to be read from the outside, with the letters standing upright and spinning like a chain. The first syllable, such as OṂ, should be connected to HŪṂ, HRĪḤ, or whatever the last syllable happens to be. As a skillful way to deal with the recitation of long mantras, the first syllable of the mantra must be visualized right in front of the spiritual life-force with the ensuing mantra following neatly after it in two or three outer rings, like a coiled snake, spinning clockwise as you chant.

Other mantra chains spin in a counterclockwise direction. With these, the syllables are visualized standing upright, beginning in front of the spiritual life-force as was the case above. The syllables should face inwards and be arranged from right to left, as if being read from the inside. Long mantras circle from the inside out, just as above, but when chanted they spin counterclockwise.

Mantra chains may spin clockwise or counterclockwise, depending on the context. Generally speaking, for male deities they spin clockwise and for female deities counterclockwise. This is not always the case, however, so you should follow the approach of your own practice text.

In certain contexts, it is taught that meditating on a guru whom you are trying to protect, or someone else you hold in high esteem, as being inseparable from the spiritual life-force is an appropriate approach to take. In others, it is said that you should visualize them as actually being present in the interior of the spiritual life-force, such as a HRĪḤ or HŪṂ, or that they should be visualized in the form of an ĀḤ or a NRI, syllables that are the essence of the life-force. There are also other profound and unique key points concerning visualizations meant to protect or repel, but these should only be transmitted in their own particular context, so I will not write about them here.

In any case, start out by repeatedly visualizing the mantra chain arranged around the seed syllable as was just described. Once the visualization is clear, recite the mantra as you concentrate on the mantra syllables rising above the seat and revolving, each with its own particular sound. This is the style of recitation that is similar to a moon and a garland of stars, which constitutes the practice of approach.

ii. The Palanquin Recitation, Like a Spinning Firebrand

The second section concerns the practice of close approach and explains a style of recitation that is likened to a spinning firebrand. In this style of practice, a second mantra chain emanates out from the chain in the heart center. Its syllables stand upright and are situated one on top of the other in a series. Resounding with the sound of its respective mantra, the top of each syllable in this uninterrupted chain touches the bottom of the next, although they are not actually joined together.

The mantra chain gradually emerges from the mouths of the wisdom being and the samaya being and enters the mouth of the female consort. It then proceeds through her body and emerges from her lotus, where it enters the path of the male consort's secret place and travels upward. As the essence of the great bliss of the awakened mind, it produces an exhilarating bliss. Finally, it dissolves back into the syllables in the center and the supreme spiritual accomplishment of the great seal is attained—the wisdom of great bliss endowed with all supreme attributes. On a temporal level as well, all the wonderful ordinary spiritual accomplishments will be attained. This includes such factors as long life, merit, glory, wealth, qualities, wisdom, fame, power, and abilities.

Next, continue to chant the mantra and visualize just as before, with the mantra revolving uninterruptedly between the bodies of the male and female consorts, spinning like a firebrand. This style of recitation should be applied to frontal visualizations as well, at which point light should be projected between you and the frontal visualization before being reabsorbed.

iii. The Recitation of Projection and Absorption, Like a King's Messenger

The third style of recitation, which is likened to the messenger of a king, relates to the practice of accomplishment. While chanting the mantra, visualize light streaming out from the mantra chain, filling the entirety of space and making pleasing offerings to all buddhas. All of their blessings and spiritual accomplishments then emerge in the form of light and dissolve into you. Imagine that this purifies the two obscurations and their habitual patterns, perfects the two accumulations, and allows you to receive all four empowerments simultaneously. This recitation brings blessings that benefit yourself.

Next, visualize light streaming forth again, this time touching all six classes of sentient beings found in the three realms. As this occurs, it purifies the negativity and obscurations associated with their karma and afflictions, as well as the ripening of suffering and all the rest of their temporary impurities. Through this, they become enlightened—their body, speech, and mind becoming the essence of the three vajras. Chanting the mantra while imagining all this constitutes the recitation of enlightened activity, which benefits others.

iv. The Recitation That is Like a Broken Beehive

The fourth type of recitation is likened to a broken beehive and relates to the practice of great accomplishment. In this approach limitless rays of light stream forth from the deity and mantra chain, purifying the entire universe into luminosity and transforming it into a pure celestial palace. All sentient beings inhabiting the universe are purified as well. Their karma, disturbing emotions, and suffering are purified, as is the conceptual fixation they have towards ordinary things. They then transform into the maṇḍala of deities. All sounds that are heard transform into the natural resounding of secret mantra, humming like a broken beehive, while all the thoughts and memories that occur in the mind transform into the play of the dharmakāya—the wisdom of bliss, clarity, and nonthought. This is the recitation of the nonduality of self and other, which should be performed within a state of nonfixation.

As there is no fixed rule dictating that one must apply these four styles of recitation concurrently, it follows that you should practice whichever of these four is emphasized in your particular practice.

e. Performing Mantra Recitation

When performing mantra recitation, it is very important not to let your mind become disturbed by distracting thoughts when in one-pointed concentration. Practice becomes uninterrupted by reciting continuously. When your mind is distracted, it doesn't matter how much you recite; apart from merely diminishing your verbal obscurations a bit, it will be very difficult to accomplish your desired goal. The great guru Padmasambhava said:

> Recite with undistracted concentration.
> Should you become distracted elsewhere,
> Even reciting for an eon will bring no result.

The rosary you use to count as you chant should have specific qualities as well. On this topic, master Padmasambhava, the second buddha, stated:

For a rosary, the best substances are jewels.
Seeds that come from trees are second best.
The lowest are clay, stones,
And the nine types of medicine.

Conch makes for peaceful rosaries
And is recommended for pacifying activities.
Golden rosaries are used for enriching activities,
While rosaries of coral accomplish magnetizing activities.

Rosaries of iron and turquoise are for wrathful activities.
Zi and agate are auspicious for various activities.
Clay and seeds are used for pacifying activities.
Apricot seeds accomplish enriching activities.

Soapberry is auspicious for magnetizing activities.
Nāga, garuda beak, and rakṣa are recommended
As rosaries for wrathful activities,
While bodhi seeds are auspicious for all.

Rosaries of bodhi tree and the kyenyen tree
Are auspicious rosaries for pacifying activities.
Mulberry and other fruit trees make rosaries
That accomplish enriching activities.

Rosaries of red sandalwood and tamarisk
Are recommended for magnetizing activities.
Teak and thorns are wrathful trees.
Rosaries of barlo tree

Are recommended for all activities.
Ivory rosaries accomplish all activities.
Clay balls make peaceful rosaries.
For enriching, stone rosaries are auspicious.

Rosaries of medicine accomplish magnetizing activities,
While rosaries of the great bone, such as skull,
Will accomplish wrathful activities.
Rosaries composed of a mixture
Are said to accomplish all activities.

Concerning the multiplication of benefits associated with these substances, the *Vajra Peak Tantra* says:

> Reciting with iron multiplies by a factor of two
> And with copper by a factor of four.
> Ru-rakṣa multiplies by twenty million,
> While pearl multiplies by a factor of one hundred.
>
> Indra's seed multiplies the practice by one thousand.
> Silver multiplies it by one hundred thousand.
> Ruby is said to multiply by one billion,
> And the bodhi seed, to do so infinitely.

The bodhi seed, also known as *putrajīva*, is the supreme rosary. It is auspicious for any peaceful or wrathful practice.

Regarding the way to string the rosary and the main bead, the *Tantra of the Natural Arising of Awareness* explains:

> For the rosary, join three, five, or nine strings,
> Symbolizing the three kāyas, five families, and nine vehicles.
> The knots are tied in three tiers, symbolizing the three kāyas.

Despite what is written here, normally it is said that the three tiers symbolize the three vajras. According to this approach, the upper bead should be blue, symbolizing enlightened mind, the unchanging wisdom of reality. The middle bead should be red to symbolize vajra speech, while the lower one should be white, symbolizing vajra body.

As for the blessing and subsequent consecration, the knowledge holder Chökyi Drakpa said, "First, you should wash your mouth and hands with clean water. Next, cleanse the rosary with the five substances of a cow and anoint it with perfume." After that, do the following:

> With the pride that you yourself are the deity,
> Coil the rosary in your left hand
> With the main bead at the top.
> Purify it into emptiness with the svabhāva mantra.
> Out of emptiness, the rosary's main bead
> Becomes the main yidam deity
> And the surrounding beads appear as the retinue.
> Then invoke, summon, and dissolve the wisdom deities.

It is said that when a rosary has been consecrated in this manner, the effects of any mantra will be multiplied one hundred thousand times.

Regarding the way to count, the great master Padmasambhava says:

> When reciting peaceful mantras,
> Count with the rosary on your index finger,
> And for enriching mantras, on your middle finger.
> For magnetizing, keep it on your ring finger,
> And for wrathful mantras, on the little finger.
> Always use your left hand;
> Don't just count with any hand.
> However, on some occasions it is taught
> That you should count using both hands,
> In which case both are used together,
> And not the right hand alone.

Sometimes, however, it is said that you should count using the thumb and ring finger on the right hand when doing wrathful practices. The first of five mantra sections found in the *Gathering of Sugatas* states:

> In all cases, holding with the thumb and index finger is recommended,
> And for wrathful practices, counting with the thumb and ring finger.

From a general point of view, an easy and effective way to practice is to hold the four fingers together, place the rosary on top of the index finger, and then count with the thumb in the form of a vajra hook. This holds for all four types of enlightened activity.

There are also samaya vows that must be observed. The great master Padmasambhava explains:

> A genuine rosary should accompany you at all times,
> Like the body and its shadow.
> This is the fundamental samaya of the rosary.
>
> Although a great many subsidiary samayas are taught,
> In brief this is what you should know:
> Do not show your rosary to others.

If you do not let it leave the warmth of your body,
Whatever you practice will quickly be accomplished.

Likewise, do not let anyone else hold it,
Especially, it is said, anyone with
Damaged samaya vows, obscurations,
Or with whom you do not share the same samaya.

Other than using it to count when reciting,
Do not hold it leisurely at inappropriate times.
Do not employ it for the sake of divination and astrology.
A rosary that has not been consecrated should never be held.

A consecrated rosary should be kept secret
And not used for other activities.
Do not place it on the ground or cast it aside.
Do not use a so-called "adulterated rosary,"
One mixed with inappropriate things.

You should not use a rosary that has been obtained from the hand of someone who has committed any of the actions with immediate retribution, nor from a butcher, samaya breaker, murderer, widow, or thief. This also applies to rosaries that have been obtained through robbery, taken from a deity's ornaments, offered to a deity by another, have an unsuitable number of beads, been burnt by fire, stepped over by an animal, or been nibbled on by birds or mice. Since it is said that using such rosaries will stain the mantra samaya vows, they should be avoided.

When engaged in recitation, the individual syllables should not be chanted too fast or too slow. The length of the syllables should not be mixed up either, nor should anything be added or left out. Do not make the recitation excessively loud or quiet. The recitation should not be interrupted by idle conversation, chanting other mantras, or any other words. The *Awesome Flash of Lightning* states:

The voice should be neither loud nor quiet,
Not fast and not slow, nor rough or weak.
Enunciate the syllables in their entirety.
There should be no distraction or idle talk,
Nor interruptions by yawning and the like.

Furthermore, the teachings of the oral instructions state that if you slip into conversation, you must subtract some numbers and go back four beads on the rosary. If you cough, go back five, three if you yawn, ten if you sneeze, and one if you spit.

There are also other forms of recitation, such as chanting wrathfully in a clear voice. Recitation can also be performed chanting softly using the lips, the tip of the tongue, and the throat, an approach referred to as "whispering recitation." Silent recitation involves reciting while holding the breath in union and focusing on the form and sound of the mantra. Mental recitation takes place exclusively in the mind. In this approach all verbal activities are given up, even holding the breath, and one focuses on the form or sound of the mantra. The secret mantras that are chanted in these ways should be practiced as they are found in the approach of each individual deity.

f. The Number of Recitations

Generally speaking, you should recite until you have attained the mundane and supreme spiritual accomplishments. However, if you merely consider the number of recitations, you should recite one hundred thousand mantras for each syllable in the mantra of the main deity of the maṇḍala and a tenth of that for each deity in the retinue. A ten percent amendment should be added to this as well. In other words, an extra ten thousand should be added to each hundred thousand mantras you chant, and an additional thousand to each ten thousand.

g. Subsequent Activities

There are three subsequent activities: 1) offerings and praise, 2) receiving the accomplishments, and 3) requesting forbearance. Activities such as making offerings and praises, the first division outlined here, should be performed once the recitation is finished and during breaks. These topics were explained above.

Receiving the accomplishments is the factor that will allow you to obtain the desired result at the conclusion of your recitation. That said, the elaborate ritual for this practice should be learned from other sources. At this point, I will explain the reception of the accomplishments that occurs at the conclusion of the recitation in one's daily practice.

You may invoke the accomplishments either by following the ritual of your particular yidam deity or through the general approach of invoking protection from the eight types of fear and so forth. Then pray one-pointedly in the following manner:

> Please grant me the spiritual accomplishments of the various actions associated with the four types of enlightened activity. Through this may I pacify circumstances that are not conducive to my practice and cause those that are conducive to develop and flourish. Grant these accomplishments so that I may magnetize those with wrong views and wrathfully conquer those who are hostile and violent. To you, the supreme yidam deity towards whom I strive, I pray that your three vajras of enlightened body, speech, and mind may purify my own body, speech, and mind, as well as the two obscurations and all my habitual patterns, to the point where none of these remain. In this way, please grant your blessings and turn my own three gates into the indestructible enlightened body, speech, and mind—the essence of the three vajras. With the supreme accomplishment of the great seal, the wisdom of unified bliss and emptiness, please bestow upon me everything I desire to attain, this very moment! Bestow upon me the attainment of the unified kāya, the body without remainder.

Imagine that praying in this manner causes all the spiritual accomplishments to stream forth in the form of light, radiating outwards from the three places of the host of deities in the maṇḍala and dissolving into your own three places. Through this, all the spiritual accomplishments that you long for are attained.

The third activity is to request forbearance. Generally, here one first expresses gratitude by making offerings and praises, and then recites the hundred-syllable mantra of Vajrasattva while thinking the following:

> Under the sway of ignorance and carelessness I have failed to realize and correctly practice the general principles of view, meditation, and conduct. This, in turn, has led to confusion and mistakes. In particular, I have failed to maintain clarity when I concentrate on the deity in development stage practice. I have done too few recitations as well, and my ritual activities have been done in an impure way. I have added things that were not needed and failed to include what

was necessary. I have also not prepared offerings, as well as the other requisites for practice, to the best of my ability. Even when I have, I have been lazy and careless. In short, I now apologize with intense sorrow and regret for all the harmful actions I have done. Please be patient and purify these acts!

With this in mind, recite the relevant verses from the bottom of your heart and request forbearance.

3. Enlightened Mind: The Practice of Luminosity

The practice of the enlightened mind symbolizes its object of purification, which is the process in which a child grows old, dies, and then comes into existence again. Dissolving the world and its beings into the protection circle and then gradually into the tip of the seed syllable symbolizes the outer and inner stages of dissolution that occur at the moment of death, as well as the dharmakāya luminosity of the death state. Arising from this state as the deity, which occurs in the breaks between sessions, resembles the existence of the intermediate state.

The various stages that comprise the process of purification are as follows. As much as possible, train in the practices of deity and mantra as explained above. When you are no longer able to continue the practice, perform the dissolution stages and then arise as the deity. First, light from your heart center causes the entire pure external universe and its inhabitants to dissolve into light and then merge into the protection circle. Next, the inner-layered elements and so forth gradually dissolve into the protection circle, which in turn dissolves into the charnel grounds. These dissolve into the celestial palace, the palace into the retinue, and the retinue into the main male and female consorts. The female then dissolves into the male, who dissolves into the wisdom being in the center of the heart. The wisdom being dissolves into the samādhi being, the seed syllable of the spiritual life-force, which itself dissolves gradually upward until reaching the tip of the syllable.

Once that vanishes, relax into a state of emptiness, a state without any sense of self and other or anything upon which to focus the mind. When in this state, nothing is perceived to be present or absent, existent or nonexistent, and every form of mental activity will have disappeared. Resting in this state eliminates the extreme of permanence.

Uttering the relevant root mantra from within that state creates a circumstance for you to arise, like a fish jumping out of the water, in the form of the yidam deity, and for the world and its inhabitants to manifest as the maṇḍala of the deity. This eliminates the extreme of nihilism. Finally, carry on with your daily activities while maintaining a continuity of practice that is like the flow of a river.

The result of purification is the manifestation of the rūpakāyas of buddhahood, which are the enlightened activities of the dharmakāya. Since the wisdom of the dharmakāya is also the essence of basic space, the rūpakāyas manifest uninterruptedly from it. This is what is illustrated by arising in the manner just described.

Everything that has been taught up to this point has emphasized the development stage. When sealed with emptiness, however, the development stage will unite with the completion stage. Here, I will briefly discuss how the two extremes are cleared away by dissolving the development stage into luminosity and then arising once again in the illusory divine form. I will also discuss how to practice the completion stage from within this state, encompassing all four aspects of its view, meditation, conduct, and fruition.

No matter how you examine the mind's innate, pure nature, you will see that it is not a concrete thing or something that can be labeled. For these very reasons, it is not a permanent entity that exists in and of itself. Yet neither is it a blank nothingness, due to the simple fact that as awareness it is unobstructed. The third alternative of being either both or neither is also not the case. Hence, the nature of mind transcends all such limitations; it is inexpressible, unimaginable, unobservable, and yet all-pervasive.

All the perceived objects that appear are just like those in a dream. As long as you do not investigate them, they are enjoyable. If analyzed, however, they are utterly insubstantial, like space. Likewise, if you examine awareness itself, the very cognition that conceptualizes all of this, it too cannot be observed in any way at all. This very nakedness, the absence of anything to identify as appearance or cognition, is itself not different from that which it perceives. This is why it is called self-existing wisdom. That is the view.

When you are in this state, do not try to concentrate, relax, or modify it with any form of effort. Without adding or removing anything, let your awareness settle naturally in its basic state and then rest vividly in this self-clarity, without focusing on any object. Not straying from this very state is the point of the unity of calm abiding and insight. That is the meditation.

If you never stray from this view and meditation, you will be able to take everything you do and perceive as the support for the wisdom of coemergent great bliss, while still remaining conscientious. That is the conduct.

Finally, once you familiarize yourself with this, the natural state of the ground will be actualized as it truly is. That is the fruition of dharmakāya, in which there is nothing left to accept or reject.

B. Subsequent Practices

From the time you dissolve into luminosity and emerge as the illusory divine form, you should be diligent in regarding all appearances, sounds, and thoughts as the play of deity, mantra, and wisdom. Likewise, you should view every movement you make, whether you are walking, sitting, or doing anything else, as the mudrā of the deity. Eating and drinking should be performed as the yoga of sustenance, with the actions of internal burning and pouring. The entire array of desired objects should be taken on as helpers for the path by not forming concepts of the three spheres. The two stages of dissolving into luminosity and subsequently emerging should also be applied to deep sleep and dreaming, respectively. Thus, you should apply yourself diligently to the yogic practices associated with both sleep and the waking state.

III

Concluding Activities

The concluding activities include the practices of offering dedication, making aspirations, and chanting auspicious prayers. At this point, these will only be mentioned briefly.

The practice of dedication should be linked with the preparatory stage of engendering the awakened mind. In that context you resolved to practice the trainings of development and completion to free all sentient beings from suffering and bring them permanent happiness. At this stage you should seal that initial pledge by dedicating the fundamental virtues you have created. If you dedicate all fundamental virtues, whether large or small, to the cause of enlightenment, their goodness will never be exhausted. The *Sūtra Requested by Sāgaramati* explains:

> When a drop of water falls into a great ocean
> It will remain until the ocean itself dries up.
> Just so, when dedicated to complete enlightenment
> Virtue will remain until enlightenment is attained.

The best way to dedicate is to do so while resting evenly in the natural state, without any thoughts of the three spheres. This is an extremely pure way to dedicate. Even if you are unable to do so in this manner, you can perform an approximation of the dedication purified of the three spheres by thinking to yourself, "I will now dedicate in the same way that the victorious ones of the past engendered the awakened mind and made their dedications and aspirations!" With that thought, recite the dedication verses found in your text.

Concerning aspiration, the great guru of Uḍḍiyana said:

For the sake of others' welfare, the awakened mind,
And motivated by faith and compassion,
I dedicate and make aspirations.

Embracing your mind-set with the awakened mind, proceed by making pure aspirations that will bring vast benefit to both yourself and others. Then recite the verses of aspiration found in your text along with any other suitable aspiration prayers, such as the "Prayer of Noble Excellent Conduct."

When uttering auspicious prayers, you should imagine that the Three Roots and Three Jewels are actually gathered before you in the sky, uttering verses of auspiciousness as a rain of flowers falls in all directions. At the same time, all the practitioners recite suitable verses of auspiciousness and scatter flowers as well. When done in this way, there is no doubt that these things will come to pass.

In this way, the path of the genuine development stage practice links the object and process of purification with the basis of purification—the nature of mind or buddha nature—and produces the experiences of clarity, purity, and stability. Moreover, to first perfect clarity, purity, and stability in the proper order and then engage in the subsequent practices in a gradual manner is the defining characteristic of definitive perfection.

At this point one might think that any other form of practice would be a mistake. There are, however, people who are unable to train progressively in the vivid presence of the deity. If this is the case, one may practice the entire ritual in a single session, inclusive of its preparation, main part, and conclusion, merely with a sense of devotion towards this ritual and its development stage. There is no doubt that this is also a valid form of practice, since our Teacher taught both the system of definitive perfection as well as that of devoted training in consideration of all the various mental dispositions of those in need of guidance.

Generally speaking, it is the very nature of things that the compassion and activity of the buddhas depend upon the interest of the student. In particular, the functioning of Secret Mantra depends entirely on the interdependent connection between the compassion of the guru and the devotion of the student; it does not depend upon anything else. All those who gained accomplishment in the noble land of India can be understood to have been liberated exclusively by encountering the path of Mantra based on such causes and conditions.

This approach of accomplishing Secret Mantra through devoted interest is also noted in the annals of the tradition. The story of Darchar, for example, describes how he chanted the recitation mantra of Vajrakīlaya incorrectly, yet still managed to be accepted directly by the yidam deity and defeat Harinanda. This is exactly what is meant in the following passage from the *Tantra of the Layman Secret Black Foe*:

> If his faith is stable, even a fool
> Will gain the accomplishment of union.

On the path of accumulation one relies on the practices of the development stage in a systematic manner, visualizing oneself as the divine form of devoted conduct. This enables the practitioner to accomplish the eight great activities and the other mundane spiritual accomplishments. Based on that, it becomes possible to attain the state of one of the knowledge holders of the desire and form realms, with all their unique qualities, such as subtlety and lightness. This, in turn, allows one to attain the body of wisdom.

Whatever the case may be, if the divine form of the energetic-mind is able to arise in an impure illusory form, the development stage will not become a meditation on anything that exists in and of itself. One will then progress to the path of joining and train in the wisdom of the four joys associated with the completion stage. Through this, a certain degree of mastery over wisdom will be attained, which will produce the stages of inner warmth, outer warmth, and so on. As one obtains empowerment for the proximate cause of the buddhas and bases one's activity on an actual or mental mudrā, one will then enter the path without hindrances connected with the actual attainment of the path of seeing.

At this point, a great degree of mastery over wisdom will be attained and the fully matured body will transform into luminosity. Nevertheless, with such a support one will still be able to make one's body appear should one wish to do so in order to benefit those in need of guidance. This is what is known as the great seal, the supreme accomplishment. Once the mind has matured into the divine form of luminosity, mastery is gained over the 1,200 qualities of the path of seeing, the first level of the noble ones. The path of cultivation is attained next, which spans from the second level up to the ninth. At this stage, abandonment and realization are gradually perfected. The tenth level is the culmination of the path, the spontaneously present knowledge holder. This form is endowed with seven qualities and appears as a vajra holder in whom the five kāyas are spontaneously present.

All of this can be applied to the framework of the four knowledge holders as well. The matured knowledge holder occurs on the path of seeing, at which point the fully ripened bodily support has yet to dissolve. Once dissolved, one becomes a knowledge holder with power over longevity. The nine levels of the path of cultivation constitute those of the knowledge holder of the great seal, while the tenth level is that of the spontaneously present knowledge holder. The phase that starts with the path of cultivation is also known as that of the unified form.

These ten levels constitute the path of training. Once an individual has reached the end of this phase, the empowerment of fruition from the great sambhogakāya maṇḍala is received. Through this, bodhicitta reverses course and, at the conclusion of this process, the two obscurations and the habitual tendencies associated with the transference of the three appearances are purified until nothing remains. Once this has come to pass, the state of a vajra holder is actualized and one comes to embody the four kāyas and five wisdoms. This is the natural state of perfect enlightenment, the indivisibility of the ground and the fruition.

> Having crossed this great ocean, the meaning of the Mahāyoga tantras,
> With the captain's ship, the lucid teachings of the guru,
> One discovers the supreme treasure of the profound meaning.
> This I now hand to those who aspire to awaken, a gift of true meaning.
>
> Perfecting this training,
> As if touched by the philosopher's stone,
> May they attain the pervasive lord heruka,
> Sealing all phenomena with the innate great bliss of unity.

In this text, I have clarified the meaning of the various practices associated with the rituals of the development stage. The command to write this treatise was made by Wangmo Rinpoche, who sustains the great levels with ease through the ten virtues and the four sections. Thinking that it would be beneficial, both to her own practice and that of others, she made this command, accompanying it with golden flowers. It was then composed by the indolent knowledge holder monk Tsewang Chokdrub. May it fill the universe with virtue and goodness and may all be virtuous!

APPENDICES

Appendix A:

Visualizing the Deity

Notes on Visualization • *by Kunkhyen Tenpe Nyima*

Start out by placing a painting or statue before you, using one made by a skilled artisan and with all the appropriate characteristics. Next, arrange offerings before it and practice the preliminaries. You can do the latter in a brief form or a more extensive one; either is acceptable. Then, according to the oral instructions of Jamyang Khyentse Wangpo (which he taught from the *Condensed Realization of the Gurus),* visualize a throne on the crown of your head. It should be held up by snow lions and piled with lotus, sun, and moon disc seats. Upon this throne imagine your kind, precious root guru in the form of the guru Vajradhara, the embodiment of all sources of refuge. Then, with great devotion, pray to him as the very essence of all the buddhas throughout the three times and offer him your body and all your possessions. Supplicate him to bless your state of being and, in particular, request his blessings so that the true absorptions of the development stage will arise in your mind this very moment. Imagine that your guru is pleased by this and smiles. He then dissolves into red light and dissolves into your crown. Once your ordinary mind and his enlightened mind have merged inseparably, rest for a while.

Once this is finished, gaze at the painting or statue placed before you. Then close your eyes and visualize the image immediately, transferring it to your own body. Train by alternating between these two steps. Once you've gotten used to the visualization, you can refine your ability by changing its size, increasing or decreasing the number of figures, visualizing the central deity and then the retinue, and so forth. You can also alternate periods of simultaneously visualizing the complete form of the deity with periods where you only focus on certain parts or ornaments.

Whichever you do, start out by focusing solely on the central deity. Starting at the tip of its crown and working your way down to the lotus seat, try to develop a clear visualization of each element: the color of its body, its face, hands and ornamentation, its clothing, the pupils of its eyes, the shape of its arms and legs, the appearance of the marks and signs, the radiation and absorption of light rays, and so on . . . work at visualizing all of these in minute detail.

The figure you are visualizing should not be a corporeal entity. It shouldn't be flat like a painting or protrude like a carving, in other words. On the other hand, it should not be a mindless entity either, like a rainbow. Rather, it should be clearly defined in every respect—its front and back, left and right sides, proportions, and so forth. Yet at the same time, it should be devoid of any sense of materiality. You should train as though it is a body of clear light, as if a deity with the wisdom of omniscience, love, and power had actually arrived.

Once you have a handle on this aspect of the practice, you can move on to sequentially visualizing its other elements—the retinue, celestial palace, the layout of the pure realm, and the protection circle. At times you can focus on the visualization as a whole, while at others focusing on specific elements.

The term "clear appearance" refers to the point at which every aspect of the supporting and supported maṇḍala circles arise in your mind with a sense of vivid clarity. This is one of the primary functions of the development stage; it is a unique method that allows one to practice calm abiding by focusing the mind on the deity. For this very reason, it is important to meditate by purposely keeping your awareness on the visualized form of the deity. Once you are familiar with this process, the five meditative experiences will sequentially arise.

—Excerpt from *Notes on the Development Stage*, pp. 41-43.

PRACTICAL ADVICE • *by Padmasambhava*

Whether you meditate on the deity in front of you or meditate on yourself as the deity, after you have received the master's oral instructions, the master should have given you, the disciple, his blessings and protected you against obstructing forces.

Next, sit on a comfortable seat and be physically at ease. Take a well-made painting of the yidam deity and place it in front of you. Sit for a short time without thinking of anything whatsoever, and then look at the image from head to foot. Look again gradually at all the details from the feet to the head. Look at the image as a whole. Sometimes rest without thinking about the image and refresh yourself. Then in this way, look again and again for a whole day.

That evening, take a full night's sleep. When you wake up, look again as before. In the evening, do not meditate on the deity but just rest your mind in the state of nonthought.

Following this, the deity will appear vividly in your mind even without your meditating. If it does not, look at its image, close your eyes, and visualize the image in front of yourself. Sit for as long as the visualization naturally remains. When it becomes blurry and unclear, look again at the image and then repeat the visualization, letting it be vividly present. Cut conceptual thinking and sit.

When meditating like this you will have five kinds of experiences: the experience of movement, the experience of attainment, the experience of habituation, the experience of stability, and the experience of perfection.

1. When your mind does not remain settled at this time and you have numerous thoughts, ideas, and recollections, that is the experience of movement. Through that you approach taking control of the mind. This experience is like a waterfall cascading over a steep cliff.

2. Then when you can visualize the deity for a short time with both the shape and color of the deity remaining vivid and clear at the same time, that is the experience of attainment. This experience is like a small pond.

3. Following this, when the deity is clear whether you meditate upon it from a long or a short distance, and when it remains for a sixth of your session without any occurrence of gross thoughts, that is the experience of habituation, which is like the flow of a river.

4. Next, no thoughts move and you are able to maintain the session while clearly visualizing the deity. That is the experience of stability that is like Mount Sumeru.

5. Following this, when you can remain for a full day or more without losing the vivid presence of the deity's arms and legs even down to the

hairs on its body and without giving rise to conceptual thinking, that is the experience of perfection.

Practitioner, apply this to your own experience!

If you sit too long with an unclear visualization of the deity, your physical constitution will be upset. You will become weary and consequently unable to progress in your concentration. You will have even more thoughts, so first refresh yourself and then continue meditating.

Until you attain a clear visualization, do not meditate at night. In general it is important to visualize in short sessions. Meditate while there is sunlight, when the sky is clear, or with a butter lamp. Do not meditate when you just have woken up or when you feel sluggish or hazy.

At night, get a full night's sleep and meditate the next day in eight short sessions.

When meditating, if you leave the session abruptly, you will lose concentration, so do it gently.

When your visualization becomes vivid the moment you meditate, you can also practice at nighttime, during dusk, and at early dawn.

In general do not weary yourself. Focus your mind on the visualization, grow accustomed to it with stability, and visualize the complete form of the deity.

—Excerpt from *Dakini Teachings* by Padmasambhava, as revealed by Nyangral Nyima Özer (transl. Erik Pema Kunzang), pp. 178-179.

Appendix B:

Topical Outline for *Ladder to Akaniṣṭha*

I. THE UNERRING CAUSE: THE BASIS FOR DEVELOPMENT STAGE PRACTICE
- A. Purifying the Habitual Tendencies Associated with the Four Types of Birth
  1. The Concise Approach of Complete Simplicity
  2. The Intermediate, Simple Approach
  3. The Extensive, Elaborate Approach
  4. The Very Extensive, Very Elaborate Approach
- B. The Three Absorptions
- C. Developing the Supportive and the Supported Maṇḍalas
  1. Visualizing the Palace
  2. Visualizing the Deity
     - a. The Ritual of the Three Vajras
     - b. The Five Manifestations of Enlightenment

II. THE UNDELUDED CONDITION: THE PATH OF MEDITATION
- A. Training on the Path According to One's Capacity
  1. Focusing the Mind on the Deity
  2. Correcting Flaws That Involve Change
  3. Parting from the Deity
  4. Bringing the Deity onto the Path
  5. Merging Your Mind with the Deity
  6. Connecting the Deity with Reality
     - a. The Four Stakes That Bind the Life-Force
  7. Bringing Experiences onto the Path
- B. The Results of the Path Linked with the Four Knowledge Holders
  1. Approach
  2. Close Approach
  3. Accomplishment
  4. Great Accomplishment

III. The Pure Fruition: Attaining the Unified State
   A. The Essence of Fruition: A General Presentation
      1. Vajrakāya
      2. Abhisambodhikāya
      3. Dharmakāya
      4. Sambhogakāya
      5. Nirmāṇakāya
   B. The Unique Presentation of Mantra

Appendix C:

Topical Outline for *Husks of Unity*

- I. THE PRELIMINARIES
  - A. The General Preliminaries
    - 1. Renunciation
    - 2. Refuge
    - 3. The Awakened Mind
  - B. The Unique Preliminaries
    - 1. Clearing Away Adverse Conditions
      - a. Expelling Obstructing Forces
      - b. Establishing the Boundary
    - 2. Gathering Positive Conditions
      - a. The Descent of Blessings
      - b. Consecrating the Offering Articles

- II. THE MAIN PRACTICE
  - A. The Practice of the Meditation State
    - 1. Enlightened Body: the Practice of the Deity
      - a. The Framework of the Three Absorptions
        - i. The Absorption of Suchness
        - ii. The Absorption of Total Illumination
        - iii. The Causal Absorption
      - b. Visualizing the Supportive and Supported Maṇḍalas
        - i. The Supportive Palace
          - *1) The Layered Elements*
          - *2) The Celestial Palace*
          - *3) The Seat*
        - ii. The Supported Deity
          - *1) The Development Rituals*
          - *2) The Characteristics of the Deity*
            - *a) Peaceful Deities*
            - *b) Wrathful Deities*
            - *c) The Blessing*

c. Invocation and Request
d. Homage, Offering, and Praise
   i. Homage
   ii. Offering
      1) *The Outer Offering*
      2) *The Inner Offering*
         a) *Medicine*
         b) *Torma*
         c) *Rakta*
      3) *The Secret Offering*
         a) *Union*
         b) *Liberation*
      4) *The Offering of Reality*
   iii. Praise
e. Training in the Deity's Appearance
   i. Clear Appearance
   ii. Stable Pride
   iii. Recollection of Purity
   iv. Bliss, Clarity, and Nonthought

2. Enlightened Speech, the Practice of Recitation
   a. Overview
   b. The Function of Recitation
   c. The Essence of Recitation
   d. Types of Recitation
      i. The Arranged Recitation, Like a Moon with a Garland of Stars
      ii. The Palanquin Recitation, Like a Spinning Firebrand
      iii. The Recitation of Projection and Absorption, Like a King's Messenger
      iv. The Recitation That is Like a Broken Beehive
   e. Performing Mantra Recitation
   f. The Number of Recitations
   g. Subsequent Activities
3. Enlightened Mind, the Practice of Luminosity

B. Subsequent Practices

III. CONCLUDING ACTIVITIES
   A. Dedication of Merit
   B. Making Aspirations
   C. Chanting Auspicious Prayers

Abbreviations

CC *Creation and Completion: Essential Points of Tantric Meditation.* Jamgön Kongtrul.

CG *bsKyed pa'i rim pa cho ga dang sbyar ba'i gsal byed zung 'jug snye ma.* dGe rtse ma h'a pandita tshe dbang mchog grub.

DE *Dzogchen Essentials: The Path that Clarifies Confusion.* Marcia Binder Schmidt, ed.

DK *sDe-dge bka' 'gyur.*

DR *rDzogs rim chos drug bsdus don.* dPal sprul o rgyan 'jigs med chos kyi dbang po.

DT *sDe-dge bstan 'gyur.*

DZ *The Practice of Dzogchen.* Tulku Thondup.

EM *Empowerment.* Tsele Natsok Rangdröl (contained in DE).

GD *bLa ma dgongs pa 'dus pa'i cho ga'i rnam bzhag dang 'brel ba'i bskyed rdzogs zung 'jug gi sgron ma mkhyen brtse'i me long 'od zer brgya pa.* 'Jigs med gling pa.

GT *sGyu 'phrul drwa las khro bo'i dkyil 'khor du bsnyen pa'i tshul gyi lhan thabs rig 'dzin dga' ston.* mKhan chen ngag dbang dpal bzang.

JG *Joyful Grove of the Vidyādharas.* Dzogchen Ponlop Rinpoche.

JL *bsKyed rim lha'i khrid kyi rnam par gzhag pa 'og min bgrod pa'i them skas* (Dodrupchen edition). 'Jigs med gling pa.

KG *dPal sgrub pa chen po bka' brgyad kyi spyi don rnam par bshad pa dngos grub snying po.* 'Ju mi pham rgya mtsho.

KN *rDzogs pa chen po mkha' 'gro snying thig gi khrid yig thar lam bgrod byed shing rta bzang po.* Nges don bstan 'dzin bzang po.

KR *bsKyed rim gyi zin bris cho ga spyi 'gros ltar bkod pa man ngag kun btus.* Kun mkhyen bstan pa'i nyi ma.

KS *rDzogs pa chen po ngal so skor gsum dang rang grol skor gsum bcas pod gsum.* Klong chen rab 'byams.

LT *bsKyed rim lha'i khrid kyi dka' gnad cung zad bshad pa.* dPal sprul o rgyan 'jigs med chos kyi dbang po.

LW *The Light of Wisdom,* vol. 2. Padmasambhava and Jamgön Kongtrül.

MM *The Mirror of Mindfulness: The Cycle of the Four Bardos.* Tsele Natsok Rangdröl.

MS *dPal gsang ba'i snying po de kho na nyid nges pa'i rgyud kyi 'grel pa phyogs bcu'i mun pa thams cad rnam par sel ba.* Klong chen rab 'byams.

MV *dBus dang mtha' rnam par 'byed pa'i bstan bcos kyi 'grel pa 'od zer phreng ba.* 'Ju mi pham rgya mtsho.

ND *Lam zhugs kyi gang zag las dang po pa la phan pa'i bskyed rdzogs kyi gnad bsdus.* 'Jam mgon kong sprul blo gros mtha' yas.

NG *Mtshams-brag Manuscript of the Rñin ma rgyud 'bum.*

NK *Rñin ma Bka' ma rgyas pa.*

NO *Yon tan rin po che'i mdzod kyi 'grel pa zab don snang byed nyi ma'i 'od zer.* Yon tan rgya mtsho. Citations list file number, then page number.

NS *The Nyingma School of Tibetan Buddhism.* Dudjom Rinpoche.

ON *gSang 'grel phyogs bcu'i mun sel gyi spyi don 'od gsal snying po.* 'Ju mi pham rgya mtsho.

PA *Pure Appearance.* Dilgo Khyentse Rinpoche.

PK *Peking bka' 'gyur.*

SC *rDzogs pa chen po sems nyid ngal gso'i 'grel pa shing rta chen po.* Klong chen rab 'byams.

SD *dPal gsang ba'i snying po de kho na nyid nges pa'i rgyud kyi rgyal po sgyu 'phrul drwa ba spyi don gyi sgo nas gtan la 'bebs par byed pa'i legs bshad gsang bdag zhal lung.* Lo chen dharma shri.

SG *Theg pa lam zhugs kyi bshags pa'i rtsa 'grel bsdus pa thar lam sgron me.* Nges don bstan 'dzin bzang po.

SS *Srog sdom gzer bzhi'i dmigs pa gnad 'gags khams gsum rol pa tshangs pa'i sgra dbyangs.* dPal sprul o rgyan 'jigs med chos kyi dbang po.

ST *Srog sdom gzer bzhi'i zin bris kun mkhyen brgyud pa'i zhal lung.* mKhan chen ngag dbang dpal bzang.

TD *Bod rgya tshig mdzod chen mo.* Krang dbyi sun, editor.

TK *Shes bya kun khyab mdzod.* 'Jam mgon kong sprul blo gros mtha' yas. Citations list volume number, then folio number.

TN *The Small Golden Key.* Thinley Norbu.

TS *Yon tan rin po che'i mdzod kyi mchan 'grel theg gsum bdud rtsi'i nying khu.* Klong chen ye shes rdo rje.

WC *rDzogs pa chen po klong chen snying gi thig le'i rtsa gsum spyi dang bye brag gi dbang bskur gyi phreng ba bklag chog tu bkod pa zab bsang bdud rtsi'i sgo 'byed skal bzang kun dga'i rol ston.* Dil mgo mkhyen brtse.

YD *Theg pa chen po'i man ngag gi bstan bcos yid bzhin rin po che'i mdzod.* Klong chen rab 'byams.

YT *Yon tan rin po che'i mdzod las 'bras bu'i theg pa'i rgya cher 'grel rnam mkhyen shing rta.* 'Jigs med gling pa.

Glossary

Abhisambodhikāya (*mngon byang gi sku*) – One of the five kāyas; encompassing all the manifestations of knowledge, love, and ability, this kāya is the basis for all the unique qualities of buddhahood. [NS 140]

Absorption (*ting nge 'dzin/samādhi*) – *See* meditative absorption.

Absorption being (*ting 'dzin sems dpa'*) – The absorption being is one of the three beings taught in development stage practice. In particular, this refers to the seed syllable or symbolic implement that is visualized at the heart center of the wisdom being. [TD 1029]

Absorption of suchness (*de bzhin nyid kyi ting nge 'dzin*) – This is the first of the three absorptions. According to Jigme Lingpa, this absorption relates to reality itself—the empty, luminous nature of mind. It also purifies the death state, the belief in permanence, and the formless realm. [JL 221] Tenpe Nyima describes the actual practice of this absorption as follows: "Start out by relaxing your mind from within; don't follow after any deluded thoughts. Mind itself is empty, yet aware—a bare reality beyond anything you can think or say. Settle for a moment in this simplicity . . . This is the absorption of suchness." He further notes that this absorption is also known as "the practice of great emptiness," "the vajralike absorption," and "the absorption of emptiness." [KR 25]

Absorption of total illumination (*kun snang gi ting nge 'dzin*) – As the second of the three absorptions, this absorption involves an impartial and unified compassion towards all beings. According to Jigme Lingpa, this compassion is the natural radiance of the empty luminosity of the first absorption, the absorption of suchness. He also states that practicing this absorption frees the practitioner from nihilistic views and rebirths in the form realm, and allows for the transformation of the intermediate state into the sambhogakāya. [JL 222] Concerning the actual practice of this absorption, Tenpe Nyima writes, "Within this state of empty clarity, meditate for a while on a nonreferential, illusory compassion towards the sentient beings who do not recognize their own innate wisdom. This is the all–illuminating absorption." He further mentions that this absorption is also known as the "practice of illusory compassion," "the heroic gait," and "aspiration–free absorption." [KR 25]

ACCOMPLISHMENT (*sgrub pa*) – Accomplishment is the third of the four divisions of approach and accomplishment. Though this stage is relevant in a variety of contexts, in terms of development stage practice accomplishment refers to the phase in which one gains mastery over wisdom. [KR 60]

AFFLICTION (*nyon mongs pa*) – A factor that upsets or disturbs the mind and body and produces fatigue. [TD 971]

AFFLICTIVE OBSCURATIONS (*nyon mongs pa'i sgrib pa*) – Concepts, such as avarice, that obstruct the attainment of liberation. [TD 970]

AKANIṢṬHA (*'og min*) [Lit. "Unsurpassed"] – 1) The eight planes of existence associated with the fourth level of meditative concentration. The gods born in this plane have reached the highest level of the form realm. This realm, which is one of the five pure realms, is referred to as such because there are no other realms of embodied beings higher than this; 2) the Densely Arrayed Realm of Akaniṣṭha (Akaniṣṭhaghandavyūha), a sambhogakāya realm located above the seventeen form realms. [TD 2529, 1103]

ALL–ACCOMPLISHING WISDOM (*bya grub ye shes*) – Quoting the *Sūtra of the Levels of Buddhahood*, Jigme Lingpa explains, "This form of wisdom is exemplified by the physical, verbal, and mental acts that are carried out by sentient beings. All-accomplishing wisdom is similar to this, as it involves the enlightened body, speech, and mind spontaneously accomplishing the welfare of sentient beings." [YT 431]

AMṚTA (*bdud rtsi*) – *See* nectar.

ANOTHER'S CHILD (*gzhan sras*) – This is one part of a twofold visualization process found in the Mahāyoga teachings of the Nyingma School. In this stage of practice, all the phenomena of saṃsāra and nirvāṇa are transformed through a complex visualization process in which the central deities of the maṇḍala "give birth" to the deities in the retinue. [LT 460]

Anuttarayoga Tantra (*rnal 'byor bla na med pa'i rgyud*) [Lit. "Unsurpassed Union Tantra"] – The fourth and highest of the four classes of Tantra. In the New Schools, this system consists of the Father Tantras, Mother Tantras, and Nondual Tantras. In the Nyingma School, this class of Tantra is equated with the three inner tantras: Mahāyoga, Anuyoga, and Atiyoga. Ju Mipham explains, "From the perspective of this approach, not only is the Causal Vehicle of the Perfections a 'long path,' but the Outer Tantras are as well. In other words, this is the true 'swift path,' the true 'Fruition Vehicle.' All other approaches are taught according to the mind-sets of disciples to lead them to this vehicle. Here, in contrast, the ultimate, definitive meaning is revealed explicitly, just as it is seen by the wisdom of the buddhas." [KG 37]

Anuyoga (*rjes su rnal 'byor*) – Anuyoga is the eighth of the nine vehicles found in the Nyingma tradition. To enter this system one first receives the thirty-six supreme empowerments: the ten outer empowerments, eleven inner empowerments, thirteen practice empowerments, and two secret empowerments. Next, one trains in the Anuyoga view until one has come to a definitive understanding concerning the essence of the threefold maṇḍala of Samantabhadra. In the meditative system of this tradition, one practices the paths of liberation and skillful means. The former involves settling in a nonconceptual state in accordance with reality or, in accordance with letters, reciting mantras to visualize the maṇḍala of deities. The latter entails arousing coemergent wisdom by relying upon the upper and lower gates. In terms of conduct, one understands all appearances and mental events to be the play of the wisdom of great bliss and, with this understanding, uses the proximate cause of being beyond acceptance and rejection to attain the fruition. Here, the fruition involves the five yogas (which are in essence the five paths), the completion of the ten levels, and the attainment of the state of Samantabhadra. [TD 3120]

Appearance, increase, and attainment (*snang mched thob gsum*) – *See* three appearances.

Approach (*bsnyen pa*) – Approach is the first of the four divisions of approach and accomplishment. Though this stage is relevant in a variety of contexts, in terms of development stage practice, approach refers to the phase in which the wisdom being "approaches" one's own state of being. [KR 60]

APPROACH AND ACCOMPLISHMENT (*bsnyen sgrub*) – *See* four divisions of approach and accomplishment.

ATIYOGA (*shin tu rnal 'byor*) – Atiyoga is the highest of the Nyingma tradition's nine vehicles. In the textual tradition of this tantric system, Atiyoga is equated with the Great Perfection, the naturally-occurring wisdom that is free from conceptual complexities and not subject to any sense of partiality or limitation. As such, it is considered the very pinnacle of all the various vehicles since it contains all of their significance. Within this Great Perfection, all the various phenomena of saṃsāra and nirvāṇa, all that appears and exists, arise as the play of naturally-occurring wisdom, apart from which nothing exists. The fundamental basis of existence, in this tradition, is this naturally-occurring wisdom. In terms of the path, there are two forms of practice: the break-through stage of innate purity and the direct leap stage of spontaneous presence. Through these two practices the four visions are brought to a state of culmination and one attains the result of this process, liberation into the very ground. Said differently, one attains the permanent state of the youthful vase body. [TD 3118]

ATTAINMENT (*thob pa*) – *See* three appearances.

AVALOKITEŚVARA (*spyan ras gzigs*) – Avalokiteśvara is the yidam deity considered to be the unified essence of the enlightened speech of all the buddhas and the embodiment of compassion. [TD 1674]

AWAKENED MIND (*byang chub kyi sems/bodhicitta*) – To desire the attainment of complete enlightenment while focusing on the welfare of others. [TD 1869]

BARDO (*bar do*) – *See* intermediate state.

BASIC SPACE OF PHENOMENA (*chos kyi dbyings/dharmadhātu*) – 1) Emptiness; 2) the empty nature of the aggregate of form and the remaining four aggregates. [TD 840]

BASIS OF PURIFICATION (*sbyang gzhi*) – There are four factors that subsume all aspects of development stage practice. Jamgön Kongtrül explains, "To engage in development stage practice, one needs to have at least some understanding of four factors: the basis, object, process, and result of purification. The basis of purification is the permanent, stable, and unconditioned basic space of phenomena—the buddha nature that thoroughly pervades all beings. This includes all the marks, signs, and other qualities of the dharmakāya, which are integral aspects of wisdom." [ND 13-14]

Bell (*dril bu*) – In the Vajrayāna tradition, the bell is a symbolic implement used to represent a number of important principles. Generally speaking, it is linked with the female principle, emptiness, and knowledge. [YT 671]

Beneficial outer empowerments (*phyi phan pa'i dbang*) – There are three groupings of empowerments linked with the peaceful and wrathful deities of the *Tantra of the Secret Essence*. The first grouping consists of the ten outer, beneficial empowerments, which prepare the student to engage in the development and completion stages. The next two groupings are the five inner empowerments of potentiality and the three profound, secret empowerments. [PA 10-12]

Blessings (*byin rlabs*) – The innate potential or strength present in the various qualities of the path of the noble ones. [TD 1885]

Bliss, clarity, and nonthought (*bde gsal mi rtog pa*) – These three factors are commonly listed as the primary forms of meditative experience (in contrast to actual realization). In particular, they are intimately connected with the nature of mind itself. Jamgön Kongtrül writes, "Wisdom energy is the mind's own nature—blissful, clear, and nonconceptual. When this becomes aware of itself, all fluctuations of the karmic winds are pacified." [TK 3, 45] In addition, as Lochen Dharmaśrī points out, these three also relate to the conceptual completion stage. He explains, "In the completion stage, the wisdom of bliss, clarity, and nonconceptuality arise from the channels, energies, and essences. [SD 35]

Blissful melting (*zhu bde*) – This term is commonly used in reference to conceptual completion stage practice, where it relates to the movement of energy in the subtle body and the subsequent experience of bliss that follows. [TK 4, 36]

Blood (*khrag/rakta*) – *See* rakta.

Bodhisattva (*byang chub sems dpa'*) [Lit. "heroic being of enlightenment"] – An individual who trains in the Great Vehicle, so-called because such individuals do not become discouraged in the face of the long duration it takes to attain great enlightenment, nor in giving away their own head and limbs out of generosity. [TD 1870]

BONE ORNAMENTS (*rus rgyan*) – Bone ornaments are symbolic ornamentation worn by certain yidam deities. Depending on the context, there are said to be either five or six types of bone ornament. The first group is presented in the *Husks of Unity* by Getse Mahāpaṇḍita. The sixfold grouping consists of bone jewels, bone lotuses, bone vajras, bone cakras, a bone eternal knot, and a bone double vajra. [TN 86]

BUDDHA (*sangs rgyas*) – One who has cleared away the darkness of the two obscurations and in whom the twofold wisdom has blossomed. [TD 2913]

CAKRA (*'khor lo*) – 1) In terms of the energetic body, the cakras are circular conglomerations of energetic channels that are supported by the central channel [TD 2209]; 2) as a symbolic implement used in development stage practice, the cakra is a circular instrument that symbolizes cutting through the afflictions. [KR 51]

CALM ABIDING (*zhi gnas*) – One of the common denominators and causes of all meditative absorptions. This form of meditation involves settling the mind one-pointedly in order to pacify mental distraction towards external objects. [TD 2384]

CARYĀ TANTRA (*spyod rgyud*) [Lit. "Performance Tantra"] – The second of the three outer tantras; the view of this tradition is similar to that of Yoga Tantra, while its conduct is equated with that of Kriyā Tantra. For this reason, it is also known as "dual tantra." [NS 271] This is also the second of the four classes of Tantra found in the New Schools.

CAUSAL ABSORPTION (*rgyu'i ting nge 'dzin*) – This absorption is the third of the three absorptions. According to Jigme Lingpa, the causal absorption purifies the consciousness present the moment one's existence is about to enter a new abode, as well as the tendency to take birth in the desire realm. [JL 221] Tenpe Nyima describes the practice of this absorption as follows: "Within a nonconceptual state, compassion will propel the mind, directing itself towards the essential nature of the mind in the form of a seed syllable, such as HŪṂ or HRĪḤ. This syllable will appear vividly in the empty expanse of space, which has no foundation. The causal absorption is also known as part of 'the single seal,' 'the causal wisdom being,' 'training in the subtle syllable,' 'the illusory absorption,' and 'the unlabelled absorption.'" [KR 25]

Causal heruka (*rgyu'i he ru ka*) – The unchanging and self aware suchness that is present as the innate potential of all beings—immutable great bliss. [TD 567]

Causal vajra holder (*rgyu'i rdo rje 'dzin pa*) – *See* causal heruka.

Causal Vehicle of the Perfections (*rgyu pha rol du phyin pa'i theg pa*) – *See* Sūtra Vehicle.

Celestial palace (*gzhal yas khang*) – In terms of development stage practice, the celestial palace is the abode of the deities. It is "immeasurable" in the sense that its dimensions and enlightened qualities cannot be fathomed. [TD 2416] According to Jigme Lingpa, "Meditating on the form of the celestial palace in boundless space allows the impure nature of one's ordinary environment to be blessed as Akaniṣṭha." [JL 221]

Central channel (*rtsa dbu ma*) – The central channel is the main energetic channel in the body, running vertically through its center. Its upper end is located at the cranial aperture on the crown of the head, while its lower end is found in the secret place (the perineum). [TD 2212]

Channels, energies, and essences (*rtsa rlung thig le*) – These three factors function as the support for consciousness, ensuring that the life remains stable and the life-force uninterrupted. Of these three, the channels are said to be like a house, the essences like the wealth contained therein, and the energies like their owner. [TD 2213]

Clarity, purity, and pride (*gsal dag nga rgyal gsum*) – These three principles are used to present the most important aspects of development stage visualization. Jamgön Kongtrül explains, "Regardless of whether you are meditating on the development stage in an elaborate or concise form, there are three factors involved. The clear appearance of the visualization purifies one's fixation towards "objective" appearances, recollecting purity eliminates the idea that it is a solid thing, and stable pride vanquishes the belief in an ordinary 'I'." [ND 15]

Clear appearance (*rnam pa gsal ba*) – Along with recollecting purity and stable pride, this is one of the primary principles of development stage practice. Jigme Lingpa explains, "The forms of the central and surrounding deities . . . should not be protruding like a clay statue or cast image, yet neither should they be flat like a painting. In contrast, they should be apparent, yet not truly existent, like a rainbow in the sky or the reflection of the moon in a lake. They should appear as though conjured up by a magician. Clear appearance involves fixing the mind one-pointedly on these forms with a sense of vividness, nakedness, lucidity, and clarity". [GD 219] *See also* clarity, purity, and pride.

CLOSE APPROACH (*nye bar bsnyen pa*) – Close approach is the second of the four divisions of approach and accomplishment. Though this phase can be discussed in a variety of contexts, in terms of development stage practice, close approach involves the merging of the enlightened mind of the yidam deity with one's own ordinary consciousness. [KR 60]

COGNITIVE OBSCURATIONS (*shes bya'i sgrib pa*) – The concepts of the three spheres, which obstruct the attainment of complete omniscience (the state of buddhahood). [TD 2860]

COLLECTED SĀDHANAS (*sgrub sde*) – The Mahāyoga teachings are traditionally divided into two groups, the Collected Tantras and the Collected Sādhanas. The latter is associated with a genre of literature known collectively as the Eight Great Sādhana Teachings. [NS 283]

COLLECTED TANTRAS (*rgyud sde*) – The Mahāyoga teachings are traditionally divided into two groups, the Collected Tantras and the Collected Sādhanas. The former includes the *Guhyagarbha Tantra*, one of the most widely studied texts in the Nyingma tradition. [NS 283]

COMPLETION STAGE (*rdzogs rim*) – Tantric practice is divided into two phases, the development stage and the completion stage. Lochen Dharmaśrī explains, "To summarize, the development stage involves transforming impure appearances into pure ones and meditating on the maṇḍala circle. In the completion stage, the aim is to realize the wisdom of bliss–emptiness." The latter, he continues, can be divided further into two approaches, the conceptual completion stage and nonconceptual completion stage. He writes, "In this stage, one either meditates conceptually on the energies, channels, and essences, or nonconceptually by absorbing oneself in reality." [SD 325] Ju Mipham summarizes this phase as follows, "All the various forms of completion stage practice bring about the manifest appearance of pure wisdom by bringing the karmic energies into the central channel, though this may be brought about either directly or indirectly." [ON 417]

CONCEPTUAL COMPLETION STAGE (*mtshan bcas rdzogs rim*) – The completion stage is divided into two categories, the conceptual completion stage and the nonconceptual completion stage. In the former, the practitioner works primarily with the subtle body—the channels, energies, and essences. As Ju Mipham points out, "This path is conceptual insofar as one must maintain mental reference points and make intentional effort, both physically and verbally." [ON 417]

CONDUCT (*spyod pa*) – *See* view, meditation, conduct, and fruition.

CURVED KNIFE (*gri 'gug*) – The curved knife is a symbolic implement that symbolizes the severing of the four demons. [KR 51]

DAILY CYCLE (*dus sbyor*) – "Daily cycle" refers to the 21,600 cycles of breathing that are said to transpire each day. [TD 1275]

ḌĀKINĪ (*mkha' 'gro ma*) – 1) A yoginī who has attained the unique spiritual accomplishments; 2) a female divinity who has taken birth in a pure realm or other similar location. [TD 298]

DEATH (*'chi srid*) – The death process is considered to be of vital importance in the Buddhist tradition, primarily because it affords a uniquely powerful opportunity to attain liberation. In terms of tantric practice, this process is purified by the completion stage. According to Tsele Natsok Rangdröl, there are outer, inner, and secret signs that mark this process. The outer signs relate primarily to the steady decrease of the body's ability to function correctly and the experiences that ensue from this decay. The inner signs have to do with the various mental states that accompany this process. The secret signs, such as the perception of smoke and mist, are associated with the mind's luminous nature. [MM 29–30] *See also* three appearances.

DEFINITIVE MEANING (*nges don*) – To specific disciples it is taught that the profound nature of all phenomena is emptiness, free from arising, cessation, and every other form of conceptual projection, and that the actual condition and nature of things is one of luminosity, beyond anything that can be thought or put into words. The definitive meaning is this nature, as well as the scriptures that teach it and their related commentaries. [TD 655]

DEFINITIVE PERFECTION (*nges rdzogs*) – *See* devoted training and definitive perfection.

DEITY (*lha*) – *See* yidam deity.

DEITY YOGA (*lha'i rnal 'byor*) – *See* development stage.

DESIRE REALM (*'dod khams*) – One of the three realms that comprise saṃsāra. The sentient beings of this realm are attached to material food and sex, primarily because they sustain themselves through the five sense pleasures. This realm is referred to as such due to the fact that this environment is home to desirous sentient beings. [TD 1414]

DEVELOPMENT AND COMPLETION (*bskyed rdzogs*) – The development stage and completion stage comprise the inner tantric path to liberation. Explaining the function of these two approaches, Lochen Dharmaśrī writes, "The development stage purifies [the idea that] the environment and its inhabitants are real entities with their own characteristics, while the completion stage purifies the subtle clinging that can occur while meditating that these are all illusory, as is the case in development stage practice." [SD 325] As Khenpo Ngaga points out, all the various categories of Tantra relate to this twofold approach. He explains, "In the Vajrayāna, there are three inner divisions—the three inner tantras. The Father Tantra emphasizes the skillful methods of the development stage and the completion stage of the subtle energies. In the Mother Tantra, the completion stage associated with the subtle essences is emphasized, in which case one relies either upon the body of another or one's own body. The Nondual Tantra stresses the view of the path of liberation alone. In actuality, however, all of these are included within the two stages of development and completion." [ST 6]

DEVELOPMENT, COMPLETION, AND GREAT PERFECTION (*bskyed rdzogs rdzogs chen*) – In the Nyingma tradition, the system of the inner tantras is said to comprise three avenues of practice—the development stage, completion stage, and the Great Perfection. These three, in turn, are associated with Mahāyoga, Anuyoga, and Atiyoga—the three inner tantras. As Dilgo Khyentse explains, "Development and Mahāyoga are like the basis for all the teachings, completion and Anuyoga are like the path of all the teachings, and the Great Perfection of Atiyoga is like the result of all the teachings." [WC 773]

DEVELOPMENT STAGE (*bskyed rim*) – Along with the completion stage, this is one of two phases that constitute Buddhist practice in the inner tantras. Explaining this approach, Ju Mipham writes, "The phases of development stage practice correspond to the way in which conventional existence develops. There are five such phases: great emptiness, illusory wisdom, the single seal, the elaborate seal, and group assembly practice. Practicing this fivefold approach *purifies* the habitual patterns of saṃsāra, *perfects* the fruition of nirvāṇa, and *matures* the practitioner for the completion stage. [ON 416]

Devoted training and definitive perfection (*mos sgom dang nges rdzogs*) – Devoted training and definitive perfection are two approaches one can take when practicing development stage meditation. According to Lochen Dharmaśrī, "Devoted training refers to the stage when one has yet to achieve a stable concentration and has the mere appearance of [true] meditation, as when one practices all the various aspects of the development stage ritual in a single practice session. Definitive perfection, on the other hand, refers to the five yogas related to the defiled paths of accumulation and joining and the four undefiled knowledge holders." [SD 35]

Dhāraṇī mantra (*gzungs sngags*) – A type of mantra in which bliss-emptiness manifests in the form of syllables, bringing the attainment of the divine form and vajra speech. [TD 2507]

Dharmakāya (*chos sku*) – One of the five kāyas; when classified into two forms, the state of buddhahood is divided into dharmakāya and rūpakāya (the form of reality and the embodied form). Dharmakāya is the actualization of what, for one's own benefit, results from the culmination of abandonment and realization. [TD 829] Explaining further, Padmasambhava writes, "The dharmakāya is the unfabricated innate nature—a profound naturalness, beyond arising and ceasing and devoid of constructs." [DE 190]

Discerning wisdom (*so sor rtogs pa'i ye shes*) – Quoting the *Sūtra of the Levels of Buddhahood*, Jigme Lingpa explains, "Discerning wisdom is like our solar system, which can be divided into distinct elements—the continents, sun, moon, and so on. Just so, discerning wisdom is the knowledge of each and every perfectly complete transcendent quality, the entire range of causes along with their results, and the genuine attainments of the listeners, solitary buddhas, and bodhisattvas." [YT 431]

Disembodied consciousness (*dri za*) – Beings in the intermediate state of the desire realm; this term literally means "scent–eater" due to the fact that these beings subsist on either pleasant or unpleasant smells, depending on their karmic propensities. [TD 1330]

Dissolution stage (*bsdu rim*) – The dissolution stage is the part of the development stage in which the entire visualization successively dissolves, to the point where nothing remains and the practitioner rests in a state of empty awareness for as long as possible. The primary function of this phase is to purify clinging to confused perceptions as being real. [LW 135]

Divine pride (*lha'i nga rgyal*) – *See* stable pride.

Dual Tantra (*gnyis ka rgyud/ubhayatantra*) – An alternate name for Caryā Tantra.

Dzogchen (*rdzogs chen*) – *See* Great Perfection.

Egg birth (*sgong skyes*) – *See* four types of birth.

Eight charnel ground ornaments (*dur khrod chas brgyad*) – The three garments (*bgo ba'i gos gsum*): elephant, human, and tiger skin; two fastened ornaments (*gdags pa'i rgyan gnyis*): human skulls and snakes; and three smeared things (*byug pa'i rdzas gsum*): ashes, blood, and grease. These also form part of the ten glorious ornaments. [TN 84]

Eight Great Sādhana Teachings (*sgrub pa bka' brgyad*) – Mahāyoga is traditionally divided into two groups, the Collected Tantras, which includes the *Guhyagarbha Tantra*, and the Collected Sādhanas. The latter division contains the Eight Great Sādhana Teachings, which comprise the ritual practices and instructions associated with eight divinities—five transcendent deities and three mundane deities. The five wisdom deities are Mañjuśrī Yamāntaka (enlightened form), Padma Hayagrīva (enlightened speech), Viśuddha (enlightened mind), Vajrāmṛta Mahottara (enlightened qualities), and Vajrakīlaya (enlightened activity). The three classes of worldly divinities are Mātaraḥ (liberating sorcery), Lokastotrapūja (mundane praises), and Vajramantrabhīru (wrathful mantra). [NS 283] These teachings have been maintained and practiced in both the Transmitted Teachings and the treasure tradition. In the former, the primary source is a cycle titled the *Fortress and Precipice of the Eight Teachings: The Distilled Realization of the Four Wise Men*. There are a great many related teachings in the treasure tradition, the most important, however, are found in the revelations of Nyang Ral Nyima Özer, Guru Chöwang, and Rigdzin Gödem. [WC 777]

Eight knowledge holders (*rig 'dzin chen po brgyad*) – The eight knowledge holders were the Indian masters entrusted with the Eight Great Sādhana Teachings: Vimalamitra, Hūṃkara, Mañjuśrīmitra, Nāgārjuna, Padmasambhava, Dhanasaṃskṛta, Rambuguhya-Devacandra, and Śāntigarbha. These individuals are also referred to as the "eight great accomplished masters" (*grub pa'i slob dpon chen po brgyad*). Details on the lives of these masters can be found in NS 475-483.

Eight measures of clarity and stability (*gsal brtan tshad brgyad*) – The eight measures of clarity and stability are used to gauge whether or not one has mastered the visualization practices of the development stage. These eight consist of the four measures of clarity (lucidity, clarity, vibrancy, and vividness) and the four measures of stability (immutability, steadfastness, complete steadfastness, and complete malleability). Once these eight measures of clarity and stability have been attained, one has reached the stage of meditation known as the experience of perfection. [JL 235]

Eight mundane spiritual accomplishments (*thun mong gi dngos grub brgyad*) – *See* mundane spiritual accomplishment and spiritual accomplishment.

Elaborate seal (*phyag rgya spros bcas*) – With the elaborate seal, one builds upon the maṇḍala that was practiced via the single seal. The focus widens from a single deity to two deities in union. Alternately, the development stage of the elaborate seal can also refer to the realization that all the hosts of thoughts are the maṇḍalas of multiple deities. [JG 31]

Empowerment (*dbang/abhiṣeka*) – In a general sense an empowerment is a tantric ritual that matures the students and allows them to engage in specific tantric practices. There are a great many divisions and descriptions pertaining to empowerment, such as those of the ground, path, and fruition. There are also unique empowerments associated with each tantric lineage and vehicle. Concerning the meaning of the term "empowerment," Jamgön Kongtrül explains that the original Sanskrit term has the literal meaning of "to scatter" and "to pour." The meaning, he explains, is that empowerments cleanse and purify the psycho-physical continuum by "scattering" the obscurations and then "pouring" the potential of wisdom into what is then a clean vessel, the purified psycho-physical continuum. [TK 3, 54] Stressing the importance of the empowerment ritual, Tsele Natsok Rangdröl writes, "Unless you first obtain the ripening empowerments, you are not authorized to hear even a single verse of the tantras, statements, and instructions. (Unauthorized) people who engage in expounding on and listening to the tantras will not only fail to receive blessings, they will create immense demerit from divulging the secrecy of these teachings. A person who has not obtained empowerment may pretend to practice the liberating instructions, but, instead of bringing accomplishment, the practice will create obstacles and countless other defects." [EM 39]

EMPTINESS (*stong pa nyid*) – The manner in which all phenomena are devoid of intrinsic existence; the true nature of things. [TD 1110]

EMPTINESS AND COMPASSION (*stong nyid rnying rje*) – These two factors are considered the basis for development stage practice. In his commentary on Jigme Lingpa's *Treasury of Precious Qualities*, Khenpo Yönga echoes this point: "Emptiness and compassion are like pillars that support the teachings. As such, they are absolutely indispensable, whether one is practicing Sūtra or Mantra. In these dark times, most tantric practitioners don't understand this point. In their version of 'the path of Mantra' emptiness and compassion are superfluous. Consequently, they meditate on the deity with a self-centered attitude. In doing things like mantra recitation, they only benefit themselves. Not only that, their anger drives them to use powerful and malicious mantras towards others. This arrogant behavior is actually a distortion of the Mantra teachings, though, a teaching for demons!" "Knowing this," Yönga continues, "realized masters of the past stressed the importance of these two factors, particularly in the context of explaining the texts of the Mantra tradition. They taught over and over again that these two are of vital importance for those who engage in the main practices of development and completion. As this is the case, we would do well not to forget it . . . Hence, all beginners who have begun practicing mantra in our tradition should take this to heart." [NO 4, 2]

ENERGY (*rlung/prāṇa*) – Energy is one element of the triad energies, channels, and essences. This factor has the nature of the five elements and completely pervades the energetic channels. [TD 2734] There are ten forms of energy: the five root energies (the life–force energy, the downwards–expelling energy, the fire–accompanying energy, the upwards–moving energy, and the pervading energy) and five subsidiary energies (the nāga–energy, the tortoise–energy, the chameleon–energy, the devadatta–energy, and the fire–energy). [JG 50]

ENLIGHTENED ACTIVITY (*'phrin las*) – Enlightened activity is one aspect of the fruitional state of buddhahood. The most common presentation of enlightened activity contains four divisions: pacifying, enriching, magnetizing, and wrathful activity. To these four, a fifth division is sometimes added, that of spontaneous activity. [TD 1771] According to Ju Mipham, enlightened activity can also be divided into supreme and mundane activities. The former, he writes, involves "planting the seed of liberation in the minds of others by granting empowerments, and through mantras, mudrās, and so forth, while the latter functions to bring others more temporary forms of happiness." [ON 559]

ESSENCE (*thig le*) – *See* channels, energies, and essences.

FAITH (*dad pa*) – Generally, three types of faith are discussed in the scholastic tradition: lucid faith, desirous faith, and the faith of conviction. The first entails a lucid frame of mind that arises in reference to the Three Jewels. The second concerns the desire to take up and reject the four truths. The third involves having conviction in the principle of karmic causality. [YD 607]

FATHER TANTRA (*pha rgyud*) – The Father Tantra emphasizes both the methods of the development stage and the energetic practices of the completion stage. In the New Schools, the Father Tantra includes the five stages of the *Guhyasamāja Tantra*. [ST 6] In the Nyingma tradition, Father Tantra is equated with Mahāyoga, the seventh of the nine vehicles. [DZ 24]

FEAST (*tshogs kyi 'khor lo*) – A uniquely effective tantric ritual for accumulating the two accumulations of merit and wisdom. This ritual involves blessing the five sense pleasures, and food and drink in particular, as wisdom nectar. This is then offered to the deities of the three roots and to one's own body, which is regarded as the complete maṇḍala of the three seats. [TD 2289]

FEMALE CONSORT (*yum*) – A female yidam deity that embodies the principle of knowledge. [TD 2585] *See also* male and female consorts.

FEMININE SEAL (*phyag rgya ma*) – The secret consort of a guru; the female embodiment of knowledge (*rig ma*) that a yogi of the Mantra tradition practices with. [TD 1733]

FIRE OF WISDOM (*ye shes kyi me dpung*) – One of the ten glorious ornaments. [TN 85]

FIVE BUDDHA FAMILIES (*rigs lnga*) – The five buddha families function as the support for the five wisdoms. The relationship between these two groups is as follows: the wisdom of the basic space of phenomena is linked with the buddha family and the Buddha Vairocana; all-accomplishing wisdom with the karma family and the Buddha Amoghasiddhi; the wisdom of equality with the jewel family and the Buddha Ratnasambhāva; discerning wisdom with the lotus family and the Buddha Amitābha; and mirrorlike wisdom with the vajra family and either Vajrasattva or Akṣobhya. [TK 2, 80]

FIVE KĀYAS (*sku lnga*) – 1) Dharmakāya (form of reality), sambhogakāya (form of perfect enjoyment), nirmāṇakāya (emanated form), svābhāvikakāya (essence form), and the unchanging vajrakāya—these five kāyas comprise the state of buddhahood. In the Nyingma School, the svābhāvikakāya may be replaced with the abhisambhodikāya (the form of complete enlightenment). Alternately, in the Nyingma tradition, this may also refer to the enlightened body, speech, mind, qualities, and activities that form the basis for the twenty-five fruitional qualities. [TD 120]

FIVE LUMINOSITIES (*'od gsal lnga*) – The five paths can be categorized in terms of the way in which the fundamental nature of things is perceived. The wisdoms associated with the perception of reality that occur at these various stages are: 1) the *luminosity of intellectual understanding* that occurs on the path of accumulation, 2) the *symbolic luminosity* that occurs on the path of joining, 3) the *true luminosity* that takes place on the path of seeing, 4) the *luminosity of training* that occurs on the path of cultivation, and 5) the *culminating luminosity*, which takes place on the path beyond training. [NO 4, 17] *See also* luminosity.

FIVE MANIFESTATIONS OF ENLIGHTENMENT (*mngon byang lnga*) – An extensive approach to development stage practice found in the Mother Tantras. According to Jamgön Kongtrül, the five manifestations of enlightenment are presented differently in the various tantric lineages. There are, however, certain elements common to these different approaches. The following presentation from the *Hevajra Tantra* mirrors Jigme Lingpa's description translated in this book. Kongtrül writes, "Developing the five manifestations of enlightenment involves the following. On top of the lotus and other elements that make up the throne, visualize that a moon disc comes out of *ali* and a sun disc out of *kali*. Resting on the center of these is a symbolic implement marked by a seed syllable. Light radiates out from this implement. Gathering back in, it coalesces into the complete form of the deity. This is what is referred to as 'the five manifestations of enlightenment.' From the moon comes mirrorlike wisdom; from the sun, the wisdom of equality; from the seed and implement, discerning wisdom; from the coalescing of all these factors, all-accomplishing wisdom; and from the complete form of the deity, the wisdom of the basic space of phenomena. This is based on the explanation of the *Hevajra Tantra*." [TK 3, 208]

FIVE MEATS (*sha lnga*) – Elephant meat, human flesh, horse meat, dog meat, and beef. In certain traditions, the latter is replaced by peacock or lion meat. [NS 146]

FIVE MEDITATIVE EXPERIENCES (*nyams lnga*) – In the tradition of practical instructions, it is said that there are five experiential stages that occur during the practice of calm abiding. First is the experience of movement, which is likened to a waterfall cascading off a cliff. Second is the experience of familiarity, which is similar to a river winding through a narrow ravine. Third is the experience of attainment, which is exemplified by a gently flowing stream. Fourth is the experience of stability, which is like a wave-free ocean. Fifth is the experience of perfection, in which one is able to rest in a state of lucid clarity, unmoved by any circumstances. This final stage is likened to the flame of a candle that is undisturbed by the wind. [TK 3, 172]

FIVE NECTARS (*bdud rtsi lnga*) – Five substances that are used as inner offerings in the Secret Mantra tradition: excrement, urine, ova, flesh, and semen. [TD 1362]

FIVE PATHS (*lam lnga*) – The path of accumulation, the path of joining, the path of seeing, the path of cultivation, and the path beyond training. [TD 2764]

FIVE PERFECTIONS (*phun sum tshogs pa lnga*) – The perfect teaching, the perfect time, the perfect teacher, the perfect place, and the perfect retinue. [TD 1718]

FIVE SUBSTANCES OF A COW (*ba byung lnga*) – Five substances that come from a cow, which must not have touched the ground: urine, dung, milk, butter, and curd. [TD 1802]

FIVE WISDOMS (*ye shes lnga*) – According to Jigme Lingpa, wisdom can be divided into twenty–five categories, as there are five different forms of wisdom present in each continuum of the five buddha families. [YT 431] More commonly, however, five forms of wisdom are taught. Dudjom Rinpoche explains that the wisdom of the basic space of phenomena is that which realizes how things really are, whereas the four subsequent wisdoms—mirrorlike wisdom, the wisdom of equality, discerning wisdom, and all-accomplishing wisdom—in their function of supporting and depending upon the former comprise the wisdom that comprehends all that exists. It has also been explained that the first wisdom mentioned above refers to the ultimate, while the latter four relate to the relative. [NS 140]

FORM REALM (*gzugs khams/rūpadhātu*) – The abodes of the first through the fourth meditative absorptions, which are located in the space above Mount Meru. The inhabitants of this realm have a body of light that is clear by nature. While they are free from passion, they still cling to form. [TD 2499]

FORMLESS REALM (*gzugs med khams/arūpadhātu*) – The four spheres of perception, from that of boundless space up to the peak of existence. In these spheres, there is no coarse form, only clear mental forms. The beings in these realms are free of attachment to form, but are attached to the state of formlessness. [TD 2503]

FOUR CLASSES OF TANTRA (*rgyud sde bzhi*) – The four classes of Tantra are Kriyā Tantra, Caryā Tantra, Yoga Tantra, and Anuttarayoga Tantra. These four divisions are commonly presented in the New Schools and subsume all tantric teachings. Though this classification system is also found in the Nyingma School, this tradition often groups the tantric teachings into the three outer tantras and the three inner tantras.

FOUR DEMONS (*bdud bzhi*) – The demon of the afflictions, the demon of the aggregates, the demon of the lord of death, and the demon of the divine son. [TD 1364]

FOUR DIVISIONS OF APPROACH AND ACCOMPLISHMENT (*bsnyen sgrub yan lag bzhi*) – There are four phases of tantric practice: approach, close approach, accomplishment, and great accomplishment. Ju Mipham explains, "Approach and accomplishment subsume all the various practices that utilize the unique methods of the Secret Mantra tradition to achieve whatever spiritual accomplishments one desires, whether supreme or mundane." [ON 534] As seen in the preceding commentaries, these classifications can be applied to the fruitional state (as in the relationship between these four and the four knowledge holders discussed by Jigme Lingpa), to mantra recitation (as discussed by Getse Mahāpaṇḍita), and also to development stage practice in general (*see* individual Glossary entries).

FOUR EMPTINESSES (*stong pa nyid bzhi*) – These four are: 1) emptiness, 2) extreme emptiness, 3) great emptiness, and 4) universal emptiness. Respectively, these four are linked with the stages of death: 1) appearance, 2) increase, 3) attainment, and 4) luminosity. [TD 1110]

FOUR JOYS (*dga' ba bzhi*) – The four joys are a common principle in the teachings on the conceptual completion stage. Though they are listed differently depending on the context, they are often presented as: 1) joy, 2) supreme joy, 3) freedom from joy (or special joy), and 4) coemergent joy. *The Great Tibetan-Chinese Dictionary* explains: "Four joys are produced when bodhicitta descends to each of the four cakras. [These four comprise] a realization associated with the yogic heat practice, which involves taking control of the subtle energies. When bodhicitta descends from the crown center, joy is produced; when it descends to the throat center, supreme joy; when it descends to the heart center, freedom from joy; and when it reaches the navel center, coemergent joy." [TD 2562]

FOUR KINDS OF ENLIGHTENED ACTIVITY (*'phrin las rnam pa bzhi*) – *See* enlightened activity.

FOUR KNOWLEDGE HOLDERS (*rig 'dzin rnam pa bzhi*) – In the Nyingma School, the four knowledge holders are used to present the various levels of spiritual attainment, from the path of training to that which is beyond training. These four are the matured knowledge holder, the knowledge holder with power over longevity, the knowledge holder of the great seal, and the spontaneously present knowledge holder. [TD 2685] It should be noted, however, that according to Jigme Lingpa's presentation above, Longchenpa maintains that the four knowledge holders encompass all five paths (rather than only taking place on the three transcendent paths, which is the position of the Zur lineage).

FOUR MANIFESTATIONS OF ENLIGHTENMENT (*mngon byang bzhi*) – According to Jigme Lingpa, the four manifestations of enlightenment comprise an approach to development stage meditation unique to the *Heruka Galpo Tantra*, in contrast to the more well-known five manifestations of enlightenment. These four are: 1) emptiness and the awakened mind, 2) the seed syllable, 3) the complete form of the deity, and 4) the placement of the seed syllable. [YT 375]

FOUR MEASURES OF CLARITY (*gsal ba'i tshad bzhi*) – *See* eight measures of clarity and stability.

FOUR MEASURES OF STABILITY (*brtan pa'i tshad bzhi*) – *See* eight measures of clarity and stability.

FOUR SEALS (*phyag rgya bzhi*) – The four seals, or mudrās, are a focal point in the meditative tradition of Yoga Tantra. These four are the activity seal of enlightened activity (karma mudrā), pledge seal of enlightened mind (samaya mudrā), dharma seal of enlightened speech (dharma mudrā), and great seal of enlightened form (mahāmudrā). [SG 335]

FOUR STAKES THAT BIND THE LIFE-FORCE (*srog sdom gzer bzhi*) – The stake of absorption, the stake of the essence mantra, the stake of unchanging realization, and the stake of projection and absorption. As Tenpe Nyima explains, "All key points of the Vajrayāna path of Secret Mantra are included in these four." [KR 59] Explaining further, Khenpo Ngaga writes, "It is traditionally said that these four stakes bring together our own ordinary body, speech, mind, and actions with the enlightened form, speech, mind, and activities of the wisdom deity. They are like stakes that bind these together . . . In other words, these key instructions on the four stakes that bind the life-force purify the three gates and actions, which seem to be obscured from the perspective of the way things appear. Consequently, enlightened form, speech, mind, and activities—the way things really are—actually manifest. This is why these four are necessary." [ST 29]

FOUR TYPES OF BIRTH (*skye gnas bzhi*) – According to tantric theory, all forms of birth fall into one of four categories: miraculous birth, heat-moisture birth, egg birth, and womb birth. Relating these four to the various forms of existence, Kangyur Rinpoche writes, "For animals and humans, any one of the four types of birth is possible, while bodhisattvas, deities, hell beings, and beings in the intermediate state are born miraculously. Spirits can take birth via the womb or miraculously." [TS 257] These four, in turn, are purified via the various types of development stage practice. Tenpe Nyima explains, "Of the four types of development stage practice, those that purify egg and womb birth accord with Mahāyoga, that which purifies heat-moisture birth accords with Anuyoga, and that which purifies miraculous birth accords primarily with Atiyoga." [KR 24] In the commentaries of Jigme Lingpa and Patrul Chökyi Wangpo, these four approaches are listed as, respectively, the very extensive, very elaborate and extensive, elaborate approaches of the Mahāyoga system, the intermediate, simple approach of Anuyoga, and the concise, completely simple approach of the Atiyoga tradition. [JL 218-229]

FOUR VAJRAS (*rdo rje rnam pa bzhi*) – According to Jamgön Kongtrül, this is one of the three most important approaches to development stage visualization, along with the five manifestations of enlightenment and the ritual of the three vajras. He explains, "To visualize the four vajras, start out by meditating on emptiness. Next, radiate light outwards from the sun disc, moon disc, and seed that are resting upon the lotus seat. Then, gathering it back in, visualize the form of the deity in its entirety, place the three syllables at its three places, and so on. This form of visualization is taught in the *Subsequent Tantra of the Assembly* and the *Two Sections*." [TK 3, 208]

FRUITION (*'bras bu*) – *See* view, meditation, conduct, and fruition.

FRUITION VEHICLE (*'bras bu'i theg pa*) – An alternate term for the Vajra Vehicle; Ju Mipham explains, "This vehicle is referred to as such because the essential fruition is seen to be present within the very ground, whereas in other systems it is believed to be something that must be attained. Hence, in this system the fruition is taken as the path in the present moment." [KG 40]

GLORIOUS MAGICAL WEB (*sgyu 'phrul drva ba*) – *See Tantra of the Secret Essence.*

GREAT ACCOMPLISHMENT (*sgrub pa chen po*) – Great accomplishment is the last of the four divisions of approach and accomplishment. Though this stage is relevant in a variety of contexts, in terms of development stage practice great accomplishment entails working for the welfare of others, primarily via the four kinds of enlightened activity. [KR 60]

GREAT GLORIOUS HERUKA (*dpal chen he ru ka*) – Though this appellation is used as a general title for wrathful yidam deities, it often refers to the deities of the Eight Great Sādhana Teachings, such as Mahottara and Viśuddha.

GREAT GLORIOUS ONE (*dpal chen po*) – *See* Great Glorious Heruka.

GREAT PERFECTION (*rdzogs pa chen po*) – This term is used in the tantric tradition of the Nyingma School, where it refers to dharmakāya (the fact that the nature of the mind lacks an essence), sambhogakāya (its clear nature), and nirmāṇakāya (its pervasive compassion). Thus, in the Great Perfection, all the qualities of the three kāyas are spontaneously *perfect*, and since this is the way all phenomena really are, it is *great*. [TD 2360]

GREAT SEAL (*phyag rgya chen po/mahāmudrā*) – 1) "Great seal" is the term given to the ultimate fruition, the supreme spiritual accomplishment; 2) this can also refer to one of the four seals taught in the Yoga Tantra. In this context, the practice of the great seal relates to the enlightened form. As such, it eliminates the temporary confusion of the all-ground consciousness and actualizes its nature, mirrorlike wisdom. [TD 1732]

GROUP ASSEMBLY PRACTICE (*tshom bu tshogs sgrub*) – A particular form of tantric practice that is often presented alongside the single seal and elaborate seal; Ju Mipham explains, "In group assembly practice, the five perfections form the basis. The main practice is then carried out via the four divisions of approach and accomplishment, which allows one to swiftly attain the states of the four knowledge holders that result from this process (in thirty-six days, for example)." [ON 536]

GUHYAGARBHA TANTRA (*rgyud gsang ba snying po*) – *See Tantra of the Secret Essence.*

HAYAGRĪVA (*rta mgrin*) [Lit. "Horse Neck"] – Hayagrīva is a wrathful divinity of the lotus family and one of the yidam deities in the Eight Great Sādhana Teachings.

HEAT-MOISTURE BIRTH (*drod gsher skyes*) – *See* four types of birth.

HERUKA (*he ru ka*) – 1) A blood-drinker; 2) Cakrasaṃvara; 3) a general term for wrathful deities. [TD 3069]

ILLUSORY BODY (*sgyu lus*) – The illusory body is referred to as such because although there are not various forms in reality, various forms appear. And though they appear, they do not truly exist. [TD 602] As a specific completion stage practice, there are three types of illusory body: the impure illusory body, the pure illusory body, and the hidden meaning—the illusory body of the energetic-mind. [DR 444] According to Jamgön Kongtrül, the most extensive treatment of this practice is found in the *Guhyasamāja Tantra*. [TK 4, 29]

Increase (*mched*) – *See* appearance, increase, and attainment.

Inner empowerments of potentiality (*nang nus pa'i dbang*) – There are three groupings of empowerments linked with the peaceful and wrathful deities of the *Tantra of the Secret Essence.* The second group consists of the five inner empowerments of potentiality, which relate to the development of the student's potential. The first and third groupings are the ten outer, beneficial empowerments and the three profound, secret empowerments. [PA 10-12]

Inner tantras (*nang rgyud*) – *See* three inner tantras.

Insight (*lhag mthong*) – Along with calm abiding, insight is one of the common denominators and causes of all meditative absorptions. It entails the observation of the specific distinguishing nature of a given object. [TD 3092]

Intermediate state (*bar srid/bar do*) – The bardo, or intermeditate state, typically refers to the state that occurs between death and a future rebirth. It can also, however, refer to the transitional periods that constitute the entire stream of existence, inclusive of birth, dreaming, meditation, death, reality itself, and transmigration. Concerning the specific completion stage practice, Dza Patrul writes (referring to the three intermediate states of death, reality itself, and transmigration), "In the first intermediate state, one brings luminosity onto the path as dharmakāya. In the second, union is brought onto the path as sambhogakāya. And in the third, rebirth is taken onto the path as nirmāṇakāya." [DR 445]

Jñānapāda (*ye shes zhabs*) – An Indian master known for his mastery of the Buddhist tantric teachings. In particular, he developed one of the two main exegetical approaches related to the *Guhyasamāja Tantra.* Jigme Lingpa writes, "The great master Buddhajñānapāda, who was accepted by noble Mañjuśrī himself, advocated the principles of clarity, profundity, and their union. Clarity is embodied in the mahāmudrā—the illusory form of the deity. Profundity lies in the enlightened mind that rests in reality, which is difficult to fathom. The indivisible union of these two is the completion stage of nondual wisdom, the nonduality of profundity and clarity." Jigme Lingpa concludes with a quote from one of Jñānapāda's texts, the *Sphere of Liberation,* about which he writes, "The terminology employed in this text is remarkably similar to that of the Great Perfection." [YT 429]

KARMIC ENERGY (*las kyi rlung*) – Jamgön Kongtrül explains this term as follows: "All of saṃsāra and nirvāṇa are said to be, by nature, energy. There are two forms of energy: karmic energy and wisdom energy. The former consists of two further divisions, the conceptual and the indivisible. Conceptual karmic energy includes the energies of ignorance, attachment, and aggression; this aspect is what must be eliminated . . . The second form of karmic energy consists of antidotes that cut the continuity of this conceptuality. This includes more authentic concepts, such as the belief in selflessness. Together, these two are referred to as 'karmic energy.'" [TK 3, 45]

KĀYA (*sku*) – This is an honorific term for body, which is often used to refer to the "body" or "form" of buddhahood, in all its various aspects. *See also* nirmāṇakāya, sambhogakāya, dharmakāya, svābhāvikakāya, vajrakāya, and abhisambodhikāya.

KHAṬVĀṄGA (*khaṭvāṅga*) – A symbolic implement that represents the severing of the three times. [KR 51]

KNOWLEDGE (*shes rab/prajñā*) – Knowledge is the factor that focuses on a specific entity, examines this object, and is then able to distinguish its essence and individual features, its general and specific characteristics, and whether it should be taken up or abandoned. Once perfected, it functions to dispel doubt. Knowledge is synonymous with the terms complete awareness, complete understanding, awakening, thorough analysis, thorough understanding, confidence, intelligence, mental functioning, and clear realization. [TD 2863]

KNOWLEDGE HOLDER (*rig 'dzin*) – In this term, "knowledge" refers to deity, mantra, and the wisdom of great bliss. One who "holds" these three, then, with profound and skillful means is a "knowledge holder." [TD 2683] In the *Chariot to Omniscience*, Jigme Lingpa points out that there are many different approaches to classifying these levels of realization. Explaining the approach advocated by Longchenpa, he writes, "The approach taken by the great Omniscient One is to link the four knowledge holders with the five paths. By stabilizing one's practice of the development stage, the mind itself matures into a divine form. Nevertheless, at this stage one does not engage the immediate cause and, hence, is unable to refine the impure elements. Such individuals are on the paths of accumulation and joining, which are associated with the matured knowledge holder."

Addressing the second and third levels, he continues, "If the physical body, the maturation [of past karma], is destroyed before they attain the supreme state on the path of joining, the practitioner will attain the great seal in the intermediate state, without having to take rebirth. The rationale is that the mind will have already matured into the form of the deity, the illusory empty form. Hence, as soon as the matured body is cast away, one will immediately attain the bodhisattva's path of seeing. On the other hand, if one reaches the supreme state with [the ordinary body] as one's basis, one will, as is said, 'attain the level of the supreme knowledge holder with power over longevity.' Said differently, the physical body itself, the support, will transform into a clear, vajra-like body." [YT 418]

It should be noted that there are different presentations of the relationship between the four knowledge holders and the five paths. Dudjom Rinpoche, for example, places all four levels of knowledge holder on the transcendent paths, the path of seeing, the path of cultivation, and the path beyond training. [NS 281]

According to Khenpo Yönga, this is also the approach taken by the masters of the Zur clan, the famed Nyingma lineage that flourished in the eleventh and twelfth centuries. He explains, "The textual lineage of the Zur clan places the four knowledge holders on the three paths of seeing, cultivation, and liberation, encompassing the ten levels upon which the noble ones train. The first two knowledge holders relate to the path of seeing. At this stage true reality is seen, but the flame of wisdom is, as of yet, unable to purify the matured body. This is the 'matured knowledge holder.' When this capacity is in place, the body transforms into a clear form, free from birth and death, which is the 'knowledge holder with power over longevity.' 'The knowledge holder of the great seal' applies to the path of cultivation and the spontaneously present knowledge holder to the state of liberation.' Concluding, Khenpo Yönga writes, "These two approaches come to the same point, however. The difference is only in terms of the point at which certain *labels* are applied, in this case that being whether or not the label 'matured knowledge holder' applies to the paths of accumulation and joining." [NO 419]

Knowledge holder of the great seal (*phyag rgya chen po rig 'dzin*) – One of the four knowledge holders, four levels of spiritual attainment that present the progression through the paths and levels of Secret Mantra in the Nyingma School. This classification subsumes the path of cultivation, referring to the form of wisdom that occurs on the unified path of training once one has arisen from the luminosity of the path of seeing. [TD 1733]

KNOWLEDGE HOLDER WITH POWER OVER LONGEVITY (*tshe dbang rig 'dzin*) – One of the four knowledge holders, four levels of spiritual attainment that present the progression through the paths and levels of Secret Mantra in the Nyingma School. This level of attainment occurs on the path of seeing, where the support present in the supreme state transforms into a clear, vajralike body, while the mind matures into the wisdom of the path of seeing and, as a result, one attains a state of freedom from birth and death. [TD 2282]

KNOWLEDGE MANTRA (*rigs sngags/vidyāmantra*) – One of three types of mantra; knowledge mantras are used primarily to accomplish the enlightened activities of a deity and the aspect of knowledge, vajra mind. [TD 2681]

KNOWLEDGE–WISDOM EMPOWERMENT (*shes rab ye shes kyi dbang*) – This empowerment is the second of the three higher, supreme empowerments, which is bestowed upon the student's mind in dependence upon the maṇḍala of the feminine seal. This purifies mental impurities and, in terms of the path, empowers the student to train in the completion stage. As the result of this empowerment, a causal link is formed that leads to the attainment of the dharmakāya. [TD 2865]

KRIYĀ TANTRA (*bya rgyud*) [Lit. "Activity Tantra"] – The first of the three outer tantras; the view of this system, in terms of the ultimate, relates to the natural purity of all phenomena, while relatively one gains spiritual accomplishments by being blessed by the pure deity. Practice in this tradition focuses on the wisdom being and mantra recitation. Its conduct involves various forms of ritual purification and asceticism. [KG 34]

LOTUS (*padma*) – As a symbolic implement used in development stage practice, the lotus signifies not being stained by faults. [KR 51]

LUMINOSITY (*'od gsal*) – The term "luminosity" is often used to refer to wisdom, the subjective counterpart to reality. As the practitioner progresses along the various paths and levels, the manner in which luminous wisdom perceives its object, reality, becomes more and more refined. [NO 4, 17] As a specific completion stage practice,

Dza Patrul explains, "There are three forms of luminosity: those of the ground, path, and fruition. The first of these is further divided into the luminosity that occurs during deep sleep, union, and death. Path luminosity is divided into fine luminosity, dense luminosity, and experiential luminosity. Finally, fruitional luminosity refers solely to that which is supreme and eternal." [DR 444] According to Jamgön Kongtrül, "The various classifications of subtle energies and the instructions on illusory body and luminosity are treated extensively and clearly in the *Guhyasamāja Tantra* and the other Father Tantras." [TK 4, 29] *See also* five luminosities and luminosity of the first intermediate state.

Luminosity of the first intermediate state (*bar srid dang po'i 'od gsal*) – The moment of death provides one of the most potent opportunities for liberation, according to the Buddhist teachings, because the dharmakāya dawns nakedly at this point and has only to be recognized for liberation to occur. Tsele Natsok Rangdröl explains, "After all the previously mentioned dissolution phases are finished, the energetic-mind will dissolve between the white and red pure essences, the A and hang, union of means and knowledge. Because of this coincidence, the dharmakāya of primordial luminosity, the noncomplex, unfabricated, coemergent wisdom of great bliss, will definitely manifest." This experience is referred to by various terms, depending on the system, but, he explains, "The general teachings common to all systems know it as the luminosity of the first bardo." [MM 45] *See also* death and three appearances.

Magical Web (*sgyu 'phrul drva ba*) – *See Tantra of the Secret Essence.*

Mahāyoga (*rnal 'byor chen po*) – Mahāyoga is one of nine vehicles found in the Nyingma tradition. In this system, one begins by maturing one's state of being with the eighteen supreme empowerments: the ten outer, beneficial empowerments, the five inner empowerments of potentiality, and the three profound, secret empowerments. In the next step, one comes to a definitive understanding of the view, which relates to the indivisibility of the superior two truths. In terms of meditation, the development stage is emphasized—the three meditative absorptions form the structure for this stage of practice, while its essence consists of a threefold process: purification, perfection, and maturation. This is then sealed with the four stakes that bind the life-force. In the completion stage practice of this system, one meditates on the channels, energies, essences, and luminosity. Then, as the conduct, one relies upon the proximate cause, which can be either elaborate in form, simple, or extremely simple, and then attains the fruition of this process—the completion of the five paths (which are subsumed under the four knowledge holders). This state of fruition is known as the unified state of the vajra holder. [TD 2052]

MAHOTTARA (*che mchog*) – The central yidam deity, associated with the principle of enlightened qualities, from the Eight Great Sādhana Teachings.

MALE AND FEMALE CONSORTS (*yab yum*) – In the Secret Mantra Vehicle, male and female deities are visualized as the embodiment of key Buddhist principles. Getse Mahāpaṇḍita explains, "Subjective appearances relate to the masculine principle of skillful means. In contrast, the object, emptiness, relates to knowledge, the feminine principle. The indivisible unity of these two is the great primordial union of everything." Discussing further, he writes, "Emptiness is seen based on appearance, while appearances arise unhindered from the expressive potential of emptiness, which itself manifests as causality. Since the truth of this is undeniable, the two truths are in union; they do not conflict with the principle of interdependent origination. You cannot attain the perfect result of nirvāṇa by utilizing just one of these while abandoning the other. Therefore, the way to bring this onto the path is to meditate on the male and female deities in union, symbolizing the indivisible union of skillful means and knowledge." [CG 50]

MALE CONSORT (*yab*) – *See* male and female consorts.

MAṆḌALA (*dkyil 'khor*) – Explaining the meaning of this term, Ju Mipham writes, "*Maṇḍa* means 'essence' or 'pith,' while *la* has the sense of 'to take' or 'grasp.' Hence, together this term means *that which forms the basis for grasping essential qualities.* Alternately, when this word is translated literally as a whole, it means *that which is wholely spherical and entirely surrounds.*"

Concerning the various types of maṇḍala, Mipham continues, "There are three types of maṇḍala, those of the ground, path, and fruition. The *natural maṇḍala of the ground of being* refers to the universe and its inhabitants being primordially present as divinities, both in terms of the support and supported . . . In terms of the path, there is the *maṇḍala of meditation*, of which there are the two forms: the symbolic maṇḍala (such as paintings, lines, arrangements, and those made from colored powder) and the true maṇḍala that is represented by these forms (enlightened body, speech, and mind). The *maṇḍala of the ultimate fruition* is composed of the kāyas and wisdoms that occur once the path has been completely traversed and one has attained the state of Samantabhadra." [ON 494]

MAÑJUŚRĪ / MAÑJUGHOṢA (*'jam dpal dbyangs/'jam dpal gzhon nur gyur pa*) – The "Gentle, Glorious, and Melodic One" or, alternately, the "Gentle, Glorious, and Youthful One"; a bodhisattva and yidam deity that personifies perfect knowledge. [TD 888]

MAÑJUŚRĪ YAMĀNTAKA (*'jam dpal gshin rje*) – The yidam deity associated with enlightened form in the Eight Great Sādhana Teachings.

MANTRA (*sngags*) – Mantras are formations of syllables that protect practitioners of the Vajra Vehicle from the ordinary perceptions of their own mind. They also function to invoke the yidam deities and their retinue. [TD 707] Explaining the etymology of the term, Dudjom Rinpoche writes, "*Mana*, which conveys the meaning of mind, and *trāya*, which conveys that of protection, become 'mantra' by syllabic contraction, and therefrom the sense of protecting the mind is derived." [NS 257] *See also* Secret Mantra Vehicle.

MARKS AND SIGNS (*mtshan dpe*) – The excellent marks and signs are physical qualities that signify the enlightened state. [TD 2306]

MASTERY OF THE THREE OBJECTS (*yul gsum gyad du gyur ba*) – According to Jamgön Kongtrül, these are three stages that refer to a practitioner's proficiency in visualization practice and the corresponding signs that manifest as a result. In the first stage, the mental visualization of the deity becomes completely clear and distinct. In the second, this visualized form actually becomes visually perceptible, and in the third, it can even be touched. [LW 113]

MATURATION (*smin pa*) – *See* purification, perfection, and maturation.

MATURED KNOWLEDGE HOLDER (*rnam smin rig 'dzin*) – One of the four knowledge holders, four levels of spiritual attainment that present the progression through the paths and levels of Secret Mantra according to the Nyingma School. This level of attainment occurs on the path of seeing, where one first gains stability in the development stage. Though the mind itself matures into its divine form at this point, the residual elements are not able to be purified. [TD 1574] *See also* knowledge holder and four knowledge holders.

Means (*thabs*) – *See* skillful means.

Medicine (*sman*) – Medicine is one of the primary offerings found in the Secret Mantra Tradition, where, along with torma and rakta, it is one of the inner offerings. In this context, medicine takes the form of "nectar that dispels the demon of dualistic thinking," which, as Getse Mahāpaṇḍita explains, symbolizes "the realization that all phenomena are equality, beyond acceptance or rejection." [CG 62]

Meditation (*sgom pa*) – *See* view, meditation, conduct, and fruition.

Meditative absorption (*ting nge 'dzin/samādhi*) – Meditative absorption has the meaning of "to truly grasp," meaning that with this mental state one is able to focus one-pointedly and continuously on a given topic or the object one is examining. [TD 1027]

Method (*thabs*) – *See* skillful means.

Miraculous birth (*rdzus skyes*) – *See* four types of birth.

Mirrorlike wisdom (*me long lta bu'i ye shes*) – Quoting the *Sūtra of the Levels of Buddhahood*, Jigme Lingpa explains, "Mirrorlike wisdom is similar to a reflection that appears on the surface of a mirror, which doesn't really exist. Reflections require no effort and are not something that can be formed. Similarly, when it comes to mirrorlike wisdom, all the various reflections of omniscience do occur, yet do not truly exist. They do not require effort, nor are they something that can be formed." [YT 431]

Mother Tantra (*ma rgyud*) – In the Mother Tantra, the completion stage associated with the subtle essences is emphasized, in which case one relies either upon the body of another or one's own body. In the New Schools, the Mother Tantra includes Naropa's Six Dharmas. [ST 6] In the Nyingma tradition, Mother Tantra is equated with Anuyoga, the eighth of the nine vehicles. [DZ 24]

Mudrā (*phyag rgya*) – *See* seal.

Mundane spiritual accomplishment (*thun mong dngos grub*) – Along with the supreme spiritual accomplishment, there are eight mundane spiritual accomplishments as well: 1) the sword that enables one to travel through the sky and space, 2) pills that allow one to be invisible and shift shape, 3) eye salve that allows one to see any worldly form as nonexistent, 4) swift-footedness, 5) the ability to extract and sustain oneself on the essences of plants and minerals (including the practice of alchemy), 6) the ability to travel to celestial realms, 7) invisibility, and 8) the ability to extract treasures from the earth and provide beings with what they desire. [TD 675]

Natural nirmāṇakāya (*rang bzhin sprul pa'i sku*) – According to Jamgön Kongtrül, the "natural nirmāṇakāya" is like a reflection cast by the sambhogakāya, referring to the five realms, kāyas, wisdoms, dharmas, and other elements that appear to tenth level bodhisattvas. In particular, this refers to the five nirmāṇakāya realms: the Unsurpassed (Akaniṣṭha, the realm of the buddha family and the Buddha Vairocana), Complete Joy (Abhirati, the realm of the vajra family and the Buddha Akṣobhya), the Glorious (Śrīmat, the realm of the jewel family and the Buddha Ratnasambhava), the Blissful or Lotus Mound (Sukhāvatī/Padmakūṭa, the realm of the lotus family and the Buddha Amitābha), and Accomplishment of Supreme Activity (Karmaprasiddhi, the realm of the karma family and the Buddha Amoghasiddhi). [TK 1, 84]

Nectar (*bdud rtsi/amṛta*) – A substance that allows one to conquer death. [TD 1362]

New Schools (*gsar ma*) – This appellation is applied most commonly to the Sakya, Kagyu, and Gelug traditions. More specifically, it refers to those who uphold the Secret Mantra tantras that were brought to Tibet in the period that began with the work of the great translator Rinchen Zangpo. [TD 3008] *See also* Nyingma School.

Nine expressions of the dance (*gar gyi nyams dgu*) – Wrathful deities are said to have nine qualities. They are captivating, heroic, and terrifying (their three physical expressions); laughing, ferocious, and fearsome (their three verbal expressions); and compassionate, intimidating, and peaceful. [JL 233]

Nine traits of peaceful deities (*zhi ba'i tshul dgu*) – To eliminate certain flaws that can occur in development stage practice, peaceful deities should be visualized as being soft, well proportioned, firm, supple, youthful, clear, radiant, attractive, and possessing an intense presence. [JL 233] In *Notes on the Development Stage*, Tenpe Nyima equates these nine traits with, respectively: 1) the purification of pride, 2) the purification of anger, 3) the purification of desire, 4) the purification of envy, 5) the purification of stupidity, 6) the elimination of ignorance, 7) the unfolding of wisdom, 8) the complete presence of the marks and signs of enlightenment, and 9) superior qualities. "The first five," he writes, "are essential qualities, while the latter four are qualities related to [particular] attributes." [KR 43]

Nine vehicles (*theg pa dgu*) – The nine vehicles comprise the path of the Nyingma School of the Early Translations. The first three vehicles are those of the Sūtra Vehicle, the exoteric Buddhist teachings: 1) the Vehicle of the Listeners, 2) the Vehicle of the Solitary Buddhas, and 3) the Vehicle of the Bodhisattvas. The next set comprises the three outer tantras: 4) the Vehicle of Kriyā, or Activity Tantra, 5) the Vehicle of Ubhaya, or Dual Tantra, and 6) the Vehicle of Yoga, or Union Tantra. The final set of three represents the inner tantric tradition: 7) the Vehicle of Mahāyoga, or Great Yoga, 8) the Vehicle of Anuyoga, or Concordant Yoga, and 9) the Vehicle of Atiyoga, or Supreme Yoga (also known as the Great Perfection). [NS 164]

Nirmāṇakāya (*sprul pa'i sku*) – 1) One of the forms of buddhahood, which arises from the empowering condition of the sambhogakāya; an embodied form that comes into existence and appears to both pure and impure disciples, working for the benefit of these beings in accordance with their attitudes. 2) A name applied to the reincarnations of great lamas. [TD 1689] Explaining further, Padmasambhava said, "Nirmanakaya is compassion born out of wisdom, magically displayed and manifest in all ways." [DE 190] Also, one of the five kāyas.

Non–Buddhist (*mu stegs pa*) – The term "non-Buddhist," which is often translated literally as "forder," is often used in a pejorative sense to refer to non-Buddhist Indian religions and philosophical schools. The original term, however, also implies certain similarities between some of these traditions and Buddhism. When it comes to the development stage, such similarities do exist between practices found in the Hindu tradition and those practiced in Buddhist Tantra. There are also important differences, however. Taking a polemic approach, Jigme Lingpa explains, "From a general point of view, the practices found in the non-Buddhist traditions do involve a tremendous amount of virtue. Nevertheless, it is nothing more than a moderate degree of virtue, insofar as these practices do not involve any sense of self-discipline. Their development stage practices are bereft of the vows of the knowledge holder and, despite their status as methods of the Secret Mantra path, they have no capacity to bring enlightenment. The specific problem is that these individuals do not grasp the interdependent link between the basis of purification and the methods that comprise the process of purification, insofar as these relate to development stage practice. Demonstrating a complete lack of understanding, in this style of development stage practice, the apparent aspect, shape, and color, for example, are believed to be permanent. This is the approach taken by the non-Buddhist schools, as well as some powerful spirits." [YT 408]

NONCONCEPTUAL COMPLETION STAGE (*mtshan med rdzogs rim*) – The completion stage is divided into two categories, the conceptual completion stage and the nonconceptual completion stage. In the latter, practice does not involve the mental reference points and visualizations found in the former, but, as Ju Mipham points out, ". . . is free from intentional effort and subtle concepts." [ON 417] The most well known traditions associated with this style of practice are those of the Great Perfection and the Great Seal.

NONDUAL TANTRA (*gnyis med rgyud*) – The third of three divisions that comprise the Anuttarayoga Tantra; Nondual Tantra stresses the view of the path of liberation. In the New Schools, this includes the Six Applications of the Kālacakra Tantra. [ST 6]

NYINGMA SCHOOL (*rnying ma'i lugs*) – This tradition, which consists of nine vehicles, is also referred to as the Secret Mantra School of the Early Translations. The teachings of this school were first translated into Tibetan during the reign of King Trisong Deutsen and were then spread by the master Padmasambhava and his followers. [TD 992]

OBJECT OF PURIFICATION (*sbyang bya*) – There are four factors that subsume all aspects of development stage practice. Jamgön Kongtrül explains, "To engage in development stage practice, one needs to have at least some understanding of four factors: the basis, object, and process and result of purification . . . The object of purification is constituted by the various factors that obscure our buddha nature. In other words, this refers to the impurities associated with the ignorance that have been incidentally confusing us from time immemorial. Just like the sun's innate capacity to give off light and the clouds that obscure it, incidental impurities temporarily obscure the innate enlightened qualities we all possess. These impurities, the afflictive, cognitive, and meditative obscurations, are the object of purification." [ND 13-14]

OBSTRUCTING FORCES (*bgegs*) – A class of malevolent spirits and ghosts. [TD 467]

OFFERING GODDESSES (*mchod pa'i lha mo*) – The eight goddesses, such as the Beautiful One (*sgeg mo*), who make offerings to the deities. [TD 857]

ONE'S OWN CHILDREN (*bdag sras*) – One part of a twofold visualization process found in the Mahāyoga teachings of the Nyingma School. In this stage of practice, all the phenomena of saṃsāra and nirvāṇa are transformed through a complex visualization process in which the central deities of the maṇḍala "give birth" to the deities in the retinue. [LT 460]

OUTER TANTRAS (*phyi rgyud*) – *See* three outer tantras.

PADMA HAYAGRĪVA (*padma rta mgrin*) – A yidam deity associated with the principle of enlightened speech (from the Eight Great Sādhana Teachings).

PATH BEYOND TRAINING (*mi slob lam*) – The fifth of the five paths; the perfection of the various qualities of abandonment and realization as they pertain to the specific context of each of the three vehicles—the attainment of the level of a foe destroyer, solitary buddha, or buddha.

PATH OF ACCUMULATION (*tshogs lam*) – The first of the five paths; this stage forms the basis for the progression to nirvāṇa, in which one gathers a vast amount of merit (that accords with liberation) and realizes selflessness through study and contemplation, albeit this realization occurs only in an abstract, conceptual sense. [TD 2293]

PATH OF CULTIVATION (*sgom lam*) – The fourth of the five paths; this stage functions as the gateway to liberation, in which one cultivates and familiarizes oneself with the nature that was realized on the path of seeing. [TD 598]

PATH OF JOINING (*sbyor lam*) – The second of the five paths; the point at which one has amassed the fundamental virtues that are the critical factors needed to transcend mundane existence, "joined" with the direct realization of the truth, grasped this truth through the knowledge that comes from meditation, and realized that phenomena lack any true nature. [TD 2030]

Path of liberation (*grol lam*) – Along with the path of skillful means, this is one of two practical approaches found in the Anuttarayoga Tantras. Ju Mipham explains, "In this phase of practice, one relies primarily upon the knowledge that comes from study, contemplation, and meditation, which allows one to come to a definitive understanding that all phenomena have been enlightened from the very beginning within the great maṇḍala of spontaneous perfection; that they are one's own innate wisdom. By meditating on this, one progresses along the path and is liberated into great equality—the maṇḍala of natural manifestation of the kāyas and wisdoms." [ON 420]

Path of seeing (*mthong lam*) – The third of the five paths; the stage of spiritual attainment in which one witnesses the true nature of reality for the first time, progressing to the level of a noble one. [TD 1222]

Path of skillful means (*thabs lam*) – Along with the path of liberation, this is one of two approaches to practice found in the Anuttarayoga Tantras. Ju Mipham explains, "In this phase of practice, one relies primarily upon certain activities to force the arising of one's innate wisdom. This results in the swift attainment of the fruition. To be more specific, one practices by relying upon the six cakras to enact a process of blazing and melting. This, in turn, generates the wisdom of bliss." [ON 419]

The various practices associated with this path are found in the tantras of both the Nyingma School and the New Schools. Listing the practices found in the tantras of the New Schools, Jamgön Kongtrül writes, "The various classifications of subtle energies and the instructions on illusory body and luminosity are treated extensively and clearly in the *Guhyasamāja Tantra* and other Father Tantras. The classifications of energetic channels and essences, on the other hand, as well as the practices of yogic heat and karma mudrā training, are treated clearly in Mother Tantras, cycles such as those of Hevajra and Cakrasaṃvara. The *Vajrayoginī* and *Saṃvarodaya Tantras* teach the trainings of dream practice and intermediate state, while transference is taught in the *Samatā* and *Caturpīṭhamahāyoginī Tantras*. In particular, the classifications of the channels, energies, and essences and the various practices, including those of yogic heat and karma mudrā, are taught in great detail and very clearly in the nondual *Kālacakra Root Tantra* and its three main commentaries [including the famed *Vimalaprabhā*]." [TK 4, 29] Patrul Rinpoche singles out the *Tantra of the Perfect Secret* and the *Heruka Galpo Tantra* as sources for these practices in the Nyingma School. [LT 472]

PEACEFUL DEITY (*zhi ba'i lha*) – *See* yidam deity.

PERFECTION (*rdzogs pa*) – *See* purification, perfection, and maturation.

PERFORMANCE TANTRA (*spyod rgyud*) – *See* Caryā Tantra.

PRECIOUS WORD EMPOWERMENT (*tshig dbang rin po che*) – The precious word empowerment is one of the three higher supreme empowerments. This is bestowed upon the student's ordinary body, speech, and mind in reliance upon the maṇḍala of ultimate bodhicitta. It purifies the impurities associated with the three gates, along with their related habitual patterns. In terms of the path, it empowers the student to train in the natural Great Perfection. As its result, a causal link is formed that leads to the attainment of the essence kāya, vajra wisdom. [TD 2271]

PRIDE (*nga rgyal*) – *See* stable pride.

PROCESS OF PURIFICATION (*sbyong byed*) – There are four factors that subsume all aspects of development stage practice. Jamgön Kongtrül explains, "To engage in development stage practice, one needs to have at least some understanding of four factors: the basis, object, and process and result of purification . . . The process of purification involves the various form yogas. Here, the five manifestations of enlightenment, the four vajras, the ritual of the three vajras, and other such visualizations are employed to purify the birth process, such as womb birth, egg birth, and heat-moisture birth. Miraculous birth is purified by visualizing instantaneously, in others words by perfecting the visualization with an instant of mindfulness . . . In short, though there are various approaches found in the Nyingma tradition and the New Schools, they are fundamentally the same in that they all purify the afflictions, the impurities of confusion." [ND 13-14]

PROFOUND SECRET EMPOWERMENTS (*gsang ba zab mo'i dbang*) – There are three groupings of empowerments linked with the peaceful and wrathful deities of the *Tantra of the Secret Essence*. Following the ten outer, beneficial empowerments and the five inner empowerments of potentiality, this third grouping consists of three empowerments that enable the student to practice the various types of completion stage, such as yogic heat, luminosity, and dream practice. These are the secret empowerment, the knowledge-wisdom empowerment, and the precious word empowerment. [PA 10-12]

PROJECTION AND ABSORPTION (*'phro bsdu*) – *See* stake of projection and absorption.

PROTECTION CIRCLE (*srung 'khor*) – A protective barrier, formed of a vajra mesh, that is erected in all directions prior to practicing a maṇḍala, making offerings, giving an empowerment, and so forth. [TD 2983]

PURE REALM (*zhing khams*) – A pure land where buddhas and bodhisattvas abide, such as the Realm of Bliss (Dewa Chen). [TD 2388]

PURIFICATION, PERFECTION, AND MATURATION (*dag rdzogs smin gsum*) – As taught in the inner tantras, it is generally considered essential to have all three of these factors present when engaging in the tantric practice of the development stage. By meditating in accordance with the processes of the birth, death, and the intermediate state (which comprise cyclic existence)—the four types of birth and so on—all clinging and appearances related to the three levels of existence are refined away and *purified*. By meditating on the pure realms, deities, and so forth (which accord with nirvāṇa) the qualities of the fruition, such as the three kāyas, are *perfected* in the ground, and the unique potential that allows for these qualities to be actualized comes into existence. In the same manner, penetrating the vital point of both purity and perfection (or, said differently, of the channels, energies, and essences in the vajra body), one is matured for the symbolic wisdom and true luminosity of the completion stage. [TD 1238]

RAKTA (*khrag*) – As a symbolic representation used in development stage practice, blood is often visualized filling a skull cup, representing the conquering of the four demons. [KR 51].

REALITY (*chos nyid/dharmatā*) – 1) The character or nature of something; 2) the empty nature. [TD 836]

RECOLLECTING PURITY (*rnam dag dran pa*) – The term "recollecting purity" refers to the symbolic associations between the features of the deity and the celestial palace and the enlightened state. Along with clear appearance and stable pride, this is one of the key features of the development stage. As Tenpe Nyima explains, development stage practice forms a link between the enlightened qualities that are present as our own fundamental nature and the state where these qualities actually manifest. He writes, "Once the experiences of clarity and stability have arisen, you should use the development stage to mature the proximate cause of the supreme spiritual accomplishment. To do this, recall the purity [of the divine form]. This will form a link with the fundamental fruition. Nevertheless, you should not fixate on the visualization as being an independent entity that really exists. In reality, it is just the natural manifestation of wisdom. The wisdom maṇḍala does not have projected features like color, shape, a face, or hands. Rather, the qualities that naturally appear with the state of buddhahood arise, from the perspective of disciples, in various symbolic forms, such as those of the support and supported, the celestial palace, and the deity." [KR 50] *See also* clarity, purity, and pride.

RESTING IN THE IMMEDIACY OF COMPLETE AWARENESS (*rig pa spyi blug su 'jog pa*) – This is one method of entering into meditative absorption. Jamgön Kongtrül explains, "There are two methods for settling the mind in a state of nonconceptual concentration: resting in the immediacy of complete awareness and resting subsequent to insight." "With the former," he continues, "having set the stage by ascertaining the view, go to a place free from anything that can harm your meditation, sit in the sevenfold posture of Vairocana, and settle your awareness in a fresh and uncontrived state. This is called 'the resting meditation of a simple yogi.'" [TK 4, 7]

RESTING SUBSEQUENT TO INSIGHT (*mthong ba'i rjes la 'jog pa*) – This is one method of entering into meditative absorption. Jamgön Kongtrül explains, "There are two methods for settling the mind in a state of nonconceptual concentration: resting in the immediacy of complete awareness and resting subsequent to insight." "With the latter," he continues, "bring to mind the view you have studied and contemplated previously and then settle in that. This is called 'the analytical meditation of the paṇḍita scholar.'" [TK 4, 7]

RESULTANT VAJRA–HOLDER (*'bras bu'i rdo rje 'dzin pa*) – The form of one's particular yidam deity with all its marks and signs vivid and complete. [CG 44]

RESULT OF PURIFICATION (*sbyang 'bras*) – There are four factors that subsume all aspects of development stage practice. Jamgön Kongtrül explains, "To engage in development stage practice, one needs to have at least some understanding of four factors: the basis, object, and process and result of purification . . . The result of purification is the actualization of the deity, which abides in the ground. This fruition, once the process of release has reached its culmination, is referred to as the 'attainment of the state of vajradhara.'" [ND 13-14]

Ritual of the three vajras (*rdo rje cho ga gsum*) – This is one method of developing the visualization of a deity. First, a seat is visualized, comprising a lotus, sun disc, and so forth. Upon this seat appears the seed syllable of the deity, from which the symbolic implement arises, marked with the seed syllable. Finally, this transforms into the complete form of the deity. [TD 822] According to Jamgön Kongtrül, this is one of the three most important forms of visualization, along with the five manifestations of enlightenment and the four vajras. [TK 3, 208]

Root mantra (*rtsa sngags*) – The primary mantra of a given yidam deity. [TD 2206]

Rudra – A powerful, violent, and malicious spirit. [TD 1315]

Rūpakāya (*gzugs kyi sku*) – The nirmāṇakāya and the sambhogakāya, which appear to those in need of guidance once the accumulation of merit has been perfected. [TD 2499]

Sādhana (*sgrub pa/sgrub thabs*) – As Mipham explains, a sādhana is "that which enables one to attain or accomplish a desired end." In terms of tantric practice, he writes, this refers to "all the various practices that utilize the unique methods of the Secret Mantra tradition to achieve whatever spiritual accomplishments one desires, whether supreme or mundane." [ON 534]

Samantabhadra (*kun tu bzang po*) – 1) That which is virtuous and good in every way, completely perfect; 2) the basic space of phenomena, dharmakāya; 3) a general term for buddhahood; 4) a particular tathāgata; 5) a particular bodhisattva; and 6) the sambhogakāya of the Bön tradition. [TD 18]

Samantabhadrī (*kun tu bzang mo*) – The female counterpart of Samantabhadra; representing wisdom, Samantabhadrī embodies the empty nature of all phenomena, the "pure spacious expanse." [NS 284]

Samaya being (*dam tshig sems dpa'/samayasattva*) – The samaya being is one of the three beings set forth in development stage practice. This is the deity that one visualizes in conjunction with the ritual of whichever yidam deity is being practiced. [TK 3, 45] According to Jamgön Kongtrül, the samaya being corresponds to the luminous, enlightened mind. This, in turn, is inseparable from the wisdom being, the dharmakāya of all buddhas. [LW 62]

SAMAYA VOW (*dam tshig*) – Along with the vows of individual liberation found in the Lesser Vehicle and the bodhisattva precepts of the Great Vehicle, the samaya vows are one of three sets of vows that form the basis for Buddhist practice. These are the vows associated specifically with the Vajrayāna. Jamgön Kongtrül explains, "The word *samaya* means 'pledged commitment,' 'oath,' 'precept,' etc. Hence, this refers to a vajra promise or samaya because one is not to transgress what has been pledged. Samaya vows involve both benefit and risk because, if kept, samaya vows become the foundation for all the trainings of Mantra. If not kept, however, all the trainings become futile." There are innumerable divisions of the samaya vows found in the various tantras. At the most fundamental level, however, one pledges to continually maintain the view of the enlightened body, speech, and mind of the buddhas. [LW 46]

SAMBHOGAKĀYA (*longs spyod rdzogs pa'i sku*) – One of the five kāyas; while not wavering from the form of reality, the dharmakāya, this form appears solely to those disciples who are noble bodhisattvas. It is also the basis for the arising of the emanated form, the nirmāṇakāya, and is adorned with major and minor marks. [TD 2818] Padmasambhava explains further, "Sambhogakāya is the enjoyment of the self-existing wisdom of awareness because the kāyas and wisdoms are present within the continuity of the innate nature of your mind." [DE 190]

SARMA SCHOOLS (*gsar ma*) – *See* New Schools.

SEAL (*phyag rgya/mudrā*) – According to Ju Mipham, the Sanskrit term *mudrā* carries the meaning of "a stamp, symbol, or seal that is difficult to move beyond. What this means is that these are unique factors that symbolize the enlightened body, speech, mind, and activities of realized beings. Once something has been 'sealed' with one of these, it is difficult to stray from the factor that is being represented." [ON 568]

SECRET EMPOWERMENT (*gsang dbang*) – The secret empowerment is the first of the three higher supreme empowerments (the other two being the knowledge-wisdom empowerment and the precious word empowerment). This is bestowed upon the ordinary speech of the student by relying upon the maṇḍala of the relative enlightened mind of the male and female teachers in union. This purifies the impurities of ordinary speech. In terms of the path, this empowers one to meditate on the energetic practices and recite mantra. In terms of the fruition, a link is formed to the attainment of the sambhogakāya and vajra speech. [TD 3006]

Secret Mantra (*gsang sngags/guhyamantra*) – Secret Mantra is the wisdom of great bliss, which protects the mind from subtle concepts through the union of empty knowledge and compassionate skillful means. It is referred to as such because it is practiced in secret and not divulged to those who are not suitable recipients of these teachings. [TD 3002] *See also* Secret Mantra Vehicle.

Secret Mantra Vehicle (*gsang sngags kyi theg pa/guhyamantrayāna*) – An alternate term for the Vajra Vehicle; Ju Mipham explains, "This system is 'secret' insofar as the profound maṇḍala of the victorious ones' enlightened body, speech, and mind is present as the innate nature of all phenomena. Nevertheless, this is inherently hidden from those who are confused and must be revealed skillfully. It is not revealed explicitly to the inferior practitioners of the lower approaches, but is transmitted secretly. Hence, it is not part of the range of experience of ordinary disciples. The term 'mantra' indicates that, in order to practice the maṇḍala of these three secrets, this nature is presented as it actually is; it is not hidden or kept secret." [KG 38]

Seed syllable (*sa bon/yig 'bru*) – As Jamgön Kongtrül explains, in the context of development stage practice, the seed syllable is the spiritual life-force of the yidam deity, "the unchanging nature of its respective family." [LW 14]

Series of three beings (*sems dpa' sum brtsegs*) – *See* three beings.

Single seal (*phyag rgya gcig pa*) – The single seal involves focusing on one principal deity. One focuses on the body of one deity that expresses the unfabricated union, and which arises together with the blissful melting of meditative absorption. Visualizing the body of the deity in this way, as nondual appearance–emptiness, is the practice of the single seal, the single mudrā. [JG 31]

Six Perfections (*pha rol tu phyin pa drug/saṭpāramitā*) – 1) generosity, 2) discipline, 3) patience, 4) diligence, 5) meditative absorption, and 6) knowledge. [TD 1698]

SIXTEEN JOYS (*dga' ba bcu drug*) – The sixteen joys are a more detailed presentation of the four joys, a common principle in both the New Schools and Nyingma teachings on the conceptual completion stage.

SKILLFUL MEANS (*thabs*) – An activity that enables one to accomplish a given outcome easily. [TD 1148] *See also* path of skillful means and Vehicle of Skillful Means.

SKILLFUL MEANS AND LIBERATION (*thabs grol*) – According to Ju Mipham, the path of Anuttarayoga Tantras can be divided either in terms of its essence or in terms of practice. The former consists of the development and completion stages, while the latter comprises the path of skillful means and the path of liberation. [ON 415]

SKULL CUP (*thod pa/kapāla*) – The skull cup is a symbolic implement that represents the ability to sustain the bliss of nonconceptual wisdom. [CG 51]

SOURCE OF PHENOMENA (*chos 'byung/dharmodaya*) – 1) a triangular shape visualized in development stage practice; 2) a symbol of the feminine principle. [TD 8401]

SO, ZUR, AND NUP (*so zur gnubs*) – Three great masters of the Nyingma School that form the source of the lineage of the Transmitted Teachings of the Nyingma School, the Secret Mantra of the Nyingma School of the Early Translations; the names of these three masters are *So* Yeshe Wangchuk, *Zur* Shakya Jungne, and *Nup* Chen Sangye Yeshe. [TD 2957]

SPIRITUAL LIFE–FORCE (*thugs srog*) – According to Jamgön Kongtrül, the spiritual life-force is the specific seed syllable of the yidam deity, "the unchanging nature of its respective family." [LW 14]

SPONTANEOUSLY PRESENT KNOWLEDGE HOLDER (*lhun grub rig 'dzin*) – One of the four knowledge holders, four levels of spiritual attainment that constitute the Nyingma School's approach of progressing through the paths and levels of Secret Mantra; this classification refers to the path beyond training and the attainment of the ultimate fruition, the spontaneous presence of the five kāyas—the state of a vajra holder. [TD 3107]

STABLE PRIDE (*nga rgyal brtan pa*) – Along with clear apearance and the recollection of purity, this is one of three key elements in the practice of the development stage. Tenpe Nyima writes, "With stable pride, the deity one is meditating on is not seen as just an image that appears to the mind. Instead, the appearance of the deity is recognized to be none other than the meditator's very own mind. Without any sense of fixation, one thinks, 'I myself am the yidam deity.' By practicing in this way, obstacles will have no effect and ego-fixation will be destroyed." [KR 49] *See also* clarity, purity, and pride.

STAGES OF THE PATH (*lam rim*) – *Stages of the Path* can refer to either one of two important early commentaries on the *Tantra of the Secret Essence*. Both were composed by the Indian master Buddhaguhya, a pivotal figure in the transmission of the Mahāyoga teachings to Tibet. These works, which are included in the Transmitted Teachings of the Nyingma School, are widely quoted in works pertaining to development stage meditation and the *Tantra of the Secret Essence*. A short biography of Buddhaguhya can be found in NS, pp. 466–467.

STAKE OF ABSORPTION (*ting nge 'dzin gyi gzer*) – One of the four stakes that bind the life-force; explaining this practice, Tenpe Nyima writes, "For the stake of absorption, start out with the three absorptions and then meditate that the environment and its inhabitants are the divine maṇḍala—empty appearances like a rainbow. Finally, complete all the various aspects of the practice, including empowerment, sealing, and so on." [KR 57]

STAKE OF ESSENCE MANTRA (*snying po sngags kyi gzer*) – One of the four stakes that bind the life-force; Tenpe Nyima explains, "For the stake of the essence mantra, focus your mind on the heart center of the wisdom being, where the absorption being—the heart essence [syllable or implement]—is encircled by a garland of mantras. Then recite the mantra." [KR 57]

STAKE OF PROJECTION AND ABSORPTION (*'phro 'du'i gzer*) – One of the four stakes that bind the life-force; Tenpe Nyima explains, "Concerning the stake of projection and absorption, while recognizing that the universe and its inhabitants are, by nature, deity, mantra, and wisdom, emanate an inconceivable number of light rays from the deity's form and the mantra chain. Ultimately, this will result in the supreme spiritual accomplishment—the accomplishment of the twofold benefit. On a temporal level, it will accomplish the four kinds of enlightened activity. White light, for example, will carry out peaceful activity; yellow light, enriching activity; and so on. It will also bring, among other things, the eight mundane spiritual accomplishments." [KR 57]

STAKE OF UNCHANGING REALIZATION (*dgongs pa mi 'gyur ba'i gzer*) – One of the four stakes that bind the life-force; Tenpe Nyima explains, "As for the stake of unchanging realization, whether in terms of deity or mantra, you should be present to the nature of the practice, which transcends the intellect. This refers to reality itself, in which all forms of dualistic fixation are inherently enlightened as the maṇḍala of vajra space—pure equality." This stake is the essence of the other three. "For this reason," he writes, "binding its essence is of the utmost importance." [KR 57-59]

SUGATA (*bde bar gshegs pa*) [Lit. "One Gone to Bliss"] – An alternate term for the buddhas who, by relying upon the path of bliss—the Bodhisattva Vehicle—progress to the blissful fruition, the state of perfect buddhahood. [TD 1368]

SUPREME SPIRITUAL ACCOMPLISHMENT (*mchog gi dngos grub*) – *See* great seal.

SŪTRA (*mdo*) – *See* Sūtra Vehicle.

SŪTRA VEHICLE (*mdo'i theg pa*) – The Buddhist teachings are often classified into two divisions, which represent two approaches to enlightenment, the Sūtra Vehicle and the Vajra Vehicle. The former is often referred to as the "Causal Vehicle" because, in this tradition, practice consists of assembling the causes that will lead to the attainment of liberation. This vehicle is further divided into the Vehicles of the Listeners and Solitary Buddhas (which comprise the Lesser Vehicle) and the Vehicle of the Bodhisattvas (the Great Vehicle).

SVABHĀVA MANTRA (*shu nya ta'i sngags*) – OṂ SVABHĀVA ŚUDDHAḤ SARVADHARMĀḤ SVABHĀVA ŚUDDHO 'HAṂ; This mantra is commonly used at the outset of development stage practice to dissolve all phenomena into emptiness (prior to developing the visualization). Tsele Natsok Rangdröl explains, "One begins the development stage with purifying into emptiness by means of the svabhāva mantra. This mantra is meant to remind the practitioner of the essence of emptiness, the original natural state of all phenomena . . . It is precisely the natural expression of this emptiness, the magical display of its unceasing cognizant quality, that emanates and manifests in the form of a celestial palace and various types of deities." [EM 88]

SVĀBHĀVIKAKĀYA (*ngo bo nyid kyi sku*) – One division of the forms (or kāyas) of buddhahood. This refers specifically to the form of ultimate basic space, which possesses a twofold purity. [TD 663]

SWORD OF WISDOM (*shes rab ral gri*) – The sword is a symbolic implement that symbolizes cutting through mortality. [KR 51]

SYMBOLIC IMPLEMENTS (*phyag mtshan*) – Symbolic implements are images, either visualized or represented in material form, that embody key principles in Vajrayāna practice. In particular, they are one expression of the principle of purity, which, along with clear appearance and pride, is one of the hallmarks of development stage practice. Explaining the significance of some of the most well known implements, Tenpe Nyima writes, "The five wisdoms are represented by the five-pronged vajra. The cakra symbolizes cutting through the afflictions. The source jewel represents desirable qualities, while the lotus signifies not being stained by faults. Unobstructed activity is represented by the double vajra. The curved knife symbolizes the severing of the four demons. The skull cup signifies sustaining the bliss of nonconceptual wisdom. The blood that fills the skull cup represents the conquering of the four demons. The sword symbolizes cutting through mortality, while the *khaṭvāṅga* represents severing the three times." [KR 51]

SYMBOLIC LUMINOSITY (*dpe'i 'od gsal*) – *See* true luminosity.

SYMBOLIC WISDOM (*dpe'i ye shes*) – *See* true luminosity.

TANTRA OF THE SECRET ESSENCE (*rgyud gsang ba snying po/Guhyagarbha Tantra*) – The most important tantra in the Nyingma School, translated by Vimalamitra, Nyak Jñānakumāra, and Ma Rinchen Chok. The full title of this twenty-two chapter text is the *Tantra of the True Nature of Reality: The Glorious Secret Essence.* [TD 574]

TĀRĀ (*sgrol ma*) – A female yidam deity whose name (Lit. "the Liberator") signifies her capacity to liberate beings from the eight forms of fear. [TD 625]

TATHĀGATA (*de bzhin gshegs pa*) [Lit. "One Who Has Passed into Reality"] – An epithet of the buddhas; this refers to one who, in dependence upon the path of reality, abides in neither existence nor peace and has passed into the state of great enlightenment. [TD 1287]

Ten glorious ornaments (*dpal gyi chas bcu*) – Ten factors related to the visualization of wrathful deities: 1-8) eight charnel ground ornaments, 9) fire of wisdom, and 10) vajra swings. [TN 85]

Ten Perfections (*pha rol tu phyin pa bcu/daśapāramitā*) – 1) generosity, 2) discipline, 3) patience, 4) diligence, 5) meditative absorption, 6) knowledge, 7) skillful means, 8) strength, 9) aspiration, and 10) wisdom. [TD 1698]

Ten signs (*rtags bcu*) – There are ten experiential signs that mark one's progress in tantric practice. Longchenpa explains, "There are ten signs that herald the basic space and wisdom becoming of one taste, which occurs once the energetic-mind enters the central channel. These ten are: 1) smoke, 2) mirages, 3) clouds, 4) fireflies, 5–6) the sun and moon, 7) blazing jewels, 8) eclipses, 9) hairs, and 10) the appearance of lights. These ten are presented slightly differently in other traditions." [MS 157]

Terma (*gter ma*) – *See* treasure.

Thirty-seven factors of enlightenment (*byang phyogs so bdun*) – The thirty-seven factors of enlightenment are qualities that occur at various stages of the Buddhist path. According to Maitreya's *Distinguishing the Middle from Extremes*, these are: 1) the four applications of mindfulness that occur on the lesser path of accumulation, 2) the four authentic eliminations that occur on the intermediate path of accumulation, 3) the four bases of miraculous power that occur on the greater path of accumulation, 4) the five faculties that occur during the first two stages of the path of joining—the stages of heat and summit, 5) the five powers that occur on the last two stages of the path of joining—the stage of acceptance and the supreme state, 6) the seven aspects of enlightenment that occur on the path of seeing, and 7) the eightfold noble path that occurs on the path of cultivation. [MV 732] These factors are often represented symbolically in development stage practice. The associations between these factors and their visualized counterparts are discussed by Longchenpa in SC, pp. 84-86.

Three absorptions (*ting nge 'dzin gsum*) – Three meditative practices that, in the Nyingma tradition, provide the framework for development stage practice: the absorption of suchness, absorption of total illumination, and causal absorption.

THREE APPEARANCES (*snang gsum*) – The three appearances are stages of the death process: appearance, increase, and attainment. An experience of luminosity, which usually goes unrecognized, follows these three stages. According to Dilgo Khyenste Rinpoche, "When the connection between the body and mind is cut, the five elements of the body—earth, water, fire, wind, and space—dissolve into each other. There are many different experiences of dissolution of the elements, depending on the individual. The most common among beings is the threefold experience called appearance, increase, and attainment." He goes on to say that during the first stage, once the breath has ceased, the white essence (related to the father's semen) descends from the forehead center to the heart center. This is experienced as a white glow and an experience of intense bliss. In recognizing the nature of this experience, which is linked with the affliction of anger, one recognizes the essence of the nirmāṇakāya. The second stage is linked with the red element (related to the mother's menstrual blood), which ascends from the navel center to the heart center. At this point one's experience is suffused with a red glow. This is related to the affliction of passion and, when recognized, is seen to be the essence of the sambhogakāya. The third stage is as follows. Once these two have merged into the heart center, consciousness dissolves. This is experienced as a state of complete darkness and is linked with the affliction of ignorance. When its nature is recognized, it is realized to be the essence of the dharmakāya. If none of these stages are recognized for what they are, an experience of emptiness then follows. [PA 41-45]

THREE BEINGS (*sems dpa' gsum*) – The three beings are the samaya being, wisdom being, and absorption being. These three embody the various aspects of the deity principle in development stage practice and are visualized successively.

THREE GATES TO COMPLETE LIBERATION (*rnam par thar pa'i sgo gsum*) – The three meditative concentrations that enable one to attain complete liberation: 1) the gate to complete liberation of emptiness, 2) the gate to complete liberation of the absence of characteristics, and 3) the gate to complete liberation of being without desire. [TD 1569]

THREE HIGHER SUPREME EMPOWERMENTS (*mchog dbang gong ma gsum*) – These three empowerments mature the student and provide access to the maṇḍala of Anuttarayoga Tantra. In order, they are the secret empowerment, knowledge-wisdom empowerment, and the precious word empowerment. [TD 853]

THREE INNER TANTRAS (*nang rgyud gsum*) – In the textual tradition of the Nyingma School, the three inner tantras comprise the final three of this tradition's nine vehicles. They are listed as the tantras of Mahāyoga, the scriptures of Anuyoga, and the key instructions of Atiyoga. [TD 1505] These three divisions are also associated with the practices of development, completion, and Great Perfection. As Dilgo Khyentse explains, "Development and Mahāyoga are like the basis for all the teachings, completion and Anuyoga are like the path of all the teachings, and the Great Perfection of Atiyoga is like the result of all the teachings." [WC 773]

THREE KĀYAS (*sku gsum*) – The two rūpakāyas (nirmāṇakāya and sambhogakāya) and the dharmakāya.

THREE MAṆḌALAS (*dkyil 'khor gsum*) – The three maṇḍalas possess a variety of meanings, depending on the context. These three frequently refer to the maṇḍalas of body, speech, and mind. In the Anuyoga tradition, these three represent the view and are presented as follows: 1) empty basic space—the *primordial maṇḍala of Samantabhadrī*, 2) wisdom—the *natural maṇḍala of spontaneous presence*, and 3) the union of emptiness and wisdom—the *fundamental maṇḍala of enlightenment*. [NS 285]

THREE OUTER TANTRAS (*phyi rgyud gsum*) – In the textual tradition of the Nyingma School, the three outer tantras are listed as Kriyā Tantra (Activity Tantra), Caryā Tantra (Performance Tantra), and Yoga Tantra (Union Tantra). These traditions are also referred to as the "Vedic Vehicles of Ascetic Practice," due to the fact that they include various ascetic practices, such as ritual cleansing and purification, that are similar to those found in the Vedic tradition of the Hindu Brahmin caste. [TD 1740]

THREE ROOTS (*rtsa gsum*) – The three roots are the three inner objects of refuge: the guru, yidam deity, and Ḍākinī. A guru is a qualified spiritual teacher who has liberated his or her own mind and is skilled in the methods that tame the minds of others. The yidam deities are the vast array of peaceful and wrathful deities and those associated with the Eight Great Sādhana Teachings. The ḍākinīs are those associated with the three abodes. The latter refers to Vajravarāhī in particular, the divine mother who gives birth to all buddhas. [KN 23]

THREE SEATS (*gdan gsum*) – In general, this refers to the presence of the aggregates and elements as the male and female buddhas, the senses and sense objects as the male and female bodhisattvas, and the limbs as the male and female wrathful deities. [TD 1342]

THREE SPHERES (*'khor gsum*) – Agent, act, and object. [TD 320]

THREE VAJRAS (*rdo rje gsum*) – *See* individual entries for vajra body, vajra speech, and vajra mind.

TORMA (*gtor ma/bali*) – Torma is one of the primary offerings found in the Secret Mantra tradition, where, along with medicine and rakta, it is one of the inner offerings. Though there are various divisions of torma, the outer torma offering consists of "the choicest types of edibles heaped upon a vessel of precious substances," which, as Jamgön Kongtrül explains, embodies "the indivisibility of basic space and wisdom." [LW 129] Explaining the significance of torma in different contexts, Dilgo Khyentse writes, "Generally speaking, torma should be viewed as the maṇḍala in the context of approach and accomplishment, as sense pleasures in the context of making offerings, as the deity in the context of empowerment, and as the spiritual accomplishments at the conclusion of a practice." [WC 743]

TRANSMITTED TEACHINGS OF THE NYINGMA SCHOOL (*rnying ma bka' ma*) – The teachings of the Nyingma School have been transmitted through two lineages, the distant lineage of the transmitted teachings and the close lineage of the treasures. In the former, the teachings of Mahāyoga, Anuyoga, and Atiyoga are preserved, respectively, under the headings of the *Tantra of the Magical Web*, the *Sūtra of the Condensed Realization*, and the Mind Class. [NS 396]

TREASURE (*gter ma*) – The teachings of the Nyingma School have been transmitted through two lineages, the distant lineage of the Transmitted Teachings and the close lineage of the treasures. In the latter, the teachings that are passed on consist of three primary categories: those that relate to Guru Padmasambhava, the Great Perfection, and the Great Compassionate One, Avalokiteśvara. [NS 396]

TRUE LUMINOSITY (*don gyi 'od gsal*) – According to Tsele Natsok Rangdröl, some refer to the various manifestations that occur during the stages of appearance, increase, and attainment as "symbolic luminosity" and the bare luminosity that follows these as "true luminosity." The reason the former is referred to as "symbolic luminosity," he explains, is because the perception of mirages, smoke, and so on are signs that the five sense consciousnesses have dissolved into the all-ground consciousness. The experience of whiteness that occurs during the stage of "appearance" signals the afflicted consciousness (the seventh of the eight consciousnesses) dissolving into the all-ground. The experience of redness that occurs during the stage of "increase" heralds the dissolution of the mental consciousness (the sixth consciousness). Once the stage of "attainment" has arrived and everything has dissolved into the basic space of phenomena, the wisdom of dharmakāya will manifest. This is true luminosity. [MM 46] This can also refer to the form of luminosity that occurs on the path of seeing, in contrast to the "symbolic luminosity" found on the path of joining. In this context, the terms "wisdom" and "luminosity" are interchangeable. *See* five luminosities for more details.

TRUE WISDOM (*don gyi 'od gsal*) – *See* true luminosity.

TWELVE DEEDS OF THE BUDDHA (*mdzad pa bcu gnyis*) – The twelve acts that are manifested by all supreme nirmāṇakāyas once they enter the world. These are: 1) descending from Tuṣita Heaven, 2) entering the mother's womb, 3) taking birth, 4) enjoying the activities of youth, 5) enjoying a retinue of queens, 6) taking ordination, 7) practicing austerities, 8) going to the essence of awakening, 9) subduing Māra, 10) attaining complete and total enlightenment, 11) turning the Wheel of the Dharma, and 12) parinirvāṇa. [TD 2334] As discussed in the commentaries translated in this book, these deeds are symbolically visualized in development stage practice.

TWO ACCUMULATIONS (*tshogs gnyis*) – The two accumulations are those of merit and wisdom. Traditionally, these two are said to lead to the attainment of the dharmakāya and the rūpakāyas, respectively. In terms of the tantric path, the accumulation of merit is often equated with the development stage, and the accumulation of wisdom with the completion stage. However, as Getse points out above, when sealed with the completion stage, the development stage also gathers the accumulation of wisdom. [CG 198]

TWOFOLD PURITY (*dag pa gnyis*) – The state of buddhahood, in which both the afflictive and cognitive obscurations have been purified. [TD 1237]

Ubhayatantra (*gnyis ka rgyud*) – Dual Tantra; an alternate name of Caryā Tantra.

Unchanging vajrakāya (*mi 'gyur rdo rje sku*) – *See* vajrakāya.

Unexcelled Yoga (*rnal 'byor bla na med pa*) – *See* Anuttarayoga Tantra.

Unified path of training (*slob pa'i zung 'jug*) – The unified path of training is one of five stages linked with the five luminosities. The five luminosities, as explained above, relate to the progressive refinement in the practitioner's perception of reality. Khenpo Yönga explains, "[These five luminosities] should be understood as: 1) the divine form of dedication linked with the path of accumulation, 2) the divine form of the energetic-mind on the path of joining, 3) the luminous divine form on the path of seeing, 4) the unified divine form of training linked with the path of cultivation, and 5) the unified divine form beyond training in the state of buddhahood." [NO 4, 17]

Unified state beyond training (*mi slob pa'i zung 'jug*) – The unified state beyond training is one of five stages linked with the five luminosities. *See* unified path of training. [NO 4, 17]

Union of development and completion (*bskyed rdzogs zung 'jug*) – The so–called "union of development and completion" seems to have been a controversial theory in Tibet. Confirming this view, Khenpo Ngaga writes, "There are those who do not accept the union of development and completion associated with deity meditation. They justify this view by saying that such an approach did not exist in the noble land of India. This, however, is not the case. There are two renowned approaches linked with the *Guhyasamāja Tantra*, one associated with noble Nāgārjuna and another with Jñānapāda. In the latter approach, it is said that, when meditating on a deity, those who have directly experienced the way things truly are 'seal the development stage with the completion stage.'" [ST 8-9]

Unsurpassed Yoga Tantra (*bla na med pa'i rgyud*) – *See* Anuttarayoga Tantra.

Vajra (*rdo rje*) – 1) That which is unchanging and indestructible; 2) an ancient Indian symbol that, of skillful means and knowledge, is used to symbolize knowledge; 3) one of the twenty-seven coincidences in Tibetan astrology; 4) an abbreviation of the Tibetan word for diamond. [TD 1438] In Vajrayāna practice, this symbolic implement is associated with a number of important principles. Generally speaking, it is linked with the male principle, compassion, skillful means, and the great bliss of unchanging reality. [YT 671]

VAJRA BODY (*sku rdo rje*) – As one of the three vajras, the vajra body is the kāya of indivisible appearance and emptiness—the purification of ordinary form. [TD 122]

VAJRADHARA (*rdo rje 'chang*) – Vajradhara is considered the sovereign lord of all families and the teacher of the tantras. It is also said that this is the form Śākyamuni took when teaching the Secret Mantra. [TD 1439]

VAJRA HOLDER (*rdo rje 'dzin pa*) – 1) Great Vajradhara; 2) Vajrapāṇi; 3) a master of the Secret Mantra; 4) Indra. [TD 1440]

VAJRAKĀYA (*rdo rje sku*) – One of the five kāyas; this refers to the indivisibility of the two rūpakāyas and the dharmakāya, showing that, while the two rūpakāyas do manifest, they have no independent existence. [TD 2065]

VAJRAKĪLAYA (*rdo rje phur pa*) – A yidam deity associated with the principle of enlightened activity from the Eight Great Sādhana Teachings.

VAJRA MASTER (*rdo rje slob dpon*) – A vajra master is a guru who either grants one empowerment into a maṇḍala of the Secret Mantra or who teaches one the liberating instructions. [TD 1442]

VAJRA MIND (*thugs rdo rje*) – One of the three vajras; according to Jamgön Kongtrül, vajra mind is linked with the dharmakāya and the union of bliss and emptiness. [LW 37]

VAJRĀMṚTA (*rdo rje bdud rtsi*) – A yidam deity associated with the principle of enlightened qualities from the Eight Great Sādhana Teachings.

VAJRAPĀṆI (*phyag na rdo rje*) – Vajrapāṇi is the condensation of the enlightened mind of all the buddhas and the embodiment of their strength, might, and power. [TD 1734]

VAJRA PRIDE (*rdo rje nga rgyal*) – *See* stable pride.

VAJRA RECITATION (*rdo rje'i bzlas pa*) – Vajra recitation is the practice of linking mantra recitation with movements of the breath. This often involves linking the inhalation, resting, and exhalation of the breath with the mental recitation of the seed syllables OṂ ĀḤ HŪṂ, while simultaneously holding the vase breath. [NO 4, 20]

VAJRASATTVA (*rdo rje sems dpa'*) – Vajrasattva is a yidam deity that is considered the sovereign lord of the hundred buddha families. He is white in appearance and sits in the vajra posture. With his right hand, he holds a vajra at his heart, and with his left, a bell at his hip. [TD 1442]

VAJRA SPEECH (*gsung rdo rje*) – One of the three vajras; according to Jamgön Kongtrül, vajra speech is linked with the sambhogakāya and the union of luminosity and emptiness. [LW 36]

VAJRAVARĀHĪ (*rdo rje phag mo*) [Lit. "Indestructible Sow"] – A semi-wrathful female yidam deity; the female counterpart of Cakrasaṃvara (*'khor lo bde mchog*). [TD 1440]

VAJRA VEHICLE (*rdo rje theg pa*) – Following the Lesser Vehicle and the Great Vehicle, the Vajra Vehicle is the third and highest vehicle in the Buddhist tradition. In particular, it contains the teachings on Buddhist Tantra. Ju Mipham explains the significance of this appellation: "In this system, one does not accept or reject illusory, relative phenomena. Instead, the relative and ultimate are engaged as an indivisible unity and one's own three gates are linked with the nature of the three vajras. Therefore, this vehicle is "vajralike" insofar as these elements are seen to be indivisible and the very embodiment of primordial enlightenment, in which there is nothing to accept or reject, hence the term 'Vajra Vehicle.'" [KG 39] *See also* Vehicle of Skillful Means, Fruition Vehicle, and Secret Mantra Vehicle.

VAJRA WISDOM (*ye shes rdo rje*) – Vajra wisdom is linked with the svābhāvikakāya and the union of awareness and emptiness. [LW 36]

VAJRAYĀNA (*rdo rje theg pa*) – *See* Vajra Vehicle.

VASE EMPOWERMENT (*bum dbang*) – The vase empowerment is a maturing empowerment that is common to both the outer tantras and inner tantras. In the latter, a maṇḍala (either one made from colored powders or painted on canvas) is used to bestow the various subdivisions of this empowerment upon the student. This includes the water, crown, and other sections. This process purifies physical impurities and, in terms of the path, empowers one to practice the development stage. In terms of fruition, a causal link is formed that leads to the attainment of the vajra body—the nirmāṇakāya. [TD 853, 2865]

VEDIC VEHICLES OF ASCETIC PRACTICE (*dka' thub rig byed kyi theg pa*) – Alternate term for the three outer tantras.

VEHICLE OF SKILLFUL MEANS (*thabs kyi theg pa*) – An alternate term for the Vajra Vehicle; Ju Mipham explains the significance of this appellation, "This approach is referred to as such due to the four characteristics of its skillful means, which are great, easy, many, and swift. With the key points of this path, afflictive and pure phenomena are not engaged from the perspective of needing to be accepted or rejected. As this is the case, they do not obscure. In addition, its methods are great insofar as they lead to the perfection of the two accumulations. In other systems, such skillful means do not exist." [KG 38]

VIEW, MEDITATION, CONDUCT, AND FRUITION (*lta spyod sgom 'bras*) – These four factors subsume the various elements involved in Buddhist practice. Jamgön Kongtrül explains one view on these four principles: "Though there are a great many divisions when it comes to the view, meditation, and conduct, they can all be applied to the individual mind. The view is absolute conviction in its actual nature, while meditation entails applying this view to one's own state of being. Conduct involves linking whatever arises with this view and meditation. Finally, fruition is the actualization of the way things are." [ND 6]

VIŚUDDHA (*yang dag*) – A yidam deity associated with the principle of enlightened mind from the Eight Great Sādhana Teachings.

WISDOM (*ye shes*) – Inborn knowing; the empty and clear awareness that is naturally present within the mind streams of all sentient beings. [TD 2593]

WISDOM BEING (*ye shes sems dpa'/jñānasattva*) – The wisdom being is one of the three beings set forth in development stage practice, that which is visualized in the heart center of the samaya being. Dza Patrul explains, "At the heart center of each of the assembly of deities you are meditating on, visualize a wisdom being that resembles the deity it inhabits, though bereft of ornamentation and implements." [SS 422] While this is the most common presentation, according to Kongtrül, meditating on the wisdom being can occur in other forms as well. It can involve visualizing a form that resembles the samaya being, as explained above, yet it can also entail meditating on a deity with a form, color, face, and arms that are different than the samaya being, or meditating on a symbolic implement that arises from the seed syllable. [TK 3, 209]

WISDOM ENERGY (*ye shes kyi rlung*) – Jamgön Kongtrül writes, "Wisdom energy is the mind's own nature—blissful, clear, and nonconceptual. When this becomes aware of itself, all fluctuations of the karmic winds are pacified." [TK 3, 45] This term is often contrasted with karmic energy.

WISDOM OF EQUALITY (*mnyam nyid ye shes*) – Quoting the *Sūtra of the Levels of Buddhahood*, Jigme Lingpa explains, "With the wisdom of equality, one internalizes the fact that all phenomena are equal, in the sense that they are all devoid of characteristics." [YT 431]

WISDOM OF THE BASIC SPACE OF PHENOMENA (*chos dbyings ye shes*) – Quoting the *Sūtra of the Levels of Buddhahood*, Jigme Lingpa explains, "The wisdom of the basic space of phenomena can be exemplified by all the forms space can take. Although space is present in these forms, by its very nature there is nothing that can be said about it; it is not manifold, but of a single taste. In the same way, though the wisdom of the basic space of phenomena is present in everything that can be known, it is ineffable. And since it isn't manifold, it is of one taste." [YT 431]

WOMB BIRTH (*mngal skyes*) – *See* four types of birth.

WRATHFUL DEITY (*khro bo*) – *See* yidam deity.

YIDAM DEITY (*yi dam/iṣṭadevatā*) – Yidams are the deities, buddhas, and bodhisattvas that form the unique support for the practices of the tantras. [TD 2565] There are a great variety of such deities, including the various classes of peaceful, wrathful, and semi-wrathful deities. Though these variations may have different appearances, this should not be taken to imply that they are fundamentally different, however. As Tenpe Nyima explains, "Though peaceful and wrathful deities may have slightly different bodies, colors, faces, hands, and so on, in terms of their compassion and enlightened activities there is no difference. They appear in accord with the inclinations of the disciple and there is no conflict between them." [KR 48] Ultimately, yidam practice is a skillful method that allows the practitioner to connect with his or her enlightened nature. For this reason, it is also important to keep the true nature of the yidam deity in mind. As Jigme Lingpa explains, "You must realize that it is your own mind, with its eightfold collection of consciousnesses, that arises as the form and wisdom of the deity. In its innate state, awareness itself is the enlightened mind—the fruitional form of the deity." [JL 235]

Yoga Tantra (*rnal 'byor rgyud*) – Yoga Tantra is the last of the three outer tantras. In this system, emphasis is placed on the internal process of meditative absorption. In terms of the path, there are two forms of practice: the practice of skillful means and the practice of knowledge. In the first, one practices deity yoga in conjunction with the four seals. In the latter, one realizes the inner reality of the mind and actualizes discerning wisdom. To supplement this internal process, external forms of ritual purification are also practiced. [SG 335]

Yogic heat (*gtum mo*) – This is one of the primary practices of the completion stage. In this practice, the vital points of the channels, energies, and essences are penetrated, thereby causing a warm bliss to blaze forth from the "a tung" at one's navel center. This blazing bliss, in turn, incinerates the impure aggregates and elements, and conquers all afflictions and concepts. In this sense, it functions in a destructive manner and causes coemergent wisdom swiftly to take birth. [TD 1046] Though this practice brings a number of temporary benefits and spiritual accomplishments, the true practice of yogic heat, as Dza Patrul explains, "is to attain the supreme spiritual accomplishment, the great seal, by undoing the knots in the central channel." [DR 444]

Zur tradition (*zur lugs*) – The Zur tradition is one of the three most prominent sublineages in the Transmitted Teachings of the Nyingma School. Citing the importance of the lineages of Nyak Jñānakumāra, Nup Chen Sangye Yeshe, and Zur Shakya Jungne in the early history of the Nyingma tradition, Dudjom Rinpoche notes that the Nyingma teachings "fell first to Nyak, fell to Nup during the intermediate period, and fell to Zur in the end." [NS 599] This lineage of masters is also known for developing some of the most unique and enduring interpretations of Buddhist scripture, especially concerning the textual lineage of the *Tantra of the Secret Essence*. An extensive discussion of this lineage can be found in NS, pp. 617-649.

English - Tibetan Translation Equivalents

English	Tibetan
absorption	ting nge 'dzin
absorption being	ting nge 'dzin sems dpa'
absorption of suchness	de zhin nyid kyi ting nge 'dzin
absorption of the spiritual warrior's gait	dpa' bar 'gro ba'i ting nge 'dzin
absorption of total illumination	kun snang gi ting nge 'dzin
acceptance [stage of]	bzod pa
accomplishment	sgrub pa
accumulation	tshogs
activity ritual	las sbyor
Activity Tantra	bya rgyud
afflicted mind	nyon yid
affliction	nyon mongs pa
agitation	rgod
Akaniṣṭha	'og min
Akṣobhya	mi bskyod pa
all-accomplishing wisdom	bya grub ye shes
Amitābha	'od dpag med
anklet	rnal 'byor bla na med pa'i rgyud
Anuyoga	rjes su rnal 'byor
approach	bsnyen pa
apricot seed	mthe'u kham
architrave	rta babs
armband	dpung rgyan
arranged recitation	bkod pa'i bzlas pa
Atiyoga	shin tu rnal 'byor
attractive	lhun sdug pa
Avalokiteśvara	spyan ras gzigs
awakened mind	byang chub kyi sems

awareness	rig pa
banner	'phan
barlo tree	bar glo shing
base	'gram rmang
basic space of phenomena	chos kyi dbyings
basis of purification	sbyang gzhi
beam	gdung ma
belt	ska rags
beneficial outer empowerments	phyi phan pa'i dbang
board	pang leb
bodhisattva	byang chub sems dpa'
bone ornament	rus rgyan
border	pha gu
bracelet	gdu bu
broken beehive	bung ba tshang zhig pa
buddha	sangs rgyas
buddha family	rigs
buddha nature	bde gshegs snying po
cakra	'khor lo
cakra of natural wisdom	rang bzhin ye shes kyi 'khor lo
calm abiding	zhi gnas
canopy	bla bre
captivating	sgegs pa
casket	sgrom
causal absorption	rgyu'i ting nge 'dzin
ceiling	thog phub
celestial palace	gzhal yas khang
central chamber	dbus phyur bu
central channel	dbu ma
central deity	gtso bo
channel	rtsa
clairvoyance	mngon shes
clarity	sang nge
clarity, purity, and stability	gsal dag brtan
clear	gsal ba
clear appearance	rnam pa gsal ba
close approach	nye bar bsnyen pa
cluster ornament	sna mchong
Collected Sādhanas	sgrub sde

Collected Tantras	rgyud sde
compassion	rnying rje
completely malleable	cir yang bsgyur tu btub pa
completely steadfast	mngon par mi 'gyur
completion stage	rdzogs rim
complexity	spros pa
conceptual fixation	zhen rtog
conduct	spyod pa
consciousness	rnam shes
continuous wheel of eternity	rtag pa rgyun gyi 'khor lo
cord	dar dpyangs
corpse	bam ro
cross over	la zla ba
crown cakra	spyi bo'i 'khor lo
curved knife	gri gug
ḍākinī	mkha' 'gro ma
definitive perfection	nges rdzogs
deity	lha
demon	bdud
development stage	bskyed rim
devoted training	mos bsgom
dharmakāya	chos sku
diligence	brtson 'grus
direct cause	dngos rgyu
disc	dkyil 'khor
discerning wisdom	so sor rtogs pa'i ye shes
discipline	tshul khrims
discrimination of phenomena	chos rnam par 'byed pa
disembodied consciousness	dri sa
dome	phyur bu
dragon	tsi pa ta
dullness	bying ba
earrings	rna cha, snyan cha
egg birth	sgong skyes
eight charnel ground ornaments	dur khrod chas brgyad
eight great charnel grounds	dur khrod chen po brgyad
Eight Great Sādhana Teachings	sgrub pa bka' brgyad
eight measures of clarity and stability	gsal ldan tshad brgyad
eightfold noble path	phags lam yan lag brgyad

elaborate mudrā	phyag rgya spros bcas
element	byung ba
empathetic joy	dga' ba
empowerment	dbang
empty sound	grags stong
enclosure	rwa ba
energetic channels	rtsa
energetic-mind	rlung sems
energy	rlung
enlightened activity	'phrin las
enlightened body, speech, and mind	sku gsung thugs
enlightenment	byang chub
equanimity	btang snyoms
essence	ngo bo, thig le
essence mantra	snying po sngags
establishing a boundary	mtshams bcad pa
eternal wheel of adornment	mi zad pa rgyan gyi 'khor lo
existence	srid pa
expelling obstructive forces	bgegs bskrad pa
experience of attainment	thob pa'i nyams
experience of familiarity	goms pa'i nyams
experience of movement	g.yo ba'i nyams
experience of perfection	mthar phyin pa'i nyams
experience of stability	brtan pa'i nyams
experiences [meditative]	nyams
external foundation	'dod snam
fearsome	'jigs rung
female consort	yum
ferocious	drag shul
fire of wisdom	ye shes kyi me dpung
firm	khril bag chags pa
five capacities	dbang po lnga
five manifestations of enlightenment	mngon byang lnga
five strengths	stobs lnga
flag	ba dan
form of luminosity	od gsal kyi sku
fortress	rdzong
four authentic eliminations	spong ba bzhi
four bases of miraculous powers	rdzu 'phrul gyi rkang pa bzhi

four correct discriminations	yang dag pa'i rigs pa bzhi
four divisions of approach and accomplishment	bsnyen sgrub yan lag bzhi
four enlightened activities	'phrin las rnam pa bzhi
four foundations of mindfulness	dran pa nye bar bzhag pa bzhi
four immeasurables	tshad med bzhi
four measures of clarity	gsal ba'i tshad bzhi
four measures of stability	brtan pa'i tshad bzhi
four modes	tshul bzhi
four stakes that bind the life-force	srog sdom gzer bzhi
four types of birth	skye gnas bzhi
four types of fearlessness	mi 'jigs pa bzhi
frontal visualization	mdun bskyed
fruition	'bras bu
Fruition Vehicle	'bras bu'i theg pa
garland	'phreng ba, chun 'phyang
generating the awakened mind	byang chub gyi sems bskyed
garuda beak	khyung mchu
great accomplishment	sgrub chen
Great Glorious One	dpal chen
Great Perfection	rdzogs pa chen po
Great Seal / great seal	phyag rgya chen po
great seal knowledge holder	phyag rgya chen po rig 'dzin
Great Vehicle	theg pa chen po
group practice	tshogs sgrub
guru	bla ma
habitual patterns	bag chags
hanging	pha gu
heat	drod
heat-moisture birth	drod gsher skyes
heroic	dpa' ba
horse ankle	rta rkang
ignorance	ma rig pa
immutable	mi g.yo ba
Indra's seed	dbang po
insight	lhag mthong
intense clarity	sang nge
intense presence	gzi byin ldan pa
interdependent origination	rten cing 'brel bar byung ba

intermediate state	bar do
intimidating	rngam pa
introspection	shes bzhin
invoke	spyan drang ba
jewel	dkon mchog
jewel knowledge holder	rin po che'i rig 'dzin
jewel necklace	do shal
jewelry	rgyan cha
karma	las
karma mudrā	las kyi phyag rgya
kīla dagger	phur pa
knowledge	shes rab
knowledge holder	rig pa 'dzin pa
knowledge holder with power over longevity	tshe dbang rig 'dzin
knowledge mantra	rig sngags
kyenyen tree	skye gnyen
lattice	zar tshags, dra ba
laughing	dgod pa
laughter	rgod pa
ledge	mda' yab, steg bu
Lesser Vehicle	theg pa dman pa
level	sa
level of the great accumulation of the wheel of syllables	yi ge 'khor lo tshogs chen gyi sa
level of the lotus endowed	padma can gyi sa
life-force	srog
listener	nyan thos
lotus	chu skyes, padma
lotus knowledge holder	padma'i rig 'dzin
love	byams pa
lucidity	gsal le
luminosity	'od gsal
lunar mansion	rgyu skar
Mahāyoga	rnal 'byor chen po
main deity	gtso bo
Maitreya	byams pa
male consort	yab
maṇḍala	dkyil 'khor

mantra	sngags
mantra garland	sngags phreng
marks and signs	mtshan dpe
master	slob dpon
maturation	smin pa
matured knowledge holder	rnam smin rig 'dzin
medicine	sman
meditative absorption	ting nge 'dzin
meditative concentration	bsam gtan
messenger of a king	rgyal po'i pho nya
method	thabs
mindfulness	dran pa
miraculous birth	rdzus skyes
mirrorlike wisdom	me long lta bu'i ye shes
moon disc	zla ba'i dkyil 'khor
moon with a garland of stars	zla ba skar phreng
mudrā	phyag rgya
mulberry	o se
mundane spiritual accomplishment	thun mong dngos grub
natural manifestation	rang snang
natural state	gnas tshul
naturally existing	rang byung
nature	rang bzhin
necklace	mgul rgyan
nectar	bdud rtsi
negativity	sdig pa
Nepal	bal yul
nine expressions of the dance	gar gyi nyams dgu
nine traits of peaceful [deities]	zhi ba'i tshul dgu
nirmāṇakāya	sprul sku
nirvāṇa	myang 'das
nondual	gnyis med
Nyingma School	rnying ma
Nyingma School of the Early Translations	snga 'gyur rnying ma
object of purification	sbyang bya
obscuration	sgrib pa
obstructing forces	bgegs
offering string	mchod phyir thogs

ornament	rgyan
ovum	khrag
pacifying, enriching, magnetizing, wrathful	zhi rgyas dbang drag
palanquin recitation	khyogs kyi bzlas pa
path	lam
path beyond training	mi slob lam
path of accumulation	tshogs lam
path of cultivation	sgom lam
path of joining	sbyor lam
path of seeing	mthong lam
patience	bzod pa
peace	zhi
peaceful deity	zhi ba
perfection	phar phyin, rdzogs
Performance Tantra	spyod rgyud
pillar capital	ka gzhu
pillar stabilizer	ka thung
pliancy	shin tu sbyang ba
post	bre spungs
potential	rtsal
practice manual	mngon rtogs
practice text	las byang
precipice	phrang
process of purification	sbyong byed
projection and absorption	spro bsdu
protection circle	bsrung ba'i 'khor lo
proximate cause	nye rgyu
pure land	zhing khams
purification	dag
purification, perfection, and maturation	dag rdzogs smin gsum
quality	yon tan
radiant	'tsher ba
rafter	phyam
railing	pu shu
rainspout vessel	shar bu spyi blugs
range of experience	spyod yul
Ratnasambhava	rin chen 'byung gnas

reality, reality itself	chos nyid
recitation	dzab, zlo ba
recitation of projection and absorption	spro bsdu'i bzlas pa
recollection of purity	rnam dag dran pa
refuge (to go for)	skyabs 'gro
renunciation	nges 'byung
request to remain	bzhugs su gsol ba
result of purification	sbyang 'bras
roof	rgya phibs
root cakra	rtsa 'khor
Ru-rakṣa	ru rakṣa
rūpakāya	gzugs sku
Samantabhadra	kun tu bzang po
samaya	dam tshig
samaya being	dam tshig sems dpa'
samaya maṇḍala	dam tshig gi dkyil 'khor
sambhogakāya	longs spyod rdzogs pa'i sku
saṃsāra	khor ba
scarf	dar
Secret Mantra Vajra Vehicle	gsang sngags rdo rje theg pa
Secret Mantra Vehicle	gsang sngags kyi theg pa
seed [syllable]	sa bon
self-awareness	rang rig
selflessness	bdag med
semen	khu
sentient being	sems can
series of the three beings	sems dpa' sum brtsegs
seven factors of enlightenment	byang chub kyi yan lag bdun
short necklace	se mo do
sign	rtags
silk streamer	dar phyang
single mudrā	phyag rgya gcig pa
single sphere	thig le nyag gcig
six limits	mtha' drug
skillful means	thabs
skirt	smad dkris
skull cup	thod pa (ka' pa la)
skylight	skar khung

soapberry	lung thang
soft	mnyen pa
solitary buddha	rang sangs rgyas
source of phenomena	chos 'byung
sphere of totality	zad par gyi skye mched
spinning firebrand	mgal me 'khor ba
spiritual accomplishment	dngos grub
spiritual life-force	thugs srog
spiritual practitioner	rnal 'byor pa
spontaneously present knowledge holder	lhun grub rig 'dzin
stake of absorption	ting nge 'dzin gyi gzer
stake of projection and absorption	phro 'du'i gzer
stake of the essence mantra	snying po sngags kyi gzer
stake of unchanging realization	dgongs pa mi 'gyur ba'i gzer
steadfast	mi 'gyur
streamer	snam bu
stronghold	mkhar
subtle concepts	mtshan ma
suchness	de bzhin nyid
sugata	bde bar gshegs pa
Sukhāvatī	bde ba can
summit [stage of]	rtse mo
sun disc	nyi ma'i dkyil 'khor
supple	ldem bag
support	rten
supported	brten pa
Supreme Son	sras mchog
supreme spiritual accomplishment	mchog gi dngos grub
supreme state	chos mchog
sūtra	mdo
sword knowledge holder	ral gri'i rig 'dzin
sword of knowledge	shes rab ral khri
symbol	brda
symbolic implement	phyag mtshan
symbolic wisdom	dpe'i ye shes
tail fan	rnga yab
tamarisk	'om bu
tassels	dra ba phyed pa

tathāgata	de bzhin gshegs pa
terrifying	mi sdug pa
that which appears to oneself	rang snang
that which appears to others	gzhan snang
thought activity	spros pa
three existences	srid pa gsum
three garments	bgo ba'i gos gsum
three gates to complete liberation	rnam par thar pa'i sgo gsum
three smeared things	byug pa'i rdzas gsum
top border	bre phul
topknot	thor cog
torma	gtor ma
transcendent conqueror	bcom ldan 'das
transmission of life	tshe lung
transmission of place	gnas lung
transmission of purification	khrus lung
treasure	gter ma
true nature	de kho na nyid
two fastened ornaments	gdags pa'i rgyan gnyis
unconditioned	'dus ma byed
unified form	zung 'jug gi sku
union	zung 'jug
unity of appearance and emptiness	snang stong zung 'jug
universe and its inhabitants	snod bcud
upper garment	stod g.yogs
Vairocana	rnam par snang mdzad
vajra	rdo rje
vajra fence	rdo rje'i rva ba
vajra knowledge holder	rdo rje'i rig 'dzin
vajra swing	rdo rje'i gshog pa
Vajra Vehicle	rdo rje theg pa
Vajrakīlaya	rdo rje phur pa
vajralike absorption	rdo rje lta bu'i ting nge 'dzin
Vajrasattva	rdo rje sems dpa'
Vajravarāhī	rdo rje phag mo
Vehicle of Skillful Means	thabs kyi theg pa
vestibule	sgo khang
vibrancy, vibrant	lhag ge
victorious one	rgyal ba

view	lta ba
visualize	bskyed pa, gsal ba, gsal gdab pa
Viśuddha Heruka	yang dag he ru ka
vivid	lhang nge ba
web	dra ba
well-proportioned	lcugs pa
wheel knowledge holder	khor lo'i rig 'dzin
wisdom	ye shes
wisdom being	ye shes sems dpa'
wisdom mudrā	ye shes kyi phyag rgya
wisdom of equality	mnyam nyid ye shes
wisdom of the basic space of phenomena	chos dbyings ye shes
womb birth	mngal skyes
wrathful deity	khro bo
Yangleshö	yang le shod
Yeshe Tsogyal	ye shes mtsho rgyal
yidam deity	yi dam
yoga	rnal 'byor
Yoga Tantra	rnal 'byor gyi rgyud
yogic heat	gtum mo
yogin	rnal 'byor pa
yoginī	rnal 'byor ma
youthful	gzhon tshul

Texts Cited

Advice of the Great Glorious One. (*Yo ga gsum gyi spyi chings dpal chen zhal lung*). Contained in *Klong chen snying thig* section of the *rin chen gter mdzod chen mo*, vol. 106. Paro, Bhutan: Ngodrup and Sherab Drimay, 1976.

Avataṃsaka Sūtra. (*Sangs rgyas phal po che zhes bya ba shin tu rgyas pa chen po'i mdo*; *buddha avataṃsaka nāma mahāvaipulya sūtra*). DK: 0044, phal chen, ka.

Awesome Flash of Lightning. (*De bzhin gshegs pa thams cad kyi gsang ba gsang ba'i mdzod chen po mi zad pa'i gter gyi sgron ma brtul zhugs chen po bsgrub pa'i rgyud ye shes rngam pa glog gi 'khor lo zhes bya ba theg pa chen po'i mdo*). NG: 369, vol. 15 (ba), Anuyoga.

Chariot to Omniscience. (*Yon tan rin po che'i mdzod las 'bras bu'i theg pa rgya cher 'grel rnam mkhyen shing rta*). Composed by 'Jigs med gling pa. Contained in *'Jigs med gling pa'i gsung 'bum*, volume 3 (ga). Bhutan: Lama Ngodrup and Sherab Demy, 1985.

Clarifying the Difficult Points in the Development Stage and Deity Yoga. (*bsKyed rim lha'i khrid kyi dka' gnad cung zad bshad pa*). Composed by dPal sprul o rgyan 'jigs med chos kyi dbang po. Contained in *dPal sprul o rgyan 'jigs med chos kyi dbang po'i gsung 'bum,* vol. 4. Chengdu, China: si khron mi rigs dpe skrun khang, 2003.

Condensed Realization. (*dGongs 'dus*). This most likely refers to *Sūtra of the Condensed Realization.*

Condensed Realization of the Gurus. (*bla ma dgongs pa 'dus pa*). Treasure revealed by Sangs rgyas gling pa. The texts of this compilation are located in various volumes of the *Rin chen gter mdzod chen mo*. Paro: Ngodrup and Sherab Drimay, 1976-1980.

Dagger Tantra. (*rDo rje phur pa'i rtsa ba*). NG: 643, vol. 35 (ci), Mahāyoga.

Dense Array of Ornaments. (*'Phags pa rgyan stug po bkod pa zhes bya ba theg pa chen po'i mdo*; *ārya ghanavyūha nāma mahāyāna sūtra*). DK: 0110, mngo sde, cha.

Enlightenment of Vairocana. (*rNam par snang mdzad chen po mngon par rdzogs par byang chub pa rnam par sprul ba byin gyis rlob pa shin tu rgyas pa mdo sde'i dbang po rgyal po zhes bya ba'i chos kyi rnam grangs; mahāvairocanābhisam bodhivikurvatī adhiṣṭhānavaipulya sūtra indrarājā nāma dharmaparyāya).* DK: 0494, rgyud, tha.

Excellent Chariot. (*sGyu ma ngal gso'i 'grel pa shing rta bzang po).* Composed by Klong chen rab 'byams. KS: vol. 2.

Fortress and Precipice of the Eight Teachings: The Distilled Realization of the Four Wise Men. (*mKhas pa mi bzhi'i thugs bcud bka' brgyad rdzongs 'phrang*). NK: vol. 13, pa.

Gateway to the Three Kāyas. (*sKu gsum la 'jug pa'i sgo*; *kāyatrayāvatāramukha nāma śāstra*). DT: 3890, mdo 'grel, ha. The cited text is spelled "*sku gsum la 'jug pa'i mdo.*" This, however, is presumably a misspelling, as there is no text in the *bka' 'gyur* that matches this citation. The text listed here is the closest match.

Gathering of Sugatas. (*bDe gshegs 'dus pa'i rgyud*). NG: 449, vol. 23 ('a), Mahāyoga.

Glorious Magical Web. (*dPal sgyu 'phrul drva ba*). Alternate title of the *Tantra of the Secret Essence.*

Glorious Secret Essence. (*dPal gsang ba snying po*). Alternate title of the *Tantra of the Secret Essence.*

Great Chariot. (*rDzogs pa chen po sems nyid ngal gso'i 'grel pa shing rta chen po*). Composed by Klong chen rab 'byams. KS: vols. 1-2.

Great Magical Web. (*sGyu 'phrul dra ba chen po*). This is presumably another alternate title for the *Tantra of the Secret Essence.*

Heap of Jewels Sūtra. (*dKon mchog brtsegs pa chen po'i chos kyi rnam grangs le'u stong phrag brgya pa*; *ārya mahāratnakūṭa dharmaparyāya śatasāhasrika grantha*). PK: 760, dkon brtsegs, tshi.

Heruka Galpo Tantra. (*dPal he ru ka'i thugs kyi rgyud gal po*). NG: 600, vol. 33 (gi), Mahāyoga.

Hevajra Tantra. (*Kye'i rdo rje zhes bya ba rgyud kyi rgyal po*; *hevajra tantra rāja nāma*). DK: 0417, rgyud, nga. This text is also referred to as the *Two Parts* (*brTag gnyis*), a common abbreviation of *The Two-Part Root Hevajra Tantra* (*dGyes pa rdo rje rtsa ba'i rgyud brtag pa gnyis po*).

Husks of Unity: A Clarification of the Development Stage Rituals. (*bsKyed pa'i rim pa cho ga dang sbyar ba'i gsal byed zung 'jug snye ma*). Included in *sgrub pa bka' brgyad kyi bskyed rdzogs zab chos thun min skor bzhugs*. Composed by dGe rtse ma h'a pandita tshe dbang mchog grub. Odiyan: Dharma Publishing, 2004.

Illusion of Manifest Enlightenment. (*sGyu 'phrul mngon byang*). Source unknown.

Guru of the Magical Web. (*gSang ba'i snying po de kho na nyid nges pa sgyu 'phrul dra ba bla ma chen po*). NG: 419, vol. 20 (wa), Mahāyoga.

Kālacakra Tantra. (*mChog gi dang po'i sangs rgyas las phyung ba rgyud kyi rgyal po dpal dus kyi 'khor lo zhes bya ba; parama ādibuddhoddhrita śrī kālacakra nāma tantrarājā*). DK: 0362, rgyud, ka.

Ladder to Akaniṣṭha: Instructions on the Development Stage and Deity Yoga. (*bsKyed rim lha'i khrid kyi rnam par gzhag pa 'og min bgrod pa'i them skas*). Composed by 'Jigs med gling pa. Gangtok, Sikkim: Dodrupchen Monastery, n.d.

Magical Web. (*sGyu 'phrul drva ba*). Alternate title of the *Tantra of the Secret Essence*.

Melody of Brahma Reveling in the Three Realms: Key Points for Meditating on the Four Stakes That Bind the Life-Force. (*Srog sdom gzer bzhi'i dmigs pa gnad 'gags khams gsum rol pa tshangs pa'i sgra dbyangs*). Composed by dPal sprul o rgyan 'jigs med chos kyi dbang po. Contained in *dPal sprul o rgyan 'jigs med chos kyi dbang po'i gsung 'bum*, vol. 4. Chengdu, China: si khron mi rigs dpe skrun khang, 2003.

Net of Wisdom. (*dPal sgyu 'phrul dra ba ye shes kyi snying po'i rgyud*). NG: 428, vol. 21 (zha), Mahāyoga.

Notes on the Development Stage. (*bsKyed rim gyi zin bris cho ga spyi 'gros ltar bkod pa man ngag kun btus*). Composed by Kun mkhyen bstan pa'i nyi ma. Delhi: Chos Spyod Publications, 2000.

Ocean of Magic. (*sgyu 'phrul rgya mtsho zhes bya ba'i rgyud*). NG: 437, vol. 22 (za), Mahāyoga.

Ornament of Clear Realization. (*Shes rab kyi pha rol tu phyin pa'i man ngag gi bstan bcos mngon par rtogs pa'i rgyan zhes bya ba'i tshig le'ur byas pa; abhisamayālaṃkāra nāma prajñāpāramitopadeśaśāstrakārikā*). DK: 3786, mdo 'grel, ka.

Ornament of the Sūtras. (*Theg pa chen po mdo sde'i rgyan gyi tshig le'ur byas pa; mahāyānasūtrālaṃkārakārikā*). Taught by Maitreya [byams pa] and transcribed by Asaṅga [thogs med]. DT: 4020, sems tsam, phi.

Pinnacle of Wisdom Tantra. (*'Phags pa sangs rgyas thams cad kyi ye shes kyi rtse mo'i rgyud kyi rgyal po chen po*). NG: 658, vol. 36 (chi), Mahāyoga.

Prayer of Noble Excellent Conduct. (*'Phags pa bzang po spyod pa'i smon lam gyi rgyal po; ārya bhadracārya praṇidhānarāja*). DK: 1095, gzugs, wam.

Recitation of the Names of Mañjuśrī. (*'Jam dpal ye shes sems dpa'i don dam pa'i mtshan yang dag par brjod pa; mañjuśrījñānasattvasya paramārtha nāma saṃgīti*). DK: 0360, rgyud, ka.

Secret Sphere of the Moon. (*dPal zla gsang thig le zhes bya ba rgyud kyi rgyal po chen po; śrī candraguhyatilaka nāma mahātantrarājā*). DT: 0477, rgyud, ja.

Seventy Stanzas on Refuge. (*gSum la skyab 'gro bdun cu pa; triśaraṇa gamana saptati*). Composed by Candrakīrti [Zla ba grags pa]. DT: 3971, dbu ma, gi.

Sphere of Liberation. (*Grol ba'i thig le zhes bya ba; muktitilaka nāma*). Composed by Jñānapāda [Ye shes zhabs]. DT: 1859, rgyud 'grel, di.

Stages of the Path. (*Slob dpon sangs rgyas gsang bas mdzad pa'i lam rim chen mo bzhugs so*). Composed by Buddhaguhya [Sangs rgyas gsang ba]. NK: vol. 23, 'a.

Subsequent Tantra of the Assembly. (*bDe gshegs 'dus pa phyi ma'i rgyud*). NG: 453, vol. 24 (ya), Mahāyoga.

Supreme Continuum. (*Theg pa chen po rgyud bla ma'i bstan bcos; mahāyānottarat antraśāstra*). Taught by Maitreya [Byams pa] and transcribed by Asaṅga [Thogs med]. DT: 4024, sems tsam, phi.

Sūtra of the Condensed Realization. (*Sangs rgyas kun gyi dgongs pa 'dus pa'i mdo chen po*). NG: 373, vol. 16 (ma), Anuyoga.

Sūtra of the Levels of Buddhahood. (*'Phags pa sangs rgyas kyi sa zhes bya ba theg pa chen po'i mdo; ārya buddhabhūmi nāma mahāyāna sūtra*). DK: 0275, mngo sde, ya.

Sūtra of the Tathāgata's Secret. (*'Phags pa de bzhin gshegs pa'i gsang ba bsam gyis mi khyab pa bstan pa zhes bya ba theg pa chen po'i mdo; ārya tathāgatācintyaguhya nirdeśa nāma mahāyāna sūtra*). PK: 760, dkon brtsegs, tshi.

Sūtra of Vast Display. (*'Phags pa rgya cher rol pa zhes bya ba theg pa chen po'i mdo; ārya lalita vistara nāma mahāyāna sūtra*). DK: 0095, mngo sde, kha.

Sūtra Requested by Sāgaramati. (*'Phags pa blo gros rgya mtshos zhus ba zhes bya ba theg pa chen po'i mdo; ārya sāgaramatiparipṛcchā nāma mahāyāna sūtra*). DK: 0152, mngo sde, pha.

Tantra of the Clear Expanse. (*rGyud kyi rtse rgyal nyi zla 'od 'bar mkha' klong rnam dag rgya mtsho klong gsal rgyud*). NG: 270, vol. 10 (tha), Atiyoga.

Tantra of the Emergence of Cakrasaṃvara. (*dPal bde mchog 'byung ba zhes bya ba'i rgyud kyi rgyal po chen po; śrī mahāsaṃbarodaya tantrarāja nāma*). DK: 0373, rgyud, kha.

Tantra of the Layman Secret Black Foe. (*dGe bsnyen dgra gsang nag po'i rgyud*). NG: 883, vol. 44 (phi), Mahāyoga.

Tantra of the Natural Arising of Awareness. (*Rig pa rang shar chen po'i rgyud*). NG: 286, vol. 11 (da), Atiyoga.

Tantra of the Perfect Secret. (*De bzhin gshegs pa thams cad kyi sku gsung thugs kyi snying po de kho na nyid nges pa ye shes mchog gi rgyud chen gsang ba yongs rdzogs*). NG: 332, vol. 14 (pha), Mahāyoga.

Tantra of the Secret Essence. (*Tantra thams cad kyi rtsa bar gyur pa sgyu 'phrul drwa ba gsang ba snying po de kho na nyid nges pa rtsa ba'i rgyud*). NG: 417, vol. 20 (wa), Mahāyoga.

Tantra of the Sun and Moon's Union. (*Nyi ma dang zla ba kha sbyor ba chen po gsang ba'i rgyud*). NG: 298, vol. 12 (na), Atiyoga.

Treasury of Precious Reality. (*Chos dbying rin po che'i mdzod*). Composed by Klong chen rab 'byams. Included in *mDzod bdun: The Famed Seven Treasuries of Vajrayana Buddhist Philosophy*. Gangtok, Sikkim: Sherab Gyaltsen and Khyentse Labrang, 1983.

Two Sections. See *Hevajra Tantra.*

Vajra Array. (*Phur pa rdo rje bkod pa rnal 'byor chen po'i rgyud*). NG: 668, vol. 36 (chi), Mahāyoga.

Vajra Peak Tantra. (*gSang ba rnal 'byor chen po'i rgyud rdo rje rtse mo; vajraśikhara mahāguhyayoga tantra*). DK: 0480, rgyud, nya.

Vast Illusion. (*sGyu 'phrul rgyas pa*). This most likely refers to one of the explanatory tantras associated with the *Tantra of the Secret Essence.*

Wisdom Guru. (*rDzogs pa chen po klong chen snying tig gi gdod ma'i mgon po'i lam gyi rim pa'i khrid yig ye shes bla ma*). Composed by 'Jigs med gling pa. *rDzogs chen skor gsum*, pp. 241-419. Kathmandu: bla ma phrin las dgon, 1999.

Words of My Perfect Teacher. (*sNying thig sngon 'gro'i khrid yig kun bzang bla ma'i zhal lung*). Composed by dPal sprul o rgyan 'jigs med chos kyi dbang po. Chengdu, China: si khron mi rigs dpe skrun khang, 1989.

Bibliography

English Language Texts

Boord, Martin. *The Cult of the Deity Vajrakīla*. Tring, U.K.: The Institute of Buddhist Studies, 1993.

———. *A Bolt of Lightning From the Blue: The vast commentary on Vajrakīla that clearly defines the essential points*. Berlin: Edition Khordong, 2002.

Dilgo Khyentse. *Pure Appearance*. Halifax: Nalanda Translation Committee, 2002.

Doctor, Andreas. *Tibetan Treasure Literature*. Ithaca, New York: Snow Lion Publications, 2005.

Dudjom Rinpoche. *The Nyingma School of Tibetan Buddhism: Its Fundamentals and History*. 2 vols. Translated by Gyurme Dorje and Matthew Kapstein. Boston: Wisdom Publications, 1991.

Dzogchen Ponlop. *Joyful Grove of Vidyādharas: Instructions on the Vajrasattva Sādhana*. Translated by Tyler Dewar. Seattle: Nalandabodhi Publications, 2005.

Guenther, Herbert. *The Creative Vision: The Symbolic Recreation of the World According to the Tibetan Buddhist Tradition of Tantric Visualization Otherwise Known as the Developing Phase*. Novato: Lotsawa, 1987.

Gyatrul Rinpoche. *Generating the Deity*. Translated by Sangye Khandro. Ithaca, New York: Snow Lion Publications, 1992.

Jamgön Kongtrul Lodrö Thaye. *Creation and Completion: Essential Points of Tantric Meditation*. Translated by Sarah Harding. Boston: Wisdom Publications, 1996.

Khamtrul Rinpoche. *Dzogchen Meditation*. Translated by Gareth Sparham. Dharamsala, India: Library of Tibetan Works and Archives, 1994.

Khenpo Namdrol. *The Practice of Vajrakilaya*. Ithaca, New York: Snow Lion Publications, 1999.

Köppl, Heidi. *Establishing Appearance as Divine.* Ithaca, New York: Snow Lion Publications, forthcoming.

Mayer, Robert. *A Scripture of the Ancient Tantra Collection: The Phur-pa Bcu-gnyis.* Edinburgh: Kiscadale, 1996.

Padmasambhava. *Dakini Teachings.* Translated by Erik Hein Schmidt. Kathmandu, Nepal: Rangjung Yeshe Publications, 1999.

———. *Advice from the Lotus-Born: A Collection of Padmasambhava's Advice to the Dakini Yeshe Tsogyal and Other Close Disciples.* Translated by Erik Hein Schmidt. Kathmandu, Nepal: Rangjung Yeshe Publications, 1996.

Padmasambhava and Jamgön Kongtrül the Great. *The Light of Wisdom.* Vol. 2. Translated by Erik Hein Schmidt. Kathmandu, Nepal: Rangjung Yeshe Publications, 1986.

Schmidt, Marcia Binder, ed. *Dzogchen Essentials: The Path that Clarifies Confusion.* Kathmandu, Nepal: Rangjung Yeshe Publications, 2004.

Snellgrove, David. *The Hevajra Tantra: A Critical Study.* London: Oxford University Press, 1959.

Thinley Norbu. *The Small Golden Key.* Boston: Shambhala, 1983.

Thondup, Tulku. *Hidden Teachings of Tibet: An Explanation of the Terma Tradition of the Nyingma School of Buddhism.* London: Wisdom Publications, 1986.

———. *Masters of Meditation and Miracles.* Boston: Shambhala, 1996.

———. *The Practice of Dzogchen.* Ithaca, New York: Snow Lion Publications, 2002.

Tsele Natsok Rangdröl. *The Mirror of Mindfulness: The Cycle of the Four Bardos.* Translated by Erik Hein Schmidt. Kathmandu, Nepal: Rangjung Yeshe Publications, 1987.

Tibetan Language Texts

Krang dbyi sun, editor. *Bod rgya tshig mdzod chen mo.* Chengdu, China: si khron mi rigs dpe skrun khang, 1988.

Kun mkhyen bstan pa'i nyi ma. *bsKyed rim gyi zin bris cho ga spyi 'gros ltar bkod pa man ngag kun btus.* Delhi: Chos Spyod Publications, 2000.

Klong chen rab 'byams. *rDzogs pa chen po sems nyid ngal gso'i 'grel pa shing rta chen po.* In *rDzogs pa chen po ngal so skor gsum dang rang grol skor gsum bcas pod gsum* by Dri med 'od zer [Klong chen rab 'byams]. Reprint of the A dzom 'brug pa chos sgar edition, 1999, vols. 1-2.

———. *dPal gsang ba'i snying po de kho na nyid nges pa'i rgyud kyi 'grel pa phyogs bcu'i mun pa thams cad rnam par sel ba*. Kathmandu: Shechen Monastery (computer version), 1998.

———. *Theg pa chen po'i man ngag gi bstan bcos yid bzhin rin po che'i mdzod.* Volume 7 of *mDzod bdun*. Gangtok: Sherab Gyaltsen and Khyentse Labrang, 1983.

Klong chen ye shes rdo rje. *Yon tan rin po che'i mdzod kyi mchan 'grel theg gsum bdud rtsi'i nying khu*. Kathmandu: Shechen Monastery, n.d.

mKhan chen ngag dbang dpal bzang. *Srog sdom gzer bzhi'i zin bris kun mkhyen brgyud pa'i zhal lung*, n.p.

———. *sGyu 'phrul drwa las khro bo'i dkyil 'khor du bsnyen pa'i tshul gyi lhan thabs rig 'dzin dga' ston*. Included in *sGrub pa bka' brgyad kyi bskyed rdzogs zab chos thun min skor bzhugs*. Odiyan: Dharma Publishing, 2004.

dGe rtse ma h'a pandita tshe dbang mchog grub. *bsKyed pa'i rim pa cho ga dang sbyar ba'i gsal byed zung 'jug snye ma*. Included in *sGrub pa bka' brgyad kyi bskyed rdzogs zab chos thun min skor bzhugs*. Odiyan: Dharma Publishing, 2004.

———. *Zhi khro dgongs pa rang grol gyi bsnyen pa'i yi ge dngos grub kun ster dpag bsam snye ma*. Included in *sGrub pa bka' brgyad kyi bskyed rdzogs zab chos thun min skor bzhugs*. Odiyan: Dharma Publishing, 2004.

rGyal sras gzhan phan mtha' yas. *dKar gling zhi khro'i dka' gnad la dpyad pa'i gsal byed skya rengs dang po*. Included in *sGrub pa bka' brgyad kyi bskyed rdzogs zab chos thun min skor*. Odiyan: Dharma Publishing, 2004.

Nges don bstan 'dzin bzang po. *rDzogs pa chen po mkha' 'gro snying thig gi khrid yig thar lam bgrod byed shing rta bzang po*. Chengdu, China: si khron mi rigs dpe skrun khang, 1997.

———. *Theg pa lam zhugs kyi bshags pa'i rtsa 'grel bsdus pa thar lam sgron me*. Chengdu, China: si khron mi rigs dpe skrun khang, 1997.

'Jam mgon kong sprul blo gros mtha' yas. *Theg pa'i sgo kun las btus pa gsung rab rin po che'i mdzod bslab pa gsum legs par stong pa'i bstan bcos shes bya kun khyab*. Kathmandu: Padma Karpo Translation Committee, 2000.

———. *Tshom bu tshogs su sgrub pa'i stong thun gsal bar spros pa tshangs pa'i nga ro*. Included in *sGrub pa bka' brgyad kyi bskyed rdzogs zab chos thun min skor*. Odiyan: Dharma Publishing, 2004.

———. *Lam zhugs kyi gang zag las dang po pa la phan pa'i bskyed rdzogs kyi gnad bsdus*. Publication data unknown.

'Jigs med gling pa. *Yon tan rin po che'i mdzod las 'bras bu'i theg pa rgya cher 'grel rnam mkhyen shing rta*. Kathmandu: Shechen Monastery, n.d.

———. *bLa ma dgongs pa 'dus pa'i cho ga'i rnam bzhag dang 'brel ba'i bskyed rdzogs zung 'jug gi sgron ma mkhyen brtse'i me long 'od zer brgya pa*. Paro, Bhutan: Lama Ngodrup and Sherab Demy, 1985.

———. *bsKyed rim lha'i khrid kyi rnam par gzhag pa 'og min bgrod pa'i them skas*. Gangtok, Sikkim: Dodrupchen Monastery, n.d.

'Ju mi pham rgya mtsho. *gSang 'grel phyogs bcu'i mun sel gyi spyi don 'od gsal snying po*. Chengdu, China: si khron mi rigs dpe skrun khang, 2000.

———. *dPal sgrub pa chen po bka' brgyad kyi spyi don rnam par bshad pa dngos grub snying po*. Chengdu, China: si khron mi rigs dpe skrun khang, 2000.

———. *dBus dang mtha' rnam par 'byed pa'i bstan bcos kyi 'grel pa 'od zer phreng ba*. Included in *'Jam mgon 'ju mi pham rgya mtsho'i gsung 'bum rgyas pa sde dge dgon chen par ma*, vol. 4. Paro, Bhutan: Lama Ngodrup and Sherab Demy, 1984.

Dil mgo mkhyen brtse. *gSang sngags kyi bskyed rim gyi gnad mdor bsdus su brjod pa rdo rje sems dpa'i dgongs rgyan*. New Delhi: Shechen Publications, 2004.

———. *rDzogs pa chen po klong chen snying gi thig le'i rtsa gsum spyi dang bye brag gi dbang bskur gyi phreng ba bklag chog tu bkod pa zab bsang bdud rtsi'i sgo 'byed skal bzang kun dga'i rol ston*. Contained in *Klong chen snying thig rtsa pod*, vol. 5. Boudhanath, Nepal: Shechen Publications, n.d.

mDo mkhyen brtse ye shes rdo rje. *bsKyed rdzogs kyi zin bris blun gtam de nyid gsal ba*. Included in *sGrub pa bka' brgyad kyi bskyed rdzogs zab chos thun min skor bzhugs*. Odiyan: Dharma Publishing, 2004.

dPal sprul o rgyan 'jigs med chos kyi dbang po. *bsKyed rim lha'i khrid kyi dka' gnad cung zad bshad pa*. Contained in *dPal sprul o rgyan 'jigs med chos kyi dbang po'i gsung 'bum*, vol. 4. Chengdu, China: si khron mi rigs dpe skrun khang, 2003.

———. *Srog sdom gzer bzhi'i dmigs pa gnad 'gags khams gsum rol pa tshangs pa'i sgra dbyangs*. Contained in *dPal sprul o rgyan 'jigs med chos kyi dbang po'i gsung 'bum*, vol. 4. Chengdu, China: si khron mi rigs dpe skrun khang, 2003.

———. *rDzogs rim chos drug bsdus don*. Contained in *dPal sprul o rgyan 'jigs med chos kyi dbang po'i gsung 'bum*, vol. 4. Chengdu, China: si khron mi rigs dpe skrun khang, 2003.

Zhe chen rgyal tshab 'gyur med padma rnam rgyal. *bsKyed rim spyi'i rnam par bzhag pa nyung gsal go bder brjod pa rab gsal nor bu'i me long*. New Delhi: Shechen Publications, 2004.

Yon tan rgya mtsho. *Yon tan rin po che'i mdzod kyi 'grel pa zab don snang byed nyi ma'i 'od zer*. Kathmandu: Shechen Monastery, n.d.

Lo chen dharma shri. *dPal gsang ba'i snying po de kho na nyid nges pa'i rgyud kyi rgyal po sgyu 'phrul drwa ba spyi don gyi sgo nas gtan la 'bebs par byed pa'i legs bshad gsang bdag zhal lung*. Kathmandu: Shechen Publications, n.d.

Tibetan Language Collections

sÑiṅ thig ya bzi. Klong chen rab 'byams *(compiler)*. Reprint of the A dzom 'brug pa chos sgar edition. Darjeeling: Talung Tsetrul Pema Wangyal, 1976.

rÑiṅ ma bka' ma rgyas pa. bDud 'joms 'jigs bral ye shes rdo rje (compiler). Kalimpong, India: Dupjung Lama, 1982-1987.

Peking bka'-'gyur (*The Tibetan Tripitaka*). Edited by Daisetz T. Suzuki. Tokyo; Kyoto: Tibetan Tripitaka Research Institute, 1955-1961.

sDe-dge bka'-'gyur. Si-tu Chos-kyi 'byung-gnas (editor). Chengdu, China: n.p., n.d.

sDe-dge bstan-'gyur. Delhi, India: Delhi Karmapae Chodhey, Gyalwae Sungrab Partun Khang, 1985.

mTshams-brag Manuscript of the Rñin ma rgyud 'bum. Thimphu, Bhutan: National Library, Royal Government of Bhutan, 1982.

Index